COURTING
FAILURE

gratefully acknowledges the
following individuals and foundations
for support of this research

LYNDE AND HARRY BRADLEY FOUNDATION

JERRY AND PATTI HUME

KORET FOUNDATION

EDMUND & JEANNIK LITTLEFIELD FOUNDATION

BERNARD AND CATHERINE SCHWARTZ FOUNDATION

WILLIAM E. SIMON FOUNDATION

BOYD AND JILL SMITH

TAD AND DIANNE TAUBE FOUNDATION

JACK AND MARY LOIS WHEATLEY

An Assessment from the Hoover Institution's
Koret Task Force on K–12 Education

COURTING
FAILURE

*How School Finance Lawsuits
Exploit Judges' Good Intentions
and Harm Our Children*

Edited by
Eric A. Hanushek

Contributions by
Williamson M. Evers and Paul Clopton
Eric A. Hanushek
E. D. Hirsch Jr.
Alfred A. Lindseth
Paul E. Peterson
Marguerite Roza and Paul T. Hill
Sol Stern
Herbert J. Walberg

EDUCATION
next
B O O K S

Stanford University
Stanford, California

www.hoover.org

An imprint of the Hoover Institution Press

Hoover Institution Press Publication No. 551

First printing, 2006
13 12 11 10 09 08 07 06   9 8 7 6 5 4 3 2 1b

Manufactured in the United States of America

The paper used in this publication meets the minimum requirements
of the American National Standard for Information Sciences—
Permanence of Paper for Printed Library Materials, ANSI Z39.48-1992. ∞

Library of Congress Cataloging-in-Publication Data
Courting failure : how school finance lawsuits exploit judges' good intentions
and harm our children / edited by Eric A. Hanushek.
        p.   cm. — (The Hoover Institution press publication series ; 551)
    Includes bibliographical references and index.
    ISBN 0-8179-4781-7 (alk. paper) — ISBN 0-8179-4782-5 (alk. paper) pbk.
    1. Public schools—United States—Finance.   2. Education—Finance—
Law and legislation—United States.   3. Educational accountability—United
States.   4. Academic achievement—Economic aspects—United States.
5. Actions and defenses—United States.   6. United States. No Child Left
Behind Act of 2001.   I. Hanushek, Eric Alan, 1943–
LB2825.C65   2006
379.1′220973—dc22   2006017909

CONTENTS

Introduction   xiii
Eric A. Hanushek

1. *Campaign for Fiscal Equity v. New York*:
   The March of Folly   1
   Sol Stern

2. The Legal Backdrop to Adequacy   33
   Alfred A. Lindseth

3. High-Poverty, High-Performance Schools,
   Districts, and States   79
   Herbert J. Walberg

4. High-Spending, Low-Performing School Districts   103
   Williamson M. Evers and Paul Clopton

5. Thorough and Efficient Private and Public Schools   195
   Paul E. Peterson

6. How Can Anyone Say What's Adequate If
   Nobody Knows How Money Is Spent Now?   235
   Marguerite Roza and Paul T. Hill

7. Science Violated: Spending Projections and the
   "Costing Out" of an Adequate Education   257
   Eric A. Hanushek

8. Adequacy beyond Dollars:
   The Productive Use of School Time   313
   E. D. Hirsch Jr.

9. Funding for Performance   329
   A Policy Statement of the Koret Task Force

Index   357

CONTRIBUTORS

Members of the Koret Task Force on K–12 Education

Williamson M. Evers, a research fellow at the Hoover Institution, is an elected trustee of the Santa Clara County (California) Board of Education. He served in Iraq as a senior adviser on education to Ambassador Paul Bremer of the Coalition Provisional Authority in 2003. Evers is a member of the White House Commission on Presidential Scholars and was a member of the National Educational Research Policy and Priorities Board in 2001–2002 and a member of the Mathematics and Science Scientific Review Panel at the U.S. Department of Education's Institute of Education Sciences in 2005–2006. He serves on panels that write mathematics and history questions for California's statewide testing system and was a commissioner on the California State Academic Standards Commission. He is co-editor of and contributor to *School Accountability*, a 2002 publication by the Koret Task Force; co-editor of *School Reform: The Critical Issues*; and editor of and contributor to *What's Gone Wrong in America's Classrooms*.

Eric A. Hanushek is the Paul and Jean Hanna Senior Fellow at the Hoover Institution. He serves as a member of the Board of Directors of the National Board for Education Sciences. His works on education policy include *Improving America's Schools: The Role of Incentives, Making Schools Work: Improving Performance and Controlling Costs*, and *Educational Performance of the Poor*. His current research involves understanding the role of teachers, programs, and funding in determining student achievement. Previously, he served as deputy director of the Congressional Budget Office. He was awarded the Thomas B. Fordham prize for Distinguished Scholarship in 2004.

Paul T. Hill, a distinguished visiting fellow at the Hoover Institution, is a research professor in the Daniel J. Evans School of Public Affairs and director of the Center on Reinventing Public Education at the University of Washington. The center develops and helps communities adopt alternative governance systems for public K–12 education. His most recent publication is *Charter Schools and Accountability in Public Education*. He edited *Choice with Equity*, an assessment by the Koret Task Force, and he contributed a chapter to *Private Vouchers*, a groundbreaking study edited by task force member Terry Moe.

E. D. Hirsch Jr., a distinguished visiting fellow at the Hoover Institution, is professor emeritus of education and humanities at the University of Virginia. He is the author of several books on education issues, including *The Knowledge Deficit, The Schools We Need and Why We Don't Have Them* and a series beginning with *What Your Kindergartner Needs to Know* that continues through each grade, concluding with *What Your Sixth Grader*

Needs to Know. He is the founder and chairman of the board of the Core Knowledge Foundation.

Paul E. Peterson, a senior fellow at the Hoover Institution, is the Henry Lee Shattuck Professor of Government and director of the Program on Education Policy and Governance at Harvard University. He has been appointed to a Department of Education independent review panel to advise in evaluating the Title I program and, in 2003, was awarded the Thomas B. Fordham Foundation prize for Distinguished Scholarship. Peterson is the editor in chief of *Education Next* and author or editor of many books on U.S. education, including *Choice and Competition in American Education, No Child Left Behind?, The Politics and Practice of School Accountability* (co-edited with Martin R. West), *The Future of School Choice, Our Schools and Our Future . . . Are We Still at Risk?, The Education Gap: Vouchers and Urban Schools*, and *Earning and Learning: How Schools Matter.*

Herbert J. Walberg, a distinguished visiting fellow at the Hoover Institution, is research professor emeritus of education and psychology and University Scholar at the University of Illinois at Chicago. He has edited more than sixty books and written about 350 articles on educational productivity and human accomplishment. He serves as a member of the Board of Directors of the National Board for Education Sciences and is one of ten U.S. members of the International Academy of Education. A fellow of several scholarly associations, he is member of six education boards and chairs two. He is co-author of *Education and Capitalism: How Overcoming Our Fear of Markets and Economics Can Improve America's Schools* and co-editor of *School Accountability*, a 2002 publication by the Koret Task Force.

Additional Contributors

Paul Clopton is a research statistician with the U.S. Department of Veterans Affairs in San Diego, a co-author of more than a hundred medical research articles, and an associate editor of the *Journal of the American College of Cardiology.* He is a co-founder of Mathematically Correct, a mathematics-education advocacy group. He serves on the review panel for California's statewide mathematics tests and is a reviewer of professional development programs for the state. Clopton previously served on the committee that drafted California's instructional framework for mathematics, the panel that recommended mathematics textbooks for statewide adoption, and the commission that oversees teacher credentialing for California.

Alfred A. Lindseth is a senior partner with the Atlanta/Washington, D.C., law firm of Sutherland, Asbill, and Brennan LLP, where he has practiced education law for more than thirty years. During his career, he has represented many states and school districts at both the trial and appellate level in complex and often controversial school finance, adequacy, and desegregation cases, including cases for the states of New York, Florida, Minnesota, Missouri, California, Arizona, Michigan, Connecticut, and North Dakota and for major urban school districts in the Atlanta, St. Louis, Knoxville, Seattle, Savannah, Charleston, and Washington, D.C., areas. His experience includes, for example, representing the State of New York in a seven-month trial challenging the adequacy of the New York City public schools and representing the State of Missouri in bringing to a close the St. Louis and Kansas City desegregation cases.

Marguerite Roza is a research assistant professor in the Center on Reinventing Public Education at the Daniel J. Evans School of Public Affairs at the University of Washington. Her research focuses on quantitative policy analysis, particularly education finance. Her recent research has investigated the spending patterns among schools in urban districts and the relation of these patterns to state and federal education spending. Her work has appeared in *Phi Delta Kappan*, the 2004 Brookings Book on Education Policy, the *Peabody Journal of Education*, and NCES's *Developments in Education Finance*.

Sol Stern is a contributing editor to *City Journal* and a Manhattan Institute senior fellow. He writes on education reform and is the author of *Breaking Free: Public School Lessons and the Imperative of School Choice*. Aside from his work in *City Journal*, his articles have appeared in the *Wall Street Journal*, the *New York Times Magazine*, *Commentary*, *Barron's,* the *New Republic*, the *New York Post*, the *Daily News*, *Newsday*, the *Village Voice*, *New York*, *Sports Illustrated*, and the *New Statesman*. Stern previously served as Director of Issues, Press Secretary, and Senior Policy Advisor in the Office of the City Council President of New York and as executive director of the New York State Commission on Juvenile Justice Reform.

INTRODUCTION

Good Intentions Captured: School Funding Adequacy and the Courts

Eric A. Hanushek

CURRENT U.S. SCHOOL POLICY discussions are deeply rooted in concerns about student performance, and one might easily conclude from media accounts that this is a new phenomenon. But the reality is that the discussions of student performance are not new. They directly follow a half century of almost continual concern about schools—a concern running from the embarrassment of segregated schools and rooted in the national wake-up call following the Soviet Union's launch of Sputnik. Perhaps the prime lesson of this lengthy period of angst about our schools has been how impervious student achievement has been to concerted efforts to change it.

In current national debates, federal legislation on accountability—No Child Left Behind Act (NCLB) of 2001—has reinforced and extended the movement of individual states to set academic standards for students and to enforce the achievement of these. This attention has focused an intense spotlight directly on student performance and has identified gaps between the desired and actual performance of students.

The accountability concerns in turn dovetail with a parallel concern about the financing of schools. From the beginning of the twentieth century, states and local governments have shared the responsibility for funding local schools. The pattern has changed throughout the century. The local share went from over 80 percent of financing around World War I to 50 percent around World War II to nearly 40 percent today. The federal share was less than 2 percent until the mid-1960s when a federal program of compensatory education under the War on Poverty began and elevated federal spending to 7–9 percent. (The federal program under the Elementary and Secondary Education Act morphed into NCLB, which itself has a strong emphasis on disadvantaged students.)

While each state differs to some extent, the general pattern of the twentieth century has been that local governments raise funds through local property taxes, and the state—using other tax instruments—distributes added funds to localities to compensate for the varying ability of localities to raise funds. As the state share has risen, the regulation and control of local schools has also tended to rise.

Perhaps the most important change in policy discussions about school finance was the introduction of court decision making into the determination of funding schemes. Following the California court case of *Serrano v. Priest*, begun in the late 1960s, most states had legal actions designed to change the method of funding local schools. From the outset, these cases stressed equity considerations, arguing that some localities—by virtue of a low property tax base, poverty, or unwillingness to support school funding—spent significantly less than other, more advantaged districts. This situation presented an equity concern, because children growing up in the wrong jurisdiction could receive an inferior education and be harmed over the long run.

The focus of these lawsuits was funding disparities across different school districts. The outcomes of these suits, argued under the separate state constitutions, were mixed, with some state courts finding disparities to be unconstitutional and others not.[1] The varying outcomes in part reflected the variation in funding schemes across states, which in turn led to differing expenditure patterns across districts. Generally, however, the lawsuits tended to increase the state share of funding, whether successful or not, because many state legislatures acted without being pressured to do so by a court judgment, and they tended to bring about more equalized funding within states (Murray, Evans, and Schwab, 1998).

Yet although these suits were motivated by the possibility of an inferior education for disadvantaged students, until recently almost no subsequent analysis investigated whether or not student outcomes were more equal after spending was equalized. In fact, the few investigations have not supported equalization in student outcomes.

The early court decisions that focused on spending equity changed, however, in the 1990s.[2] Even with equal spending across a state, some have argued that children may not be getting enough education. Kentucky is usually identified as the birthplace of the modern era of cases (*Rose v. Council for Better Education*, 1989). Alabama (*ACE v. Hunt*, 1993), however, best

1. An early suit in federal court, *Rodriguez v. San Antonio*, was brought under the Fourteenth Amendment to the U.S. Constitution, but the U.S. Supreme Court ruled in 1973 that state funding arrangements were not a federal constitutional violation.

2. A number of court cases also argued "tax equity," that some jurisdictions had to maintain a higher tax rate than others in order to have comparable spending. In general, state constitutions discuss educational requirements but do not focus on such taxpayer equity.

epitomized this situation, where the spending across districts was equal, but students were performing at the bottom of the nation in terms of achievement levels.[3] This example of an equitable system performing poorly led to a new legal and policy view, now described as "adequacy."

Adequacy dovetails directly with accountability. The standards and accountability movement focuses on how much students are achieving relative to the standards, or goals, for the students. NCLB codified the requirement for regular assessment and reporting of student performance. A ubiquitous outcome of accountability systems is an explicit statement of the performance deficit—that is, how many students have not reached proficiency by the state's standards.

The natural extension of this finding of low student performance is an assessment of why this might be. And the answer as asserted in the new round of court cases dealing with adequacy is that resources are insufficient to support the achievement standards. Thus, a variety of parties have sued states to compel them to provide adequate funding so that all students can achieve the state standards.[4]

The court cases reflect concern about student performance, but they ignore uncertainty about how to improve the schools. The simple fact is that it is unlikely the courts will solve this problem. And while governors and legislatures have yet to solve it, judicial intervention clearly makes the tasks of the legislatures more difficult.

3. For example, Alabama was in the bottom 20 percent of the nation in fourth grade reading in 1992.

4. Related discussions and suits have been leveled at the federal government, claiming that NCLB is an unfunded mandate and that the federal government should fully fund the schools to meet the requirements of NCLB. On April 20, 2005, the National Education Association (NEA) filed suit against the U.S. Department of Education (*Pontiac v. Spellings*) to obtain the greater funding for schools that the NEA thought necessary to meet accountability standards. See Munich and Testani (2005) and Peyser and Costrell (2004).

Simply put, solutions require more fundamental changes. They will not come with doing the same thing over and over again.

The Nature of the Lawsuits

The adequacy lawsuits stem from interpretations of state constitutions and from questions about whether existing funding is consistent with the educational requirements specified in the constitution. As described below, state constitutions generally call for the broad and nondiscriminatory provision of education to children but do so with vague language that allows a range of interpretations. When deficits in knowledge persist and when the legislature does not seem to be effectively improving the state of education, it is an open invitation for the courts to enter. They are encouraged to do so by self-interested parties, heavily weighted toward current school personnel and toward other advocates who would like to see state spending slanted more toward schools.

Nonetheless, the separation of powers and responsibilities across the branches of government places limits on how far the courts can go in setting policies aimed at improving student achievement. The textbook on American government emphasizes the separation of powers and distinct roles for the executive, legislative, and judicial branches. The political branches (executive and legislative) develop regulations and programs to accomplish their mandates under the constitution, raise funds that are needed to support them, and administer their operation. The judiciary is charged with assessing whether the mandates of the state constitution are being met along with interpreting whether laws are constitutional. Of course, the finance lawsuits highlight the possibility for conflict, a conflict that has become apparent as courts appear to be increasingly willing to direct legislatures on the appropriate details of school funding.

A clear statement of the basic issues comes from the Texas Supreme Court, which included the following caution in its 2005 decision:

> [W]e must decide only whether public education is achieving the general diffusion of knowledge the Constitution requires. Whether public education is achieving all it should—that is, whether public education is a sufficient and fitting preparation of Texas children for the future—involves political and policy considerations properly directed to the Legislature. (*Neeley v. West Orange-Cove*)

Of course there can be disagreement over where to draw the line about what is constitutionally required—and the courts in different states have taken what appear to be very different views on this. There is, for example, no way that anybody could believe that the line drawn in Texas (*Neeley v. West Orange-Cove*) was comparable to that drawn in New York (*CFE v. New York*). And indeed the analysis that follows (chapters 1 and 2) gives insight into both the politics of court decisions and their legal basis.

Without drawing our own line—which would be considerably different from the *CFE* line or the Wyoming line (*Campbell v. Wyoming*)—it is possible to assess some of the implications of the court's entry into these decisions. An important element, often ignored in the legal proceedings, is the difficulty of defining "adequate" in an operational way that can be a court enforceable standard. Specifically, *all* available evidence indicates that translating an adequacy standard into a funding standard seriously distorts reality to the point where actual harm is possible.

At one level, it seems difficult to oppose the lawsuits. After all, who favors inequitable education? Or, perhaps worse, who favors inadequate education? In point of fact, it is possible to support the goal of a solid education while believing that the court cases and judicial decisions are not leading to good policy. The first concern is about the ability of the courts to make effective policy. The second is whether there is any evidence to support the effectiveness of the courts in making judgments.

There is no denying that serious educational problems exist and that our society would be better off if it could improve our schools. Similarly, because of the persistence of the problems, there is no denying that the political branches, for all their rhetoric, have not succeeded in solving our educational shortcomings after decades of effort. If there is one thing that comes through in this, it is that repeating the past approaches is unlikely to succeed.

Court Capacity

Dissatisfaction with our schools is not a new phenomenon. When the Soviet Union placed the first astronaut into space, a central concern was whether our schools were effective and, specifically, whether the math and science instruction was sufficiently good. The ensuing debate led to a variety of changes in schools, but identifying progress in our schools was more difficult. Even early on, if anything, there was worry about the decline of the schools (Congressional Budget Office 1986). After a quarter century of debate and action, an official government commission concluded in *A Nation at Risk* (National Commission on Excellence in Education 1983) that the nation's schools had to make fundamental changes if we were to continue to compete internationally.

Having a federal commission provide an unqualified statement of problems solidified the permanent position of school quality issues on the national policy agenda. It also led to license for the schools to pursue even grander versions of the policies they thought would work, including substantial increases in the resource investments in our schools (Peterson 2003).

The one thing that has become readily apparent over this long period of concern about schools is that student achievement is difficult to move. By most measures, both within the United States and internationally, the performance of U.S. students has remained stubbornly flat in the face of resource and policy adjustments by the public schools (Peterson 2003).

This pattern of achievement has made it clear that education is a very complicated undertaking. Simple conclusions such as "lack of resources is the fundamental factor driving low achievement" have been contradicted by the evidence: dramatic increases in resources have not led to improvement in the performance of our students. Even when policies are driven by evidence of each program's efficaciousness, the inability to implement them broadly and effectively has stymied progress.

Perhaps no other policy area sees the clash between commonsensical arguments and reality that education does. The conventional wisdom in a wide range of policy domains has not held up well against the evidence (Moe 2001).

This short historical overview brings us back to the issue of whether the courts can effectively use their powers to improve student achievement. For the most part, the courts have focused on resource issues when addressing any identified shortcomings of the schools. Specifically, if a state's financing of schools is found to be unconstitutional by reason of not providing for adequate outcomes, courts tend to order more resources. At times the ruling is general, as with the court finding that New York City schools should receive an additional $5.63 billion a year in operating funds. At times it is more specific such as the South Carolina judge's opinion that the state should provide universal preschool education.

But, again, history suggests that pursuing these simple approaches—as we have for at least four decades—is unlikely to bring about significant change in student outcomes. If the shortfalls in student achievement are the *raison d'être* for the resulting court orders, the remedies are unlikely to solve the problem. Nothing suggests that more of the same will suddenly become effective.

The complexity of education has two relevant components. First, simple answers just do not exist. If there were some simple, easy-to-institute programs or policies that would lead to the dramatic improvements in performance that are often sought, it is reasonable to believe that policy would be moving toward them without the intervention of the courts. None, however, are apparent. Second, in the face of uncertainty, it is important to experiment with different programs and policies and to evaluate which work in different circumstances. In other words, it is necessary to invest in knowledge about new approaches.

This complexity is difficult for the courts to deal with. The courts do not have expertise in the details of schooling. Nor do they have any easy way to launch and monitor an ongoing set of policy changes and experiments.

The complexity contributes to the concentration of the courts on the resources available for schools. The resources are readily identified. It is also possible to monitor and enforce any court orders.

If a court acknowledges the uncertainty about the underlying relationship between resources and achievement, it has difficulty crafting a remedy to ensure that the schools meet its interpretation of a constitutionally adequate level of student achievement. Similarly, while the logic of shortfalls in performance points to the court's focus on student achievement, a remedy written just in terms of outcomes cannot be easily enforced. After all, unless the courts want to believe that the schools are malicious—withholding the underlying knowledge of how to improve schools—there is no obvious way to order the schools to improve student performance. To enforce such an order, the court would have to know that the schools are not using the best approaches, as opposed to simply being confused about the best approach.

A policy of experimentation, on the other hand, takes the court into a specialized but highly uncertain area of program design and evaluation. These are also not things the court can easily deal with.

Courts are unlikely to step out of the arena of education. Education is after all a primary activity of the states. But the courts need humility, recognizing that their instant analysis in the course of a lawsuit is unlikely to find an approach that has eluded governors and legislatures in their fevered attempts to improve the schools. Even when the courts develop more expertise through years and decades of court supervision of school funding, there is, as we show below, little evidence that they are better positioned to improve the schools. Along with humility, the courts might develop more suspicion about the "answers" that are readily provided by self-interested parties in the schools. A natural conclusion is that court involvement should concentrate on the performance of the schools while stopping short of telling the political branches how they should go about meeting requirements (including the amount of resources that must "constitutionally" be devoted to schools).

The Outcomes of Court Actions

The adequacy court cases are a fairly new development, but they follow a line of equity cases that have been pursued over a longer time period. In fact, it is frequently difficult to distinguish between adequacy and equity cases because the arguments tend to merge together over time. The New Jersey funding case (*Abbott v. Burke*), for example, began in the 1970s with a pure funding equity focus but, as it has remained in the courts for decades, has taken on the character of an adequacy case. In its latest incarnation in the courts, a set of designated districts has received enormous spending, largely motivated by notions of poor student outcomes.

Yet after decades of court cases on school funding, little effort has been made to assess the effect of court involvement on student outcomes. The analyses that do investigate the outcomes of court actions in specific states find little support for the argument that the courts have had a positive effect on achievement (Downes 1992; Flanagan and Murray 2004; Downes 2004; Cullen and Loeb 2004; Duncombe and Johnston 2004). Further, Hanushek and Somers (2001) find that narrowing the distribution of spending across schools, in part motivated by court actions, has not led to a decrease in the variation of labor market outcomes for the students.

The direct evidence on outcomes and adequacy later in this volume (chapters 4 and 7) similarly gives no indication that providing "adequate" resources leads to improvement in student outcomes. This includes the results of funding changes in New Jersey, the current record setting case with three decades of court involvement.

Districts having adequate funding according to the methods presented to the courts might even do worse than districts with inadequate funding. Such findings of course tell us much more about the complexities of education and the shortcomings of some common research approaches than about what sensible school policies might be.

The simplest summary is that *no* currently available evidence shows that past judicial actions about school finance—

either related to equity or to adequacy—have had a beneficial effect on student performance.

The reason is now unfortunately quite obvious. Measures of school resources do not provide guidance either about the current quality of schools or about the potential for improving matters. The standards and accountability movement is the result of decades of confusion and disappointment about how resources translate into student outcomes. Shortcomings in student achievement should not be used as a justification for making the same mistakes again.

What Follows

This book provides relevant data for the consideration of adequacy court cases. The design is to bring together a series of important "data points" that highlight issues in assessing the adequacy of school finance. The analysis in these chapters forms the foundation for the conclusions and recommendations of the Koret Task Force on K–12 Education that conclude the book.

Many people look upon the courts as apolitical, entering into disputes in order to adjudicate conflicts under the law. Sol Stern's history of the New York City legal battles (chapter 1) dispels this view. The Campaign for Fiscal Equity understood the politics of the courts and exploited them at every opportunity. And the record makes clear that the New York City case is the result of a well-orchestrated political campaign in which the plaintiffs mobilized the courts and public opinion to achieve their goal—increasing the funding of city schools.

The plaintiffs in adequacy suits understand the importance of politics in designing and executing their cases. The commonly held view of the courts as being above politics gives the plaintiffs the moral high ground, which in turn allows them to develop public opinion in ways that not only influence the courts but also the legislatures that frequently must deal with court judgments. Indeed, the hope of the plaintiffs is often that they get the defense to argue the case as a purely constitutional matter and not as the political contest that it is.

The legal issues surrounding the cases are profound. Alfred Lindseth (chapter 2) analyzes how the adequacy cases represent not only a strained issue of constitutional jurisprudence but also a break with the rules of evidence. On constitutional issues, the disjuncture between the vague provisions of state constitutions and the elevated court judgments on outcome standards is clear. A review of a variety of cases shows little relation between constitutional provisions and court rulings. It is difficult, for example, to ignore the Wyoming court's willingness to interpret a requirement for an "efficient" system as a requirement for the school system to be "visionary and unsurpassed."

Nonetheless, the larger issue is how these court cases blaze new territory in terms of consideration of causation. The plaintiffs seldom, if ever, address whether differences in achievement are caused by resource shortfalls. Yet the courts are comfortable with making a determination that places all responsibility for performance on the schools and their funding.

The educational disadvantages often faced by minority students and by students from low-income families are well known and thoroughly documented. But as Herbert Walberg (chapter 3) shows, low achievement is not inevitable for disadvantaged students. Nor is it the case that school resources dominate the ability of disadvantaged students to climb above expectations. Substantial numbers of schools demonstrate that it is possible to "beat the odds." A simple demonstration of this in South Carolina contributed to a recent lower-court ruling that further resources for the public schools were not a constitutional requirement for an adequate education.

The schools that do well tend to stay on top over time. It is not simply a statistical artifact that some schools for disadvantaged students do well. Studies of the schools that do well with disadvantaged students show that they have common programs and that this is not random. Their common characteristics are ones of structure and do not just relate to the provision of extra resources.

History also provides substantial evidence about "pure resource solutions." Williamson Evers and Paul Clopton (chapter 4) trace the results of a selection of notable districts where the districts were given carte blanche to dream. Kansas City has received justified notoriety for the lack of outcomes after a federal judge gave them license to spend whatever was needed of state money to make the district attractive. Less known are the tales of Sausalito, California; Cambridge, Massachusetts; the District of Columbia; and New Jersey's Abbott Districts. Each has shown that funding per se has been tried in different locations and has not achieved its purpose.

When we are confronted with such examples, it is natural to say "well, of course we would not do anything as stupid as that." Yet in schools that have few incentives for performance and even have incentives that drive them in the opposite direction, it is not enough just to call for better spending. After all, these schools do not have experience with better spending. (Nor do courts show an ability to monitor spending to ensure achievement results.)

The comparisons of performance between public and private schools have been controversial, but as Paul Peterson discusses (chapter 5), the cost advantages of private schools are much clearer. Nearly all studies of performance show that private schools produce achievement at least as high as that of public schools, and some suggest a substantial advantage for private schools. But they do this at lower cost—perhaps 40 percent lower on average compared with public schools. A number of things contribute to these lower costs. Teacher salaries are lower, schools are smaller, and administration is simpler. However, Peterson also suggests that private schools involve students more actively in the educational process—what he calls co-production. Co-production, getting the other participants in education to work in conjunction with the schools, is not something that costs extra.

Private schools that must attract students have a direct incentive to keep costs low. This leads them to find ways to produce outcomes efficiently. And this leads them to mobilize the resources at their disposal, including the students. Private schools do not have any special advantage over public schools other than the incentive to produce achievement efficiently.

Marguerite Roza and Paul Hill (chapter 6) ask a deceptively simple question: does funding within districts follow the pattern they argue for in the lawsuits? Specifically, a primary element of adequacy cases is the discussion of increased resource requirements for teaching disadvantaged students. Mounting special compensatory programs very likely requires extra funds, but it would be nice to confirm that districts allocate the funds they have in a compensatory way—just as they say is required. Unfortunately, when resources are traced to individual schools, it becomes clear that large disparities in funding exist within districts *and* that these disparities do not follow the identified needs.

If districts do not spend the funds they have in the way they indicate is needed, how should we interpret it? There seem to be two logical answers. Either they do not actually track funds and know where they go, or they make explicit anticompensatory allocations, even though they argue compensatory spending patterns are necessary. There is little reason to believe that any added funds for adequacy would be spent more in line with the arguments about needs if the existing—and scarcer—funds are not.

The analysis by Eric Hanushek (chapter 7) considers the available methods of the costing out studies, that is, studies that purport to calculate how much an adequate education would cost. On careful analysis, the studies turn out to be more politics than science. The studies, frequently done by consultants who are commissioned to do them by self-interested parties, always presume that simply doing more of the current practice (with the commensurate additions to resources) will yield the desired student outcomes—but they never provide a convincing analysis to support that claim. In fact, while these are advertised as "cost" studies, none effectively deals with any inefficiencies that might currently exist in a state's schools. Indeed, some of the studies explicitly choose the most expensive way of running a program rather than the more natural, least expensive way. In application, the biased choices of the consultants systematically inflate the resources needed to accomplish their chosen objective, while completely ignoring any possible change in incentives or operations of schools.

The cost studies are incapable of providing the guidance that is sought, because they do not provide an objective and reliable answer of the cost of meeting educational standards. It is not just a matter of errors in the commission of the studies but instead a matter of inability to provide a scientific answer to the underlying adequacy question. Nevertheless, they do serve the purposes of the interested parties that tend to contract to have the studies done, because courts have shown a willingness to write their specific findings into their orders.

One of the fundamental features of schools, as highlighted by E. D. Hirsch (chapter 8), is the significance of the time constraint on schools. Most of the court discussion of adequacy cases concentrates on resources, as if resource constraints were the most basic issue thwarting higher achievement. Yet time and its use are much more fundamental. There is little demonstration that effective use of school time costs more than ineffective use. Indeed scientific study has made it clear that the curriculum that is offered in a school has a significant effect on student learning. Yet the best curricula do not necessarily cost more than less effective ones.

The questions of curricula and use of time interact importantly with student background. Disadvantaged students, whose low achievement is frequently used to motivate the legal actions, are particularly sensitive to the character of the curriculum and specifically to the provision of a broad knowledge base, because they frequently come to school with less educational help from the family. Moreover, disadvantaged students are more prone to move from school to school, making a common curriculum across schools very important so that continuity of education can be maintained in the face of mobility. These are not things that are commonly found in the schools serving disadvantaged students. Nor are they things that cost added money.

Koret Task Force Conclusions

The Koret Task Force on K–12 Education has assessed the current state of both court and legislative actions to bring America's students up to twenty-first century standards. The simple summary is that the courts have not pushed schools toward these outcomes, and are unlikely to do so in the future. None of this says that governors and legislatures are generally moving things in desirable directions. The outcomes of their small and cautious steps, even if successful, are not going to match our aspirations.

Attaining the outcomes that we want, and need, as a nation will take more fundamental changes than simply throwing more resources at the problem. We have already tried that solution.

We have added substantial resources—a tripling in cost-adjusted per-student spending since 1960—without getting measurable improvement in student outcomes. In fact, this past record makes it clear why we cannot find a scientific solution to what an adequate education costs.

The changes that are likely to move us toward having a world class schooling system are conceptually straightforward even if difficult to institute.

First, *we need a strong accountability system* that identifies and rewards good performance in our public schools. Until recently, many parents and policymakers have not been able to determine the quality of their schools, making it impossible to assess policy and actions.

Second, *incentives have to be aligned with performance.* If we do not reward success and deal strongly with failure, we should not be surprised that performance does not change when we just add resources while staying with our current systems. There are many ways to change incentives for teachers and schools, some of which are included in No Child Left Behind and in individual state accountability systems. Nonetheless, an important arrow in the reform quiver is the use of wider parental choice of schools. It seems crucial to mobilize consumer demand to influence change in the schools. Importantly, while normal political forces can thwart the accountability regimes of states by minimizing their effects, the current self-interested actors cannot stand up to a lack of clients. These actors must address performance issues if parents have a choice and can leave a low-performing school.

Third, *the operations and activities of schools must be transparent.* Everybody who is interested in schools and their performance must be able to understand what their schools are doing both in relation to outcomes and to programs and policies. It is impossible for policymakers or parents to control their schools constructively without being able to know what the schools are doing and why. Two separate components are relevant: resource transparency and programmatic transparency. Nobody outside the schools today knows where resources come from, how much is spent at individual schools, where teachers come from, or how teachers are allocated to schools. Informed decision making requires this information. Neither is it known what programs are being used and why. While calls for using scientifically proven programs are now common, many schools continue to use scientifically discredited curricula.

Improvement is a necessity. If our country is to maintain and improve its economic performance and the well-being of society, the unacceptable and unchanging pattern of student achievement must be altered. This change will, by historical experience, be difficult. But we know with some certainty that more of the same will not work.

References

Congressional Budget Office. 1986. *Trends in educational achievement.* Washington, D.C.: Congressional Budget Office.

Cullen, Julie B., and Susanna Loeb. 2004. "School finance reform in Michigan: Evaluating Proposal A." In *Helping children left behind: State aid and the pursuit of educational equity*, ed. John Yinger, 215–249, 251–281. Cambridge, MA: MIT Press.

Downes, Thomas A. 1992. "Evaluating the impact of school finance reform on the provision of public education: The California case." *National Tax Journal* 45, no.4 (December): 405–419.

———. 2004. "School finance reform and school quality: Lessons from Vermont." In *Helping children left behind: State aid and the pursuit of educational equity*, ed. John Yinger, 284–313. Cambridge, MA: MIT Press.

Duncombe, William, and Jocelyn M. Johnston. 2004. "The impacts of school finance reform in Kansas: Equity is in the eye of the beholder." In *Helping children left behind: State aid and the pur-*

suit of educational equity, ed. John Yinger, 148–193. Cambridge, MA: MIT Press.

Flanagan, Ann E., and Sheila E. Murray. 2004. "A decade of reform: The impact of school reform in Kentucky." In *Helping children left behind: State aid and the pursuit of educational equity*, ed. John Yinger, 195–214. Cambridge, MA: MIT Press.

Hanushek, Eric A., and Julie A. Somers. 2001. "Schooling, inequality, and the impact of government." In *The causes and consequences of increasing inequality*, ed. Finis Welch, 169–199. Chicago: University of Chicago Press.

Moe, Terry M., ed. 2001. *A primer on America's schools*. Stanford, CA: Hoover Institution Press.

Munich, John R., and Rocco E. Testani. 2005. "NEA sues over NCLB: The bucks are big, but the case is weak." *Education Next* 5, no.4 (Fall): 10.

Murray, Sheila E., William N. Evans, and Robert M. Schwab. 1998. "Education-finance reform and the distribution of education resources." *American Economic Review* 88, no.4 (September): 789–812.

National Commission on Excellence in Education. 1983. *A nation at risk: The imperative for educational reform*. Washington, D.C.: U.S. Government Printing Office.

Peterson, Paul E., ed. 2003. *Our schools and our future: Are we still at risk?* Stanford, CA: Hoover Press.

Peyser, James, and Robert M. Costrell. 2004. "Exploring the costs of accountability." *Education Next* 4, no. 2 (Spring): 23–29.

1

Campaign for Fiscal Equity v. New York: The March of Folly

Sol Stern

IN MAY 1993 a class action lawsuit was filed in state court in Manhattan alleging that Governor Mario Cuomo and the state legislature were denying "thousands of public school students in the City of New York their constitutional rights to equal educational opportunities, and their right to an education that meets minimum statewide educational standards." In their complaint the lawyers for the plaintiffs (two dozen New York City public school children and their parents) didn't explain *why* the city wasn't able to offer a minimally acceptable education to its children, other than claiming that the state's level of funding for city schools was both "inequitable" and "inadequate."

Thirteen years and more than $50 million in court costs and lawyers' fees later, *Campaign for Fiscal Equity (CFE) v. New York* is still being vigorously litigated. In February 2005 the trial judge who presided over the case from day one ordered the state to provide the city with an additional $5.6 billion in annual operating costs above New York City's $15.7 billion education budget. As expected, the state appealed the judge's decision and—for the third time—the case is now winding its way slowly up through the state's appellate system. Even if the court of appeals (the state's high court) upholds the trial court's ruling, it's not at all clear that New York City schoolchildren will ever see any extra money because of the judicial proceedings. The state faces combined budget deficits of more than $6 billion over the next few years, and some knowledgeable observers in Albany have suggested there could be a constitutional crisis if the courts try to force the legislature to appropriate money it does not have. Moreover, elected officials know that in the thirteen years since the *CFE* case was filed, per-pupil education spending in New York City's public schools has doubled as a result of the normal give and take of the legislative and political process (State Education Department 1993, 2004). They also must realize that this huge spending binge had very little effect on student learning.

Unfortunately, that stubborn fact hardly registered throughout a judicial proceeding whose underlying premise was that increased spending leads to better academic outcomes for children. Like so many of the other adequacy cases around the country, *CFE v. New York* is based on the fantastical notion (as chapter 7 of this volume demonstrates) that a court, or indeed any education expert, can determine the exact level of school spending that will magically produce an "adequate" education for all our children. The pursuit of this fantasy over thirteen years has produced a perversion of the judicial process, featuring junk science in the courtroom. Instead of producing better schools, the *CFE* case has only managed to divert public attention away from the serious task of school reform and stands as a paradigmatic example of what is wrong with the nation's education adequacy movement.

Birth of a Movement

Sometime during the 1991–1992 school year, Robert Jackson became mad as hell and finally decided—just like Howard Beale, the character played by Peter Finch in the movie "Network"— that he wasn't going to take it any more. The African American trade union official was then the elected president of Community School Board 6 in the Washington Heights section of Manhattan. All three of his daughters attended schools in the predominantly minority district, which were among the most overcrowded and rundown in the city. "The situation was disgraceful; the schools were falling apart," Jackson recalls. Then, as if to rub salt in the wound, the district had to absorb budget cuts imposed in the middle of the school year by the supposedly "child friendly" administration of David Dinkins, the city's first black mayor. As a result, Jackson's board had to lay off badly needed guidance counselors and school aides.

Jackson came to the painful conclusion that despite many years of devoted community service and parent activism he hadn't been able to effectively use the political process to alleviate the awful conditions in his district's schools. That's when it occurred to him that the only way to beat the system was to sue it. Jackson was aware of some of the cases around the country in which activist state or federal courts ordered legislators and other elected officials to spend more money on the schools with the purpose of helping disadvantaged children. And as luck would have it (or perhaps it was destiny) the attorney who won one of the biggest of those lawsuits happened to be serving as the part-time lawyer for the District 6 school board. He was a forty-seven-year-old Yale Law School graduate and self-described "child of the 60s" named Michael Rebell.

In the 1979 case known as *Jose P. v. Ambach*, Rebell charged in federal court that the New York City Board of Education was failing to provide disabled children with equal access to all education services. The court agreed and ordered the city to create a very expensive, rules-driven special education system for those children. Rebell and several other plaintiffs' lawyers were assigned to oversee day-to-day compliance with the consent decree accepted by the city.

Jose P. illustrated both the dangers of judicial activism and the law of unintended consequences. Under the supervision of Rebell and the other lawyers, special education morphed from what had been intended as a compassionate plan for educating the small number of truly disabled children into a dysfunctional bureaucracy responsible for the education of over 150,000 students. Thousands of children with classroom behavior problems were dumped into special education classes. To make matters worse, under this flawed process 15 percent of the total student population were consuming over 25 percent of the city's total education budget. One way to understand what the *Jose P.* consent decree wrought is that the effective lawyering Michael Rebell delivered for his special education clients meant that money was being drained away from all the mainstream students in Community District 6 where Rebell now served as the school board's lawyer.

But Robert Jackson wasn't interested in the contradictions of the twelve-year-old *Jose P.* case. The only issue on his mind at that moment was that the children in Washington Heights were, in his words, "getting screwed." Moreover, neither the state legislature nor the "progressive" administrations of Governor Mario Cuomo or Mayor David Dinkins seemed capable of mustering the political will to tackle the problem. Out of desperation, Jackson went to his board's talented lawyer and asked him if there wasn't some way to get the fiscal plight of District 6's schools into the courts. Rebell certainly agreed with Jackson's objective. Nevertheless, he warned that "this is a long shot" (Rebell 2004).

Rebell was referring to the legal precedent established in the case of *Levittown Union Free School District v. Nyquist,* a lawsuit brought in the late 1970s by a coalition of revenue-poor school districts on Long Island, and subsequently joined by New York City and four other big city school districts. The plaintiffs claimed that there were "great and disabling" disparities in education funding among school districts in violation of the state constitution. New York's court of appeals eventually ruled in 1982 that the constitution could not be interpreted as requiring equal education funding. After all, the constitution's education article consisted entirely of the following sentence: "The legislature shall provide for the maintenance and support of a system of free common schools, wherein all the children of this state may be educated." In a rare display of restraint that seems almost quaint by today's standards, the state's highest court declared that while reducing or ending funding disparities in education might be a grand idea, it was up to the legislature, not the judicial branch, to address the issue.

This led Rebell to calculate (as any competent lawyer would have) that the courts were unlikely to entertain a lawsuit based on a "fiscal equity" standard. But Jackson continued to badger Rebell, insisting that the children of Washington Heights couldn't wait. "Fiscal equity" or not, wasn't the condition of the district's schools a moral outrage that called out for a legal remedy? Faced with Jackson's determination, Rebell at least agreed to look more closely at the case law.

Rebell quickly realized that while the court of appeals had rejected an unequal funding claim in *Levittown*, it nevertheless hinted that it might consider one based on what it called "gross and glaring *inadequacies*" (italics added). It was a narrow window of opportunity for a creative litigator. Perhaps a case could actually be made that the resources available to District 6's schools were "inadequate" to provide even the most minimally acceptable level of education, therefore violating the intent of the constitution's education article.

Thus the school year that began in extreme frustration for Robert Jackson ended with a ray of hope. He now had a lawyer experienced in education litigation willing to take the plight of the district's schools into the courts. Rebell and Jackson then partnered in founding a new activist organization to help raise the substantial amounts of money needed for the legal battles to come and to mobilize public support. The partners understood that this would be a political case, indeed a race case, and would be won as much by the force of public opinion and emotion as by the strength of the arguments or evidence offered in the courtroom. Despite knowing that the courts were not going to consider a claim based on "equity," they nevertheless named their group the Campaign for Fiscal Equity (CFE). It was a brilliant stroke. "Campaign for Fiscal Adequacy" might have been more accurate, but too neutral sounding to stir up public opinion. On the other hand, who amongst the public would remain unmoved by the cause of "fiscal equity," that is, equal opportunity for disadvantaged minority schoolchildren?

By the time Rebell and Jackson began planning their lawsuit, a large swath of New York City's elite opinion makers, including the political and education establishment and the media, already believed that the city's schoolchildren were the victims of an unfair education funding system. There was some truth in that perception. For the 1991–1992 school year, New York City spent an average of $7,495 per student, compared with the statewide average of $8,241. The average for the state's four other large city districts (Rochester, Syracuse, Buffalo, and Yonkers) was $8,493, while the suburban districts spent an average of $9,115 per pupil (State Education Department 1993, 41). Moreover,

while the city had 37 percent of the state's students it was receiving only 35 percent of the education aid dollars. Almost
every observer agreed that the state's multilayered formulas for
deciding the amount of aid given to each district were irrational
and incomprehensible.

But while the spending gap was real enough, it soon became
wildly exaggerated in the public imagination. To some degree
this was due to the publication in 1991 of Jonathan Kozol's run-
away bestseller, *Savage Inequalities*, one of the last half century's most influential education books (although for all the
wrong reasons). Kozol managed to convince millions of Americans that the spending disparities between inner city minority
schools and middle class white schools were caused by institutional racism and accounted for the academic achievement gap
between black and white children. Thus the key to improving
the education of minority children seemed simple and obvious—
pour lots more money into urban schools. *Savage Inequalities*
was heralded by *Publishers Weekly* as a major political event.
For the first time in that venerable publication's 129 years, ad-
vertising pages were dropped to run excerpts from the book. The
publisher was also moved to write a front page open letter to
President George H. W. Bush, arguing that "we will have to
spend money, and a lot of it, to bring genuine equality to our
schools."

In one chapter Kozol writes movingly about New York City's
underfunded schools. But instead of comparing the per-pupil
spending figures for the city with the average for suburban districts, or for other big city districts, and therefore demonstrating
gaps in the range of 7 percent to 20 percent—as in the above
official figures—Kozol only focused on the disparities between
spending in New York City and gilded suburbs like Great Neck
and Rye, which ranked among the richest school districts in the
country. That allowed him to create a heartbreaking comparison

between a typical poor black New York City child, allegedly worth only six thousand dollars for his education, and the white suburban child worth sixteen thousand dollars or more, and leading to what was indeed a "savage" spending gap.

In both *Savage Inequalities* and its 1995 successor, *Amazing Grace*, Kozol described the once beautiful and successful Morris High School in the Bronx as "one of the most beleaguered, segregated and decrepit secondary schools in the United States. Barrels were filling up with rain in several rooms. . . . Green fungus molds were growing in the corners" of some rooms, and the toilets were unusable. Kozol wrote that it would take at least $50 million to restore Morris's decaying physical plant and suggested that the white political establishment would never spend that much money on a ghetto school. The city actually did spend more than $50 million to restore Morris High School after the publication of *Savage Inequalities*, though Kozol had not a word to say about it when discussing Morris in the second book. Of course the newly gleaming building had no perceptible effect on the academic performance of the students.

Kozol's books were chock full of such inaccuracies and distortions, yet their spectacular commercial success reflected the extent to which the author had touched a public nerve. Many influential New Yorkers came to believe that malign neglect, if not outright racism, must be at the root of the problems in their own city's schools. Naturally, the same people also concluded that the solution meant spending more money. And when Michael Rebell filed a lawsuit demanding that the state spend a lot more money for the schools, such people were also inclined to believe, even before hearing any evidence in the courtroom, that the case of *CFE v. New York* was part of the country's historic civil rights struggle and in the same tradition as *Brown v. Board of Education*.

In Judge DeGrasse's Courtroom

Michael Rebell filed his lawsuit against the state in June 1993, in Supreme Court, New York County ("supreme court" is actually the designation for New York's district trial courts, while the highest court of review is called the court of appeals). The thirty-page complaint alleged that New York City public school students were denied "their constitutional rights to equal education opportunities, and their right to an education that meets minimum statewide educational standards." Rebell acknowledged that the court of appeals had already denied a similar challenge to the state's education funding system in *Levittown v. Nyquist*, but then went on to argue that the high court had "specifically left open the possibility of reconsidering that holding if it could be shown in a future case—as it will he here—that the state's financing scheme had reached the point of 'gross and glaring inadequacy,' and that students are being denied an education which meets minimum statewide standards."

Listed plaintiffs were the Campaign for Fiscal Equity Inc.; fourteen out of the city's thirty-two community school boards; Robert Jackson and his three daughters; and another twenty public school children and their parents. The defendants included the state of New York; Governor Mario Cuomo; Commissioner of Education Thomas Sobol; the state comptroller; the state's commissioner of taxation and finance; and the majority and minority leaders of both houses of the legislature. The complaint specified four "causes of action." Rebell alleged, first, that the defendants were violating the education act of the state constitution in failing to provide the city's schools with adequate funds to achieve minimal education standards; second, that the state was denying the plaintiffs equal protection rights under the Fourteenth Amendment to the United States Constitution; third, that the state was violating the plaintiffs' rights under the antidiscrimination clause of the New York Constitution; and fourth, that the state was violating Title VI of the Civil Rights Act of 1964 prohibiting racial discrimination in education.

As lawyers usually do in class actions, Rebell had fired off a scattershot of allegations and causes of action, hoping that after the state's lawyers inevitably moved to dismiss the complaint and challenged the standing to sue of the various plaintiffs, and after the lower court's rulings on those motions were appealed all the way up to the court of appeals, there would be at least one solid cause of action and some plaintiffs left standing.

It was a long gauntlet for CFE to run just to get to a hearing of the facts in a trial court. Still, the odds were already somewhat better than a "long shot" (as Rebell had once described the lawsuit's prospects to Robert Jackson). Moreover, reinforcements were arriving almost every day to support the lawsuit, including some of the city's leading educational foundations and advocacy groups. And of course, rising public concern about the alleged "savage inequalities" of urban schooling couldn't hurt.

The odds were also improving for CFE because of the political realities of the venue in which the case was filed. Not to put too fine a point on it, but Supreme Court, New York County, is in many ways a wholly owned subsidiary of the Manhattan Democratic Party. Each judge in the courthouse is at least vetted, and often selected, by the party's county leader.

Even though the position of judge is ostensibly an elected position, current election law provides no open party primary that a prospective candidate can enter. Instead candidates are picked at county judicial conventions dominated by the party leadership. Those selected are then placed on the ballot as the party's candidate for the office of judge. An editorial in the *New York Daily News* (September 15, 2005) characterized this arrangement as follows: "This thoroughly rotten and discredited process, where handpicked delegates act like trained seals for the party bosses, supporting their candidates of choice, is unique in the nation. It excludes any participation by voters and lets pols alone choose who will populate the bench of New York's most important trial court."

In Manhattan, a one-party town, the Democratic judicial candidates never have to face a Republican opponent. Thus there is no political diversity among the supreme court justices. While judicial bias is not necessarily an issue in most criminal and commercial cases, the reality is that no one gets on the bench who would be likely to question the standard Democratic Party approach to public policy issues, including education.

When Michael Rebell's complaint was filed with the court clerk, it was randomly assigned to the courtroom of Judge Leland DeGrasse, another fortuitous moment for CFE. DeGrasse and his wife, Carol Huff, also a judge, were both elected to the New York Supreme Court in 1988, after previously serving on the civil court. They were two of three black candidates for supreme court openings handpicked that year by county Democratic boss Herman (Denny) Farrell, who rammed his choices through the party judicial convention. (The candidates then ran unopposed in the general election.) Farrell made no bones about it: he told reporters he had chosen the three judges to maintain the existing "racial balance" on the court. Thus, in a highly charged case with racial overtones, the presiding judge owed his appointment to the local Democratic Party boss who had a strong interest in more state aid dollars coming to the city.

In Judge DeGrasse's courtroom the state, as expected, moved to dismiss the entirety of Rebell's complaint, asserting that the plaintiffs had failed to state a cause of action under existing case law. The state also challenged the standing of the fourteen local school districts to sue the state. Judge DeGrasse agreed with the state in part, ruling that the school districts had no standing and throwing out the claims under the state's antidiscrimination article and, partly, under federal Title VI. However, CFE got the big breakthrough it was looking for. The judge let stand the heart of the complaint, namely that the state was violating the education article of New York's constitution by not providing city schoolchildren with "adequate" funds to provide a minimally acceptable education.

The appellate division, the next rung on the appeals ladder, thought otherwise. That court's majority said this case was déjà vu all over again, that none of the legal issues had really changed since the court of appeals ruled in the *Levittown* case that the constitution did not prohibit disparities in education funding. The appellate division judges couldn't see how CFE was raising claims substantively different from those made by the Levittown plaintiffs more than ten years earlier. That is, despite all the talk about "adequacy," the complaint was really still basically about equality. (And equality was the rallying cry CFE was mobilizing around outside of the courtroom.) Thus the court overruled Judge DeGrasse and granted the state's motion to dismiss all of CFE plaintiffs' claims.

As expected, that decision was then appealed by CFE to the court of appeals. On June 13, 1995, the high court reversed the appellate division. The majority agreed with CFE that the complaint about city schools being underfunded in this case was substantially different from the one put forward by the school board plaintiffs in *Levittown*. The court also reaffirmed what it had only hinted at in *Levittown*—that the education article *did* establish a constitutional requirement that children receive adequate resources for what the court now was calling a "sound basic education." Thus the plaintiffs' claims along those lines had to be put to a factual test in a trial court. The high court never did get around to enumerating what the academic contents of a "sound basic education" might be, except to offer the trial court a vague test to consider. It was whether students were able to obtain the skills in reading and other subjects needed to "vote in elections" and "serve as jurors." Michael Rebell later characterized the high court's vagaries on the issue of what constitutes a constitutionally adequate education as "putting out a first draft of its constitutional definition, soliciting a reaction and input from the judge, the lawyers and the expert witnesses at trial" (Rebell 2004).

Thus, after an expensive two-year legal journey through the appeals process, *CFE v. New York* came back to Judge De-Grasse's courtroom to work on the "second draft" (which would take six more years to complete). By this time, however, the political complexion of the case had also changed radically. In 1994 Mario Cuomo was defeated for reelection by George Pataki, a sometimes moderate, sometimes conservative, upstate Republican. There's no way of knowing how the *CFE* lawsuit might have developed if Governor Cuomo had still been the main defendant. The fact that the broad coalition of support developing around CFE also happened to be part of Cuomo's liberal political constituency might have led the governor to look to settle the case, rather than slug it out for years in the courts. But the new lead defendant in the case was driven by exactly the reverse political considerations. Governor Pataki's strongest supporters were upstate Republicans, already chafing at paying the highest state taxes in the country. They certainly expected the governor to play hardball against what they saw as an attempt to use the courts to make an end run around the political process and force them to pay even higher taxes—all to support a big city education system they regarded as hopelessly dysfunctional.

Another new player in the case was Attorney General Dennis Vacco, swept into office with Pataki in 1994, and sharing with the governor the same upstate Republican political base. As the officially designated lawyer for the state, the attorney general's office was in charge of defending the *CFE* case. Vacco took to the task aggressively. To supplement his own office's somewhat inexperienced legal staff, he hired Sutherland, Asbill, and Brennan, a top tier law firm from Atlanta, Georgia, that had defended states and school districts in similar cases around the country. Bringing in the Atlanta firm (which dispatched a half dozen lawyers to New York) made sense in vigorously defending the governor's position. But from a political perspective it added fuel to the bonfires the plaintiffs started when they decided to play the race card in and outside the courtroom.

In the meantime CFE was building up its own front line legal forces. Michael Rebell scored a major coup when he secured the pro bono services of Simpson, Thacher, and Bartlett, one of the city's (and the nation's) largest and most prominent corporate law firms, with five hundred lawyers on staff. The firm's managing partner, Richard Beattie, was a past president of the New York City Board of Education and remained an important behind-the-scenes player in the city's education politics. In fact, Beattie headed a mayoral commission in the early 1980s that exposed some of the systemic failings of the special education regime that Michael Rebell had helped impose on the schools. Clearly Beattie didn't hold that against Rebell. Instead he enthusiastically offered his firm's immense resources for the battle to bring more education dollars to the city. Six Simpson, Thacher, and Bartlett partners and twenty associates then put in thirty-three thousand hours on the case over the next eight years. Lower-level summer associates and paralegals would add another twenty-three thousand hours. Rebell also signed up five more lawyers who worked directly for CFE.

Leading the Simpson, Thacher, and Bartlett team, and working almost full time on the *CFE* case, was one of the firm's top litigators, Joseph F. Wayland. For the Columbia law school graduate, the case became a passion and a cause. As a product of the public schools, Wayland seemed guilt ridden that he now sent his own young children to one of the city's elite private schools. He sometimes referred to his own version of the "savage inequalities" by comparing the education his children were getting with the education available to poor, minority kids condemned to the city's decrepit public schools. "My kids get small class sizes, multiple specialists, well trained teachers, great support staff," he once told me in a telephone interview (2004). "It costs more than $20,000 and they don't even need it." Wayland was genuinely moved by the injustice of it all, so much so that he broke down and cried as he spoke about the case to a conference of educators organized by Schools Chancellor Harold Levy. The crowd was so moved it gave Wayland a standing ovation.

With all the expensive and high-powered legal talent assembled in Judge DeGrasse's courtroom on both sides, the pretrial discovery process dragged on for more than four years. It took so long that while the lawyers were still wrangling over depositions of expert witnesses, another statewide election was held in November 1998. Once again the political dynamics of the case were changed. Governor Pataki was reelected handily, but Attorney General Vacco suffered an upset defeat at the hands of Elliot Spitzer, a New York City Democrat and a former prosecutor. Taking office while the *CFE* case was still in the pretrial phase, Spitzer fulfilled his professional obligation to vigorously defend the case for the Republican governor. He decided to keep the Atlanta lawyers on the state's legal team and continued to give them a free hand in the courtroom.

Yet Spitzer faced a political problem. The CFE coalition was also part of his own political base and had just helped him get elected. The last thing the new attorney general needed was to be perceived by many of his voters and supporters as being in cahoots with the heartless Republican governor fighting against a fair shake for the minority children of New York. This became even more of a problem a few years later as Spitzer set his eyes on the Governor's mansion.

Spitzer tried to solve his political dilemma by essentially putting a gag order on his own defense team. The Atlanta lawyers, as well as the attorney general's office's regular career lawyers, were told never to respond publicly to CFE attacks emanating from inside or outside the courtroom. All public comment about the case from the defendant's side was controlled by Spitzer's spokesperson. Throughout the trial, even under extreme provocation, the defense lawyers hardly commented at all. Since the case was fought on the streets and in the media as much as in the courtroom, this became a serious handicap for the defense team. At least in the trial phase, the state of New York was defending the *CFE* case with one hand tied behind its back.

At the beginning, when the idea of a lawsuit against the state was just a gleam in Robert Jackson's eyes, a script might have been written casting this as a classic American underdog story of two powerless but civic-minded idealists taking on the powerful Empire State. But by the time the trial drew near, the roles had been largely reversed. With an annual budget that would soon reach $3 million and underwritten by some of the big national philanthropic foundations, CFE had grown into a legal, political, and public relations juggernaut. A dozen or so major political and community organizations and trade unions—above all, the powerful United Federation of Teachers—actively collaborated with CFE. The local political and educational establishments, even including Republican Mayor Rudy Giuliani, were also on board.

CFE had not just one, but two, high-powered public relations firms working the media and generating a constant stream of favorable comment about the "fiscal equity" cause and the plaintiffs' lawyers. When an important expert for the plaintiffs was about to testify, one of the PR firms would release the testimony to the press a day early, to help spin the coverage. This tactic worked like a charm. On the morning that SUNY-Albany Professor Hamilton Langford testified for the plaintiffs about the negative effect of low salaries on the city's ability to recruit qualified teachers, to take one instance, the *New York Times*, *Newsday*, and the *Daily News* ran almost identical stories—presenting the professor's data and quoting plaintiffs' lawyers on the import of the testimony. Defense lawyers could offer no comment, not only because they hadn't yet heard the expert's presentation, but also because of the attorney general's gag order.

But the truth is that the New York media didn't need all that much prodding to cast the case as a contest between good and evil. Reporters profiled CFE's lawyers as selfless heroes working for the common good of all the schoolchildren. However, the media showed no curiosity about the fact that Michael Rebell was wearing two hats during the trial. In one courtroom he was charging that the city's students as a whole were not getting enough money from the state. But at the same time he was still representing clients in the continuing *Jose P.* case in which he continued to press for diverting even more resources from the school budget toward special education.

On the other hand, several reporters and columnists slimed the private Atlanta law firm representing the state. *New York Times* columnist Bob Herbert hinted that the lawyers from "down South" were racists because they had previously defended cities and states fighting desegregation suits. Herbert attacked the visiting attorneys for taking in "millions of taxpayer dollars . . . to undermine the interests of the ethnic minorities and newly arrived immigrants" in New York City's public schools. Douglas Feiden, a reporter for the *Daily News*, used the Freedom of Information Law to obtain the bills submitted to the state by the Atlanta firm. He then blasted Attorney General Spitzer for allowing the "Dixie barristers" who were brought here to defend the "indefensible" to stay in expensive hotels, and to bill the taxpayers more than $8 million for their legal work, including fees of up to $270 an hour (*Daily News*, March 11, 2001). (Neither Herbert nor Feiden commented when Simpson, Thacher, and Bartlett and CFE petitioned the court after the trial—unsuccessfully—to recover fees and expenses totaling $21 million, including a rate of $550 an hour for Joseph Wayland.)

As the trial finally opened almost seven years after Michael Rebell filed his first complaint, CFE's biggest advantage was that it was still in Judge DeGrasse's courtroom. It wasn't supposed to be, at least not according to the court's official administrative rules at the time. The rules state that after the discovery process each case is put into a new pool and then assigned randomly for trial among another group of judges.

However, during a conference on discovery issues a year before the trial opened, Judge DeGrasse casually announced, "I will have the case for trial."

One of the Atlanta lawyers, Alfred Lindseth, voiced his surprise. "I think I heard you say that you've got the case," he said.

"I will have it," Judge DeGrasse confirmed.

The following exchange then ensued:

MR. LINDSETH: Okay. That's been approved. I haven't seen an order or anything.

THE COURT: Well, there has been no order. There was a conversation with the administrative judge.

MR. WAYLAND: Okay

MR. LINDSETH: Okay.

THE COURT: You don't mind, do you?

MR. LINDSETH: I don't know that there's much I could do about it, your honor.

(Conference transcript, 4–19, October 16, 1998)

The Show Trial

Early on the morning that the trial opened, Robert Jackson led a group of more than a hundred parents and children from District 6 on an eleven-mile march down Broadway from Washington Heights to the southern tip of Manhattan. They then joined a CFE rally in progress in front of the supreme court building. The courtroom was completely packed with CFE supporters, with many more gathered outside the courthouse.

Those who got inside heard Joseph Wayland play the race card thirty seconds into his opening statement. Addressing the black judge directly (there was no jury) Wayland compared the case to *Brown v. Board of Education* and accused Governor Pataki of "echo[ing] what we heard a generation ago when the governors stood on the schoolhouse steps to say that the courts have no business addressing the wrongs of segregation." Further, Wayland said that "the effect of the constitutional wrong visited upon the children of New York City is no less insidious than the harm that the Supreme Court condemned in Brown against the Board of Education." And just to make sure that Judge DeGrasse understood who he was dealing with on the defendants' side, Wayland said that "the Attorney General has hired Georgia counsel. They have defended lots of cities and states against claims that their education systems were unconstitutionally segregated . . ." (Trial transcript, 4, October 12, 1999).

The court didn't rebuke Wayland for this thinly veiled accusation of racism against opposing counsel. From that moment, DeGrasse made little effort to establish a neutral atmosphere in the courtroom. Plaintiff lawyers and CFE enjoyed virtual free rein to play the race and poverty themes to the media, and through the media to the public. The nine-month trial seemed part political carnival and part show trial. The CFE worked with the Board of Education, for example, to troop minority high school students into the courtroom almost every day, ostensibly to teach them how democracy and the court system work, but in reality to keep the purported beneficiaries of a pro-CFE ruling always in the judge's eye—and the media's as well. A steady stream of visitors from the school-system hierarchy also thronged the courtroom. At one session, Schools Chancellor Harold Levy theatrically stormed out after a state witness dared claim that the city had enough money to run the schools if the funds were used effectively.

Judge DeGrasse allowed the plaintiffs to parade to the witness stand almost anyone with an opinion about the matter at hand. For example, United Federation of Teachers (UFT) President Randi Weingarten and Chancellor Levy were allowed to testify that, of course, the system needed a lot more money—despite their obvious institutional interest in the trial's outcome.

But the judge suddenly turned excessively legalistic when the state sought to submit an outside consultant's study it had commissioned purporting to objectively analyze how much a "sound basic education" in New York City should actually cost. This "costing out" study was done by a well-regarded independent research firm called Management Analysis and Planning (MAP) and relied mainly on the same "professional judgment" method that had been used in education funding cases in other states. As MAP's president, Dr. James Smith, explained to the court, a diverse panel of twelve professional educators (teachers, administrators, fiscal officers), all of them from outside the city, constructed an "adequate" budget for an education system with demographic characteristics similar to New York's, and then compared it with the real city school budget. The MAP panel's major finding: "The financial resources available to New York City Public Schools are adequate to provide the state-specified 'opportunity of a sound basic education.'"

The CFE lawyers objected to admitting the MAP report into the record, citing various case precedents disallowing an expert witness from testifying concerning the findings of another expert. According to Joseph Wayland, permitting Dr. Smith to report would be the equivalent of permitting hearsay testimony, since only Dr. Smith, but not the members of the professional judgment panel, was available for cross-examination by the plaintiffs. (Wayland was a little more colorful in a phone interview. He called the MAP study "bullshit" and said there was "no science" behind it.) Judge DeGrasse agreed with the CFE lawyers that the professional judgment report was mere "hearsay" and chucked it out.

The fight over the MAP study was a telling moment, not because admitting it would have made any difference in the Judge's deliberations. It wouldn't have. Nor was it that the court had wrongly rejected a high-level scientific study that was capable of answering the fundamental question supposedly at the heart of the case—how much money does it actually take to deliver a "sound basic education" to all the children of New York City? The costing out study was admittedly unscientific. However, the haste with which Joseph Wayland moved to throw it out (not even being content to raise questions through cross-examination about the "science" behind such studies) reflected the sheer opportunism of the CFE lawyers and the fundamental bias of the judge. Within three years the same lawyers would come back to the courtroom brandishing a costing out study by the same MAP and the same Dr. Smith and insisting that it proved that the city schools had to have an extra $5.6 billion in operating funds. And this time Judge DeGrasse agreed.

In 2001, Judge DeGrasse ruled decisively in CFE's favor. While declining to specify any amount at this point, he said that the state must substantially boost its funding for New York City schools so that the city could hire lots more qualified teachers, reduce class size (one of the judge's policy favorites), and fix up school buildings, among other improvements. This presumably would allow all students an opportunity for that elusive "sound basic education" while preparing them for their roles as productive citizens in our democracy, including "voting in elections" and "serving on juries." Swelling a chorus of acclaim in the city, the *New York Times* hailed the judge's 180-page opinion as "carefully argued." But it was mostly a rehash of the plaintiffs' lawyers' own arguments. DeGrasse accepted almost every piece of evidence that the plaintiffs presented—even personal and subjective opinions—yet consistently rejected scholarly evidence offered by the state.

One example will suffice. In his opinion, Judge DeGrasse writes that "plaintiffs offered probative evidence that the totality of conditions in crumbling facilities can have a pernicious effect on student achievement." And what might this evidence be? DeGrasse cites this witness-stand rumination from former state Education Commissioner Thomas Sobel, once a named defendant but now a witness for the plaintiffs: "If you ask the children to attend school in conditions where plaster is crumbling, the roof is leaking and classes are being held in unlikely places because of overcrowded conditions, that says something to the child about how you diminish the value of the activity and of the child's participation in it and perhaps of the child himself." Sobel continued, "If you send a child to a school in well-appointed facilities that sends the opposite message. That says this counts. You count. Do well."

DeGrasse found this pop psychology persuasive. But he quibbled endlessly with a rigorous statistical study by education economist Eric Hanushek, which demolished the hypothesis that there is a causal relationship between schools in disrepair and poor student performance. And he performed extraordinary legal jujitsu to evade one of the most powerful contentions in the state's case: that so dysfunctional was the existing New York City educational system that corruption, fraud, and waste were bleeding it of money that should be going into the classrooms— and that therefore the school system should be required to clean up its act before anyone entrusted it with a single additional taxpayer dollar. DeGrasse opined that any fraud or waste in the city's school system was really the state's fault, since school districts are legal creations of the state and subject to state regulation. Therefore, even if New York City's educational system was shown to be squandering money with shameless abandon, that would be irrelevant to the question of whether the city's schools have sufficient funds.

Astonishingly, even as the trial moved along, CFE's argument that more money would improve New York City's public schools was receiving a real-life test—not that anyone in the courtroom noticed. From 1997 to 2002, total spending on the city's public schools rocketed from $8.8 billion to $12.5 billion— or about 25 percent in inflation-adjusted dollars. That brought per-pupil spending in the city almost to twelve thousand dollars, well above most districts in the state and the nation. Most of the extra funding, moreover, went for precisely the budget items that Judge DeGrasse believed would lift student achievement. Class size in the early grades fell from an average of twenty-five to twenty-one students; the schools hired thousands of new teachers; and all city teachers won salary hikes of 16 to 21 percent. Indeed, according to the New York City Independent Budget Office, total spending for the city's schools has more than doubled since the *CFE* lawsuit was filed in 1993. (As almost everyone studying the issue agrees, New York now receives a proportion of all state aid that matches its percentage of all students in the state.) Yet the results were underwhelming. More than half of the city's children still can't read at grade level, and only

15 percent of New York City students graduated with a Regents diploma.

The state appealed Judge DeGrasse's 2001 decision, and the lawyers took yet another two-year sojourn through the appeals process. Once again the appellate division overturned the trial court. The four-judge majority still took a very minimalist view of the education article of the constitution. Unfortunately for the state the court majority also carelessly declared that the constitution only required the state to guarantee students the equivalent of eighth or ninth grade academic skills. This set off a firestorm of protest, with CFE supporters and editorial boards denouncing the judges for saying, in effect, that it was acceptable for the schools to train kids for nothing better than jobs flipping hamburgers at McDonald's. Even Governor Pataki had to demur.

After the political storm over the eighth grade or "hamburger flipping" standard, it was almost inevitable that the court of appeals would reverse the appellate division and uphold Judge DeGrasse. In 1982 the high court had allowed only that the education article of the constitution *might* be interpreted as requiring "adequate" resources for a minimal level of education. Then in its first review of the *CFE* lawsuit it upped the ante to a "sound basic education," defined as providing all students with the skills to vote and serve on juries. Now it proclaimed that all students must have the opportunity "for a meaningful high school education, one which prepares them to function productively as civic participants," and defined that as meeting the new higher graduation standards established by the Board of Regents. The lone dissenter on the court of appeals, Judge Read, declared that the court had put itself into the position of "judicial overseer of the legislature" and predicted that there would be decades of similar litigation initiated by school districts throughout the state.

If the court of appeals was unimpressed by the fact that the city was now spending $5 billion more a year on the schools than when it last reviewed the case, you would think that the justices might say exactly how much more money would be required to meet the new standard they had just established. But in their only concession to the separation of powers, the judges tossed that hot potato back to the legislature and the governor. The court said the state must now determine "the actual cost" of providing an opportunity for a "meaningful high school education" for all children in New York City.

The March of Folly

Little wonder that the legislature found itself paralyzed over how to deal with the court of appeals' ruling. In its total focus on the fiscal condition of the New York City schools, the court paid no attention to the fact that the state of New York was now $4 to $6 billion in the red. The governor and members of the legislature, representing real taxpayers (particularly those from upstate) couldn't afford such a luxury. But even if the governor and the legislature had agreed to make the court ruling its highest budgetary priority, it's not clear how they might have proceeded. As public policy, the court's premise is somewhat absurd. No magic level of funding can be determined a priori to guarantee all children a "meaningful high school education," any more so than a level of defense spending that guarantees the military a victory in Iraq.

However, while Albany dithered CFE gladly stepped into the breach. It now commissioned its own costing out study to decide how much money it would take to meet the court mandate. Without any apparent embarrassment, one of the two research organizations that CFE hired (at $1 million) to find the magic number was MAP, the same MAP whose study CFE lawyers moved to exclude from the trial. MAP's president, Dr. James Smith, said in a telephone interview with the author that the "professional judgment" method in the costing out study commissioned by CFE was essentially the same one he had used for the trial.

Moreover, in the costing out study done for CFE, the financial calculations for New York City were prepared by two professional judgment panels consisting exclusively of administrators, principals, and teachers on the payroll of the city's Department of Education. Not surprisingly the DOE employees were very generous with the taxpayers' money. Based partly on the panels' assumption that class size in the early grades must go down to thirteen students and that there must be full pre-K programs for all children, resulting in the hiring of thousands of extra teachers, the preliminary costing out report concluded that city schools must get yet another $3.7 billion a year in operating funds above the $13 billion the city was then spending. (Another $8 billion was proposed for capital funding.) According to Dr. Smith, the numbers were then tweaked upward at the urging of Michael Rebell. The final number was $5.6 billion in added operating funds for New York City. However, the final costing out report contained one rather large caveat inserted by Dr. Smith: it was that the recommended billions of dollars in new funding was "not based on an exact science" and that "different assumptions can lead to different results."

Considering the state's looming budget deficit, CFE's $5.6 billion claim left upstate legislators gasping. Ultimately, it made Albany even less likely to voluntarily comply with the court of appeals ruling. Meanwhile Governor Pataki had appointed his own task force to provide recommendations for meeting the ruling. The governor's commission hired Standard & Poor's to do yet another costing out study, which in turn used an alternative method called the "successful schools" model. (See chapter 7 for more detailed discussion of various costing out methods.) Based on Standard & Poor's study, the governor's commission then concluded that the city schools could actually provide a "sound basic education" for a few billion dollars less than what the plaintiffs were demanding.

Nevertheless, no action was taken by either the legislature or the governor on either of the two reports. In July 2004 the parties were summoned back to Judge DeGrasse's courtroom to discuss the fact that the state had failed to repair the constitutional violation as ordered by the court of appeals. Still, Judge DeGrasse wasn't ready to order an appropriate judicial remedy just yet. Instead he ordered the parties to yet another hearing in front of a panel of three "referees" to determine the exact amount of money that the state would have to come up with to achieve constitutional "adequacy." DeGrasse's appointees to the panel included a retired New York judge who is the father of a former president of the Board of Education and prominent supporter of CFE, another former New York Supreme Court judge, and the former dean of Fordham University Law School.

The referees' panel held several days of hearings in the fall of 2004. CFE presented arguments and expert witnesses in support of the $5.6 billion figure recommended in the MAP/American Institute of Research (AIR) report (and notwithstanding the report's own caveat about the process not having much to do with "exact science"). But there was a new twist introduced at the masters' hearing. For the first time during the ten years of the *CFE* case, the city of New York was suddenly at the table as a party to the proceedings. Even though the city's education budget for the 2005–2006 fiscal year was likely to top $17 billion, Mayor Michael Bloomberg and Schools' Chancellor Klein testified under oath that they couldn't get the job done without at least another $5.4 billion a year in state funding. Annual expenditures for the city's schools would then reach $22 billion, or about twenty thousand dollars a student. That, in turn, would come close to fulfilling Joseph Wayland's dream of having all public school students receive as much in education funding as his own children receive attending elite private schools.

Mayor Bloomberg's sudden emergence as a determined claimant for the $5.6 billion grand prize seemed, however, to contradict much of what he had previously stood for as an education reformer. Upon gaining control of the school system in 2002–2003, Bloomberg consciously avoided making an argument for more money as the key to school improvement. To the contrary, at a time when the school budget was still a mere $13 billion, he said the problem was a dysfunctional and uncompetitive system and that the city had enough money to run good schools if it used the money effectively.

More troubling still was the "civil rights" spin that Bloomberg and Klein now put on their new money demands. Taking a page out of Joseph Wayland's opening remarks at trial, Klein gave speeches in black churches arguing that it would violate the spirit of the historic *Brown v. Board of Education* decision if the state failed to provide the additional $5.4 billion in education funding. Yet as a private attorney in the 1980s, Joel Klein represented the state of Missouri in one of the nation's original fiscal adequacy lawsuits. In court Klein argued that pouring more money into Kansas City's schools was not the answer to the education woes of its largely minority students. The court found otherwise, but Klein turned out to be right. Twelve years and $2 billion later, almost all parties agreed that Missouri's experiment in judge-ordered school financing was a costly failure.

To no one's surprise the referees' panel of old New York legal hands ruled unanimously that New York City should get a huge bonanza, intended to finally make sure that its children receive that elusive "sound basic education." Pulling together elements from all the costing out studies presented, the referees recommended to Judge DeGrasse the number $5.63 billion, not a penny less, not a penny more. After yet another hearing in his courtroom, Judge DeGrasse agreed. He ordered the state to pay up, but without setting any deadlines or penalties for noncompliance. The state then announced that it would appeal, partly on the grounds that the New York Constitution may actually prevent the judicial branch from ordering the legislature to appropriate any specific amount of money.

In March 2006 the appellate division ruled on the state's appeal. But the 3 to 2 decision was so muddled that it left both sides claiming victory. Writing for the majority, Presiding Justice John Buckley seemed to be trying to square the circle. On the one hand, his opinion said that the state should provide the city with somewhere in a range of $4.7 billion to $5.6 billion in increased funding. On the other hand, the court also seemed to affirm the state's position that only the legislature can appropriate money.

There is no way of knowing how this thirteen-year legal circus will end in the courts. It's hard to imagine that after encouraging the litigation of this case two times, the court of appeals might concede that it actually never had the power under the constitution to enforce a specific fiscal remedy. On the other hand, most upstate legislators would need to be chained and sent to jail before agreeing to impose on their constituents the whopping tax increases that would be needed to cover $5.63 billion in new funds for the city they hate anyway. So perhaps the *CFE* case ends in a constitutional crisis. Or New York's likely next governor, Elliot Spitzer, steps in and uses his influence with his liberal New York City constituents to negotiate a compromise settlement.

Either way, we already know quite a bit about the lessons *CFE v. New York* teaches. Perhaps the main one is that the strategy of using the courts to short circuit the political system to get better educational opportunities for the children always looks more promising at the beginning than at the end. It seems like almost another lifetime since Robert Jackson, out of genuine frustration as a parent, thought about suing the state to bring relief to his own children's schools. Since then dozens of lawyers and judges have logged thousands of hours and spent tens of millions of dollars, in an adversarial process designed to get at the truth. Yet we are no closer today to answering the question supposedly at the heart of the case—how many dollars does it take to create schools that work well and produce results for most of the city's children? And the children are also not much closer to obtaining a better education despite all the years of litigation.

In the meantime, and while all that energy was consumed in the courtroom, and so many smart people wasted their time trying to answer an unanswerable question, the political process that Robert Jackson once despaired of, has, willy-nilly, moved along. Between the actions of elected officials in Albany and in New York's City Hall, the amount of money going to the city's schools has almost doubled. It happened through the give and take of democratic politics, as flawed as that politics is in New York, rather than by having a judge arbitrarily impose spending increases on unwilling taxpayers. In fact, Robert Jackson himself played a part in this political process. In 2001 he was elected to the New York City Council, where he voted to increase spending on the schools. And now he is the chairperson of the council's education committee, where he will presumably have even more influence on the city's education policies.

Public School 287 in District 6, the school that all three of Robert Jackson's daughters attended, benefited greatly from the same political process over the years. According to the Department of Education Web site, per-pupil expenditures for the school are now close to fourteen thousand dollars, which is higher than 90 percent of the schools in the state, and almost twice as much as when Jackson was president of the school board. Mr. Jackson still thinks that the children of Washington Heights are getting a lousy education. He's right, of course. But it still hasn't occurred to him that perhaps the premise of the wasteful lawsuit he filed thirteen years ago—that is, that more money equals better student outcomes—was wrong from the start. Nor has it occurred to Michael Rebell, who has now left CFE to take a position as the director of the new Campaign for Educational Equity at Teachers College, Columbia University, where he promises to bring this wrongheaded and counterproductive crusade to inner city school districts throughout the country.

Sources

Trial Transcript: *Campaign for Fiscal Equity v. New York State.* 1999. Supreme Court of the State of New York, County of New York.

The State Education Department, *Statewide Profile of the Educational System.* 1993 and 2004 Reports.

Michael Rebell. 2004. Speech to the Public Education Association, Center for Educational Innovation.

2

The Legal Backdrop to Adequacy

Alfred A. Lindseth

K–I 2 EDUCATIONAL FINANCING systems in almost twenty states have been declared unconstitutional by state courts because such states are not providing sufficient funding for the "adequate" education guaranteed by their constitutions.[1] The result

---

1. *Rose v. Council for Better Education*, 790 S.W.2d 186 (Ky. 1989); *McDuffy v. Secretary, Executive Office of Education*, 415 N.E.2d 516 (Mass. 1993); *Roosevelt Elementary School District v. Bishop*, 877 P.2d 806 (Ariz. 1994); *Campbell County School District v. Wyoming*, 907 P.2d 1238 (Wyo. 1995); *Claremont School District v. Governor*, 703 A.2d 1353 (N.H. 1997); *Abbott v. Burke*, 798 A.2d 602 (N.J. 2002); *DeRolph v. State*, 677 N.E.2d 733 (Ohio 1997); *Campaign for Fiscal Equity v. New York*, 100 N.Y.2d 893 (N.Y. 2003) (hereinafter "*CFE II*"); *Montoy v. State*, 278 Kan. 769, 102 P.3d 1160 (2005) (hereinafter "*Montoy II*"); *Lakeview School District v. Huckabee*, 91 S.W.3d 472 (Ark. 2002); *Columbia Falls Elem. School Dist. No. 6, et al. v. The State of Montana*, No. 04-390 (Mt. S. Ct. March 22, 2005); *Harper v. Hunt, Op. of Justices*, 624 So.2d 107 (Ala. 1993); *Brigham v. State*, 692 A.2d 384 (Vt. 1997); *Sheff v. O'Neill*, 678 A.2d 1267 (Conn. 1996); *Hoke County Bd. of Educ., et al v. State of North Carolina*, 599 S.E.2d 365 (2004); *Seattle Sch. Dist. v. Steele*, 585 P.2d 71 (Wash. 1978); *Pauley v. Kelly*, 255 S.E.2d 859 (W. Va. 1979);

has been court orders in many states requiring significant increases in education spending and judicial supervision of the school financing system for many years and even decades into the future, as the courts act as superlegislatures on matters affecting K–12 education. Since "adequacy" is both a legal and factual concept, it is essential that educators, school finance experts, lawyers, legislators, and others considering issues of adequacy in education have an understanding of the legal principles and trends underlying and informing the concept.

The "adequacy movement" reached its peak in New York where a Manhattan trial judge, relying on the state's constitutional obligation to provide "free common schools," ordered the state legislature to increase funding for the New York City public schools by $23 billion over the next five years, including $5.63 billion a year for operations.[2] This is a 45 percent increase over current per-pupil expenditures, already among the highest in the nation, and will bring per-pupil spending in the city's public schools to over $17,000 a year, approximately twice the national average.[3] New York is not alone when it comes to such deci-

---

Abbeville County School District, et al v. The State of South Carolina, Case No. 93-CP-31-0169 (Ct. Common Pleas, 3rd Jud. Cir., S.C., Dec. 29, 2005); and *Bradford v. Maryland*, No. 94340058/CE 189672 (Cir. Ct., Baltimore City, June 30, 2000).

2. *Campaign for Fiscal Equity v. State of New York, et al.*, Index No. 111070/93 (Sup. Ct. New York County, March 22, 2005). In 2006 the appellate division modified the trial judge's order, and ordered the legislature to increase annual K–12 appropriations for the operations of the city schools by an amount between $4.7 billion to $5.6 billion, plus an additional $9.179 billion for capital spending. *Campaign for Fiscal Equity, Inc., et al. v. The State of New York, et al.*, 6915 Index 111070/93 (App. Div., 1st Dept., N.Y., March 23, 2006). If the legislature appropriates the lowest amount permissible under the court order, annual per-pupil spending in the New York City public schools would still be almost twice the national average.

3. *Quality Counts*, Education Week 25, no. 17, Jan. 5, 2006, at 98 (hereinafter "*Quality Counts 2006*"). In 2002–2003 the average per-pupil expenditures for the nation were $8,041.

sions. In Kansas, for example, a state court trial judge enjoined any further spending on education until the legislature appropriated enough resources to close the achievement gap between poor and minority students and white, middle-class students, an admirable goal, but one which no large school system in the country has yet managed to accomplish.[4] In Wyoming, the Supreme Court ordered the legislature to provide enough money to local school districts to enable them to furnish an education that is the "best" and is "visionary and unsurpassed."[5] While 2005 has seen some pushback from the courts, particularly in Texas, judicial control over educational policy and appropriations remains either the reality or potential future in many states.

This chapter consists of four parts. Part 1 describes the development of school finance case law, including how the courts have moved far beyond their traditional role in ensuring equal opportunity and are now deciding issues of educational funding and policy historically reserved for the legislative branches of government. Earlier federal court desegregation and state court equity cases, which were based on proof of disparate or discriminatory treatment, have now been almost entirely superseded by state court "adequacy" cases that require no such proof.

Part 2 examines the perversion of time-honored legal principles in educational adequacy cases. Instead of courts minimizing their interference with the policymaking and appropriation powers of its coequal branches of government, the courts in sev-

---

4. *Montoy v. State*, Case No. 99-6-1738, 2004 WL 1094555 (Kan. Dist. Ct., May 11, 2004), at 10 (hereinafter referred to as "*Montoy T.C.*"). On occasion, other trial court decisions in the case will also be referred to as "*Montoy T.C.*," but will be followed by the date of the decision, *e.g.*, "*Montoy T.C.*, Dec. 3, 2003 order."

5. *Campbell County School District v. State*, 907 P.2d 1238, 1279 (Wyo. 1995) ("*Campbell I*"); *Campbell County School District v. State*, 19 P.3d 518, 538 (Wyo. 2001) ("*Campbell II*").

eral states have done just the opposite. Ignoring separation of powers considerations, they have approached adequacy lawsuits in a such a way as to substantially usurp the power of the legislature. Under the guise of "interpreting" vague constitutional language often devoid of qualitative language, a number of courts have ratcheted up the constitutional standards to the point where few, if any, states can now meet them. At the same time, the concept of legal causation has been eroded to the extent that many states are, as a practical matter, held strictly liable for low student performance outcomes with little or no proof that such performance has been caused by insufficient state funding of K–12 education. The result has been to make it very difficult for states to defend against adequacy claims, regardless of how much of the public treasury they devote to education. For example, all five of the highest spending states in the nation on a per-pupil basis—New York, New Jersey, Massachusetts, Vermont, and Wyoming—have had their school financing systems struck down by the courts in an adequacy case.[6]

Part 3 describes and analyzes the legal and practical problems faced by the courts as they become more and more enmeshed in what are essentially political decisions and seek to enforce orders that ignore political and financial realities. As a result, the relationship between the judicial and legislative branches in several states has become severely strained.

Finally, part 4 examines 2005 court decisions in Texas and Massachusetts, which rejected the activist role of the courts that has characterized adequacy cases since the early 1990s, and instead applied long-standing principles of judicial deference to reasonable, non-arbitrary choices made by legislative bodies.

---

6. *See* footnote 1.

1. The Courts—from Protecting Equal Rights to Dictating Educational Policy and Spending

Adequacy cases are the new kid on the block when it comes to school finance litigation. To understand them, it is useful to examine how the courts got into the business of school finance in the first place and how such court decisions have evolved to the present state of affairs.

Federal Court Desegregation Cases

K–12 education in the United States has traditionally been a state and local responsibility. Before the 1950s, even the involvement of state government was minimal and nearly all important decisions about elementary and secondary schools and their funding were made locally. Neither the federal government nor the courts were involved in any meaningful way. This all changed in 1954 with the landmark decision of the Supreme Court in *Brown v. Board of Education* declaring state-mandated racial segregation of schools unlawful.[7] Since then the courts have been an important institutional player in America's public schools.

After *Brown*, the role of the courts in education expanded exponentially for several decades. Starting in the late 1950s and continuing into the 1990s, court orders governing the desegregation of schools were commonplace as the federal courts, often faced with vigorous opposition from local and state officials, took remedial action to eliminate racially segregated schools, integrate faculty and staff, and ensure the equal allocation of resources. In the early 1970s, civil rights advocates also began to push for extraordinary funding and programs for predominantly

---

7. *Brown v. Board of Education*, 347 U.S. 483 (1954).

poor and minority schools. In response, several federal courts ordered both states and local school districts to make substantial expenditures to enhance the quality of education offered in predominantly minority schools.

Such court-ordered educational enhancements began with the *Milliken v. Bradley* case involving the Detroit schools, and led to such remedies often being referred to as "*Milliken II* remedies."[8] These "educational enhancement" remedies were justified as desegregation remedies on two grounds: First, the additional programs and funding would make the schools more attractive to nonminority students and aid in attracting or retaining a more racially mixed student body. Second, increased spending would improve the achievement levels of black children who, because of their substandard education in segregated schools, trailed behind those of white children and better prepare them for integrated schools.[9]

The most notorious example of such remedies was the *Missouri v. Jenkins* case involving the desegregation of the Kansas City, Missouri, public schools. In a series of orders beginning in 1986, a federal court ordered the state and local school district to spend about $1.5 billion over and above regular school expenditures to improve the quality of education offered in the school district of 37,000 pupils.[10] The court's orders were based on a previous finding by the court that black children in the school district were performing below the national average on nationally normed tests. To bring test scores up to the national average, the court literally gave the local school officials a "license to dream."[11] They did exactly that, spending hundreds of

8. *Milliken v. Bradley*, 433 U.S. 267 (1977).

9. *Id.* at 283–287; *Missouri v. Jenkins*, 515 U.S. 70, 84 (1995) ("*Jenkins III*").

10. *Jenkins v. Missouri*, 639 F.Supp. 19, 23-24 (W.D.Mo. 1985), *aff'd as modified by*, 807 F.2d 657 (8th Cir. 1986), *cert. denied* 484 U.S. 816 (1987).

11. *Jenkins III*, at 79–80.

millions of dollars of court-ordered funding for such things as new state-of-the-art facilities; a 2,000-square-foot planetarium; a 25-acre farm with an air-conditioned meeting room for 104 people; a Model United Nations wired for language translation, broadcast-capable radio and television studios; movie editing and screening rooms; a temperature-controlled art gallery; a 3,500-square-foot dust-free diesel mechanics room; an 1,875-square-foot elementary school animal room for use in a zoo project; and so on.[12] Besides ordering funding for magnificent facilities, the court made every school in the district a magnet school, ordered significant raises for teachers, and added teachers and staff, thousands of computers, early childhood development programs, and before- and after-school tutorial programs.[13] Unfortunately, none of this court-ordered largesse led to better scores by the school district's students on nationally normed tests, which was the whole purpose of the increased spending in the first place.[14]

The beginning of the end for *Milliken II*-type remedies came in 1995. In the Kansas City case's third trip to the Supreme Court, the Court ruled, in *Jenkins v. Missouri (Jenkins III)* that improving the educational offerings at a school to attract white pupils from outside the district, absent grounds for an interdistrict remedy, was beyond the remedial powers of the courts.[15] It also held that a desire to raise the test scores of black students to the national average was not enough to justify the court's extensive remedial orders without proof such substandard

12. *Id.,* at 79.

13. *Id.,* at 76–80.

14. *See* expert report of Dr. John Murphy introduced during 2001 unitary hearing in *Berry v. School District of Benton Harbor*, Civil Action No. 4:67-CV-9 (W.D. Mich. 2001). Dr. Murphy was the court-appointed monitor of the Kansas City, Missouri, School District from 1997 to 2000.

15. *Jenkins III* at 98–99.

scores were attributable to earlier illegal segregation.[16] Following *Jenkins III*, the court orders in the Kansas City case, as well as similar cases against other states, were either dismissed or phased out as it became difficult for plaintiffs to prove that low achievement was causally linked to the earlier de jure segregated school system that had ended decades ago.[17] This ended the efforts of civil rights groups to convince the federal courts to order local and state authorities to increase K–12 education funding in order to increase the quality of education. By then, however, the main battleground had already shifted to the state courts.

State Court Litigation

In the early 1970s, concurrent with their efforts in federal courts, plaintiffs also began to pursue litigation in state courts— first, to divide the education funding "pie" more equitably among school districts, and, second and more recently, to substantially increase the size of the "pie" to provide for an "adequate" education in every school district.

Equity Cases

Education funding systems in most states have historically relied mainly on the local property tax to pay for schools. Because of often large disparities in the property tax bases of wealthy and poor districts, this practice resulted in large disparities in per-pupil funding among school districts in many states. In the early 1970s, plaintiffs began to file lawsuits to require states to equal-

16. *Id.* at 101–102.

17. *E.g.*, *Jenkins v. School District of Kansas City, Missouri*, No. 77-0420-CV-W-DW (W.D. Mo. Aug. 13, 2003). Since the 1995 *Jenkins III* decision, federal court decisions requiring *Milliken II* remedies have also been phased out or dismissed in Yonkers, New York; Detroit and Benton Harbor, Michigan; Little Rock, Arkansas; and Ohio's largest cities.

ize the per-pupil funding among school districts, reasoning that the school district a child resides in should not determine the quality of the education he or she receives. One of plaintiffs' first efforts took place in federal court in a case involving Texas' education funding system. However, in *Rodriguez v. San Antonio*, the United States Supreme Court rejected plaintiffs' claim, holding that education is not a fundamental right under the federal Constitution and that classifications based on wealth were therefore not suspect classes.[18] This meant that the Texas system of funding education would not be strictly scrutinized by the Court but would instead be judged under the more lenient standard of whether the system had any rational basis. The court ruled that reliance on local property taxes satisfied the rational basis test and dismissed the case.[19] The *Rodriguez* decision had nationwide effect, and ended plaintiffs' efforts in the federal courts to equalize spending among school districts.[20]

Undeterred, plaintiffs proceeded to file lawsuits in state courts based on state constitutional provisions guaranteeing equal rights. There they enjoyed more success. Unlike the federal Constitution, most state constitutions specifically require some level of free public education. As a result, the courts of some states have ruled that education is a fundamental right under their constitutions, and that state educational funding systems are therefore subject to the higher test of strict scrutiny. It was these two rulings that had eluded plaintiffs in *Rodriguez*. As a consequence, funding systems that relied mainly on a local property tax to fund schools have been struck down in a number

18. *San Antonio Independent School District v. Rodriguez*, 411 U.S. 1 (1973).

19. *Id.* at 54–55.

20. *Rodriguez* addressed funding differences between school districts and not schools. The equality of funding of schools within a school district is important in school desegregation cases, and the federal courts have not hesitated to address such inequalities.

of states.[21] Such cases have become known, in the vernacular of those involved in school finance, as "equity" cases.

Because of these equity cases or the legal threat they presented, many states changed their school finance formulas to include some kind of equalizing mechanism. Such changes have generally taken the form of state school funding formulas that provide less state funding to property-rich districts and more state funding to property-poor districts, thereby reducing disparities in the amounts spent per student in the school districts of the state. As a result, intrastate funding disparities among school districts have been significantly reduced, although hardly eliminated (Murray, Evans, and Schwab 1998).

Equity suits are still being filed in some states, usually as part of an adequacy lawsuit, contending that significant funding disparities among school districts still exist or that disparities previously alleviated by reform to the state financing system have once again raised their ugly heads.[22] However, despite the persistence of these suits, the main focus of current school finance litigation is on the "adequacy" count—the desire to expand the pie rather than reallocate it. There are several reasons for this shift in focus.

First, plaintiffs' record of success in equity cases was mixed. A well-known plaintiffs' attorney estimates that, despite an initial flurry of proplaintiff equity decisions in the early 1970s, plaintiffs have won only seven equity cases compared with fifteen losses (Rebell 2001). A good example is in New York. An equity case was filed in that state in 1974 by several property-

21. *E.g.*, *Serrano v. Priest*, 557 P.2d 929 (Cal. 1976).
22. *E.g.*, *Douglas County School District, et al v. Michael Johanns, et al.*, Doc. 1028, No. 017 (District Court of Douglas County, Neb. 2003); *Williston Public School District No. 1, et al. v. State of North Dakota, et al.*, Civil No. 03-C-507 (Dist. Ct., Northwestern Judicial Circuit. 2003); *Committee for Educational Equality, et al v. State of Missouri, et al.*, Case No. 04CV323022 (Circuit Ct. of Cole County, Mo. 2004).

poor districts. In 1982, after several appeals and a lengthy non-jury trial, the New York Court of Appeals rejected plaintiffs' equal protection claims under both the state and federal constitutions.[23] It was only a decade later when plaintiffs returned to court asserting that the New York City schools were not "adequate" that they were successful.

Second, even in states where plaintiffs won equity suits, they did not always turn out to be the panacea plaintiffs intended. *Serrano v. Priest* in California is a good example.[24] *Serrano* was plaintiffs' first big victory in the equity arena and led to greater spending parity among California's 1,200 school districts. But the insistence on equity eliminated much of the incentive that local communities had previously had to tax themselves to support education and was one of the factors driving California voters to approve Proposition 13, which severely limited the amount of property taxes that could be levied in the state (Fischel 2004). The result of this and other factors, including an economic downturn in many parts of the state, has been a financial disaster for California's schools. In its financial commitment to K–12 education, California has gone from the top to the bottom of the fifty states in a little over one generation due, at least partly, to the *Serrano* decision. In 1977 when *Serrano* was decided, California was one of the highest spending states on education in the country. By 2003 it had sunk to forty-third in per-pupil expenditures, when adjusted for regional cost differences. Even perennially low-spending Alabama spent more.[25]

Finally, such suits are not supported by many school districts, some of which may be pitted against others in their fight for the state education dollars. In contrast, every school district in an adequacy case stands to gain as the funding pie is ex-

23. *Bd. of Educ. v. Nyquist,* 57 N.Y.2d 27, 50 (N.Y. 1982).
24. *Serrano v. Priest,* 557 P.2d 929 (Cal. 1976).
25. *Quality Counts 2006.*

panded. As pro-adequacy author Peter Shrag points out: "Advocates of the adequacy idea argue, quite correctly, that unlike equity, adequacy can be a winner for all schools. It does not require redistribution" (Shrag 2003). Therefore, adequacy suits have become very popular among powerful segments of the community, including the public school establishment, union leaders, many parents, and local taxpayers who believe that further state aid will lessen their tax burden.

Adequacy Cases

Their proponents claim adequacy suits are merely an extension of *Brown* in the fight for equal opportunity, but these suits are in fact quite different from either the federal court desegregation cases or the state court equity cases that preceded them. The objective of earlier school finance cases was to ensure that equal educational opportunities were made available to children regardless of their race or the wealth of the school district in which they lived. Such decisions were based either on the equal protection clause of the Fourteenth Amendment or on similar provisions in state constitutions requiring equality or uniformity, and, as such, involved equal protection issues traditionally handled by the courts. Adequacy cases are another animal entirely. They have their roots not in equal protection, but in the so-called education clause of most state constitutions. No discrimination or inequities need even be alleged, much less proved, for a plaintiff to prevail in an adequacy case.[26]

26. School districts that are the focus of adequacy cases are often funded at higher levels than the average school district in the state. For example, both the St. Paul and Minneapolis, Minnesota, School Districts brought adequacy lawsuits against the state of Minnesota even though at the time they were among the highest spending school districts in the state on a per-pupil basis. In the Missouri adequacy case, the City of St. Louis School District has intervened to assert adequacy claims, even though it is one of the highest spending school districts in the state. Plaintiffs continue to pursue more funding in the

Nearly every state constitution has an "education clause" that requires the state or its legislature to provide some form of free public education to the children of the state. Generally, this constitutional requirement is couched in very vague language, for example, a "thorough and efficient" system of education,[27] "a system of free common schools,"[28] "free instruction,"[29] or "suitable education."[30] Such language gives little guidance on what quality or level of educational resources are required. Therefore, traditionally decisions as to how much of the state's treasury to appropriate for education have been left up to the legislature. In the absence of objective standards in the wording of the constitutions themselves, there are no discernable standards by which a court can reasonably determine if the legislature is performing its duty. The courts would simply be substituting their judgment about the level of education required, and correspondingly its cost, for that of the legislature. Therefore, unless the constitution itself contains "judicially discoverable and manageable standards" on which a court can base its decision, the general rule of law is that issues of educational policy and spending are "political questions" over which the courts have no jurisdiction.[31]

For this reason a number of state courts have held that judicial intrusion into these legislative prerogatives is a violation

---

New Jersey adequacy case even though New Jersey spends more per pupil than any other state and the school districts that are the target of the suit spend substantially more than the next highest spending districts in the state. Similarly, if the remedy ordered by the court in New York is funded by the legislature, New York City's public schools will enjoy per-pupil funding of several thousand dollars more than that of the average school district in New York.

27. Minn. Const. Art XIII, §1.
28. N.Y. Const. Art XI, §1.
29. Neb. Const., Art. VII, §1.
30. Kan. Const., Art. 6, §6.
31. *Committee for Education Rights v. Edgar*, 672 N.E.2d 1178 (Ill. 1996); *Baker v. Carr*, 369 U.S. 186, 209 (1962).

of the doctrine of separation of powers, the system of checks and balances that is the bedrock of our constitutional system of government. Courts in Illinois,[32] Florida,[33] Rhode Island,[34] Nebraska,[35] Pennsylvania,[36] and Arizona[37] have decided that the language of their respective constitutions does not provide "judicially manageable and discoverable standards" sufficient for a court to decide on the proper level of education required. Accordingly, these courts have dismissed adequacy cases, ruling that such issues are political questions reserved for the legislative branch of government and beyond the power of the courts to decide.

However, court decisions dismissing adequacy cases because they involve political questions have been in the minority, especially in recent years. Most courts facing this issue have rejected arguments based on the doctrine of separation of powers and undertaken to decide whether the education being funded is, in their view, adequate.[38] Many people, including plaintiffs, believe that the courts' increasing willingness to enter into what was formerly the political arena is the unintended result of what has become known as the "Standards Movement." Beginning in the 1990s, many states responded to criticism that poor and minority children were the victims of "low expectations" by adopting rigorous academic outcome standards and then hold-

32. *Committee for Education Rights v. Edgar.*

33. *Coalition for Adequacy and Fairness in School Funding v. Chiles*, 680 So.2d 400 (Fla. 1996).

34. *City of Pawtucket v. Sundlun*, 662 A.2d 40 (R.I. 1995).

35. *Douglas County School District, et al v. Michael O. Johanns, et al*, Case No. 1028-017 (Dist. Ct. Douglas County, Neb., May 14, 2004). (Trial court dismissed adequacy count of complaint on separation of powers grounds. The decision is on appeal.)

36. *Merrero v. Commonwealth*, 709 A.2d 956 (Pa. 1998).

37. *Crane Elementary School District v. State*, Case No. CV2001-016305 (Sup. Ct. Maricopa County, Ariz. Nov.25, 2003) (Appeal pending).

38. *See* footnote 1.

ing school districts, schools, and students accountable for meeting these standards through statewide testing programs. Even though such outcome standards often reflect ambitious goals with no relation to the minimum standards of the state constitution, adequacy plaintiffs and the courts have seized on them as the heretofore missing "judicially manageable and discoverable standards" that are a prerequisite for court intervention (Rebell 2001; Heise 2002; Gorman 2001). As discussed further in part 2, not only has the advent of the standards movement resulted in fewer of these cases being dismissed as beyond the power of the courts to decide, but it also has had the effect of raising the standard for adequacy to often ambitiously high levels. As a result, plaintiff groups have been particularly successful in the last decade, at least until 2005. Since 2000, plaintiffs have succeeded in adequacy suits in New York, Arkansas, Kansas, Montana, North Carolina, and to a lesser extent, South Carolina.[39] Emboldened by this string of successes, plaintiffs' groups in a number of other states have also filed adequacy lawsuits which have yet to be finally decided.[40] Although plaintiffs suffered significant setbacks in 2005, when the highest courts of Texas and Massachusetts dismissed adequacy cases after trials on the merits,[41] there is little doubt that adequacy suits are here

39. *Id.*

40. *Douglas County School District, et al v. Michael Johanns, et al,* Doc. 1028, No. 017 (Dist. Ct. of Douglas County, Neb. 2003); *Williston Public School District No. 1, et al v. State of North Dakota,* et al, Civil No. 03-C-507 (Dist. Ct., Northwestern Judicial Circuit. 2003); *Committee for Educational Equality, et al v. State of Missouri, et al,* Case No. 04CV323022 (Circuit Ct. of Cole County, Mo. 2004); *Lobato, et al. v. The State of Colorado, et al.,* Case No. 05CV4794 (Dist. Ct. Denver, Colo. 2005); and *Oklahoma Education Association, et al v. State of Oklahoma, et al,* Case No. CV-2006-2 (District Ct. of Oklahoma County, Okla. 2006).

41. *Shirley Neely, et al v. West Orange-Cove Consolidated Independent School District, et al,* Case No. 04-1144 (Tex. 2005) (hereinafter "*West Orange-Cove*"); *Hancock, et al v. Commissioner of Education, et al,* Case No. SJC-09267 (Sup. Jud. Ct. Mass., Feb. 15, 2005) (hereinafter "*Hancock*").

to stay and will be an important part of the school finance land-
scape for years to come.

2. A "Presumption" of Unconstitutionality

In assuming the power to decide these traditionally political issues in the first place, the courts have strayed outside of their
traditional role. At most these constitutional provisions should
be read as establishing the minimum level of education required,
leaving maximum discretion in the legislature to decide whether
or not it wants and is willing to pay for a level of education
higher than the constitutional minimum. Indeed, the court decisions themselves speak of requiring only a "minimally adequate" or "basic" education, suggesting that once that floor is
reached or exceeded, the court no longer has a role to play.[42]
But in practice, these principles are often ignored when it comes
to actually specifying the quality of education or the funding levels that will satisfy the court. The reality is that many state courts
only pay lip service to these principles while in fact making evidentiary findings and setting goals for educators that require
much more than a minimum or basic education. For example,
speaking out of one side of their collective mouths, the New York
courts hold that the constitution only requires "minimally adequate" schools, but out of the other side, order funding levels for
schools intended to meet perhaps the highest academic standards in the country. In ordering billions of dollars of additional
annual payments to New York City, the trial court relied on a
costing out study conducted on behalf of the plaintiffs. The goal
of the study was to enable all students to meet the Regents
Learning Standards, which were described, even by plaintiffs'
witnesses, as "rigorous," "world-class," and exceeding notions

---

42. *Campaign for Fiscal Equity v. State of New York, et al*, 86 N.Y.2d 307,
317 (1995) (hereinafter *CFE I*).

of "basic literacy and verbal skills," the standard first enunciated by the New York Court of Appeals.[43] There seems little doubt that in New York the courts are setting education policy and spending, not enforcing constitutional minimums.

Some argue that education is a fundamental right, and that legislative enactments are therefore not entitled to deference but should be judged under a strict scrutiny standard. However, few courts have relied on this legal principle to justify their sweeping decisions. First, education has not been found to be a fundamental right in most states facing adequacy lawsuits. Second, even in those states where it is a fundamental right, the courts have been reluctant to justify their intrusion into legislative prerogatives by applying a strict scrutiny standard. Instead, they have found such a standard inappropriate in light of the public policy issues before them and the constitutionally based authority of the legislature over appropriations. For example, in the Kentucky adequacy case, the court held that education was a fundamental right but also held that the presumption of constitutionality was substantial and that legislative enactments were entitled to great weight.[44]

In summary, presumptions of constitutionality and deference to legislative choices often give way in adequacy litigation to what amounts to a presumption of unconstitutionality, coupled with little, if any, deference to the work of the legislative branches. The two main reasons for this development are discussed below.

43. *CFE*, Report and Recommendations of the Judicial Referees, Nov. 30, 2004; American Institute for Research and Management Analysis and Planning, Inc., *"The New York Adequacy Study: 'Determining the Cost of Providing All Children in New York an Adequate Education,'"* Vol. 1—Final Report, March 2004, at x, 4 (hereinafter "AIR/MAP Study"); CFE trial record, Transcript at 1108, 1715, 4993–4995, 9210, 9976, 10545; Plaintiffs exhibits 1587, 1588, 2064; Defendants' exhibits 10202, 15470A, 19017A.

44. *Rose v. Council for Better Education*, 790 S.W.2d at 209.

The Conversion of Ambitious Goals into Legal Requirements

In some states, the courts have set the standard of adequacy so high that few, if any, states could meet it. In setting the standard, the beginning point for any court inquiry should be the language of the education clause of the state constitution. Unfortunately, the words used in nearly every state constitution are so vague and general that they offer little practical guidance to someone who must actually formulate a workable definition. As discussed, state constitutions commonly use words like "thorough," "efficient," "free common schools," and "free instruction" in describing the kind of education required.[45] For this reason, the courts' interpretation of what such words mean is what counts. Although they often resort to the minutes, speeches, and other records of the constitutional conventions to divine a more specific definition of what level of education the framers of the constitution intended, the courts are often writing on a largely blank slate. Whether such interpretations have strong or weak support in the constitutional language or record is of little importance since the court's decision is final and is not appealable to any higher authority. This has led to court-imposed standards bearing little or no relation to the words of the constitution itself.

The trend in recent years has been to use student achievement standards set by the state, either directly or indirectly, to measure adequacy and therefore how much money is required to attain it.[46] The courts have moved in this direction despite recognition by at least one of them that "caution should be exercised" in relying on student outcome measures because (1) they are influenced by a "myriad of factors" beyond state fund-

45. *See, e.g.,* footnotes 27–30.
46. This has spawned a cottage industry of consultants who purport to "cost-out" how much money it will take for students to actually achieve at such levels. *See* Hanushek (2005).

ing and (2) such standards may be higher than the constitution requires.[47] The results have been legal standards of adequacy in several states set at very high levels, reflecting ambitious academic goals set by the states for their students to strive for, thereby ensuring court control for many years into the future. Even in cases where the courts have relied more on ensuring that appropriate resources are provided than on achieving particular student outcomes, the bar has been set at an extraordinarily high level. Three cases illustrate this point.

New York

Because it involves the nation's largest school system and astronomical amounts of money, the most notable case to date has been *Campaign for Fiscal Equity v. the State of New York* *("CFE")*. In *CFE*, the courts had before them a relatively weak constitutional provision that simply required the state of New York to provide "a system of free common schools" without specifying any particular level or quality of education.[48] The case was at first dismissed, but New York's Court of Appeals in *CFE I* reversed and remanded the case for trial, ruling that New York's constitution guaranteed a "sound basic education" requiring "minimally adequate" resources.[49] *CFE I* signified a relatively low constitutional minimum, but on remand, the trial court ruled this meant that the state was required to provide an education that would produce an "engaged, capable voter" with the "intellectual tools to evaluate complex issues, such as campaign finance reform, tax policy and global warming. . . ."[50] It held that the education provided in the New York City public schools did not meet this standard and that insufficient funding was the rea-

47. *CFE I*, at 317.
48. N.Y. Const., Art. XI, §1.
49. *CFE I*, at 318.
50. *CFE*, 187 Misc. 2d 1, 14 (Sup. Ct. New York County 2001).

son, despite the fact that New York City was then the highest spending of the nation's ten largest urban school districts, spending over $10,000 a year per student.[51] Although an intermediate appellate court reversed the trial court on both the facts and the law, the New York Court of Appeals reversed again and reinstated the trial court's decision in *CFE II*.[52] After the state legislature was unable to agree on a remedy, the trial court ordered the legislature to increase New York City's annual funding for operations by $5.63 billion a year to more than $17,000 a student. Although the appellate division later modified the trial court's order regarding funding, the legislature remains under court order to appropriate an additional $4.7 billion to $5.6 billion per year for the city's public schools.[53]

While the New York Court of Appeals in *CFE II* specifically disavowed reliance on the Regents Learning Standards,[54] perhaps the highest state academic standards in the nation, the trial court nevertheless relied on cost studies that used such high standards as its measure of adequacy. Consequently, the court process in New York has converted the words of the New York Constitution requiring only "free common schools" into a court-imposed constitutional requirement that the state provide the highest-quality education in the country and spend double what the rest of the nation is spending to provide it. To put the amounts ordered by the court in perspective, New Jersey is currently the highest spending state in the country on K–12 education at $12,568 per student for the 2002–2003 school year.[55] In the words of one commentator, the trial judge in *CFE* "had

51. *Id.* at 67–68, 82; CFE Trial Record, Defendants' Exhibit 19118.

52. *CFE*, 744 N.Y.S.2d 130 (1st Dept. 2002). This intermediate appellate court decision was reversed by the New York Court of Appeals in *CFE II* (*see* footnote 1).

53. *See* footnote 2.

54. *CFE II*, at 907.

55. *Quality Counts 2006*.

become completely unmoored from the text [of the constitution] and was sailing in purely policy waters" (Dunn and Derthick 2005).

Kansas

The Kansas courts have also suggested a standard so high that the legislature is unlikely to satisfy it, no matter what it does or how much money it spends. In December 2003 in *Montoy v. Kansas*, the trial judge held that the Kansas system of financing schools was unconstitutional because it failed to provide sufficient funding for the "suitable education" required under the Kansas constitution.[56] When the legislature failed to agree on remedial legislation, the court enjoined any further funding of the public schools in Kansas. As part of his order, the trial judge set forth a list of what the legislature would have to do for him to approve any new funding plan and to lift his injunction to allow the reopening of the schools. One requirement was that the new funding plan "must provide resources necessary to close the 'achievement gap.'"[57] In other words, Kansas had to meet a standard of achievement no other state has even come close to achieving for the trial judge to find its educational finance system constitutional.

In 2005, the Kansas Supreme Court affirmed the order of the trial court, and ordered the Kansas Legislature to appropriate an additional $853 million over the next two years, also threatening to enjoin school spending if its demands were not met.[58] Although stating in its 2005 decision that appropriate outcomes would play an important role going forward, the court in 2006 dismissed the case after the legislature responded with $755

56. *Montoy v. State*, Case No. 99-C-1738 (Dist. Ct. Shawnee County, Kan., Dec. 2, 2003).
57. *Montoy v. State*, 2004 WL 1094555 (Kan. Dist. Ct. 2004) at 9.
58. *Montoy v. State*, No. 92032 (S. Ct. Kan. June 3, 2005) at 19.

million in additional aid, without any discussion of whether such an increase was sufficient to achieve desired outcomes. That decision, it stated, would have to be made in a separate lawsuit challenging the newly enacted legislation.[59]

Wyoming

The decisions of the Wyoming Supreme Court have been even more radical. In 1995, in *Campbell County School District v. Wyoming*, the court, relying on constitutional language requiring a "thorough and efficient" and "complete and uniform" education, held that these words meant that the state was obligated to furnish and pay for the "best" education.[60] The court found that the existing education system failed to meet this lofty standard and ordered the legislature to enact a remedy.[61] The legislature responded by substantially increasing school funding, but in 2001 the court found the legislative response insufficient. The court reiterated that, in its view, the Wyoming Constitution requires the "best" education.[62] It embellished its earlier opinion by holding further that such education had to be "visionary" and "unsurpassed," and ordered the legislature once again to dramatically increase spending.[63]

As a result, Wyoming has increased spending to the point that, when adjusted for cost of living differences, it now has the fourth highest per-pupil expenditures in the nation.[64] The constitutional standard, as dictated by the Wyoming courts, has had the practical effect of removing all discretion from the legislature to decide on the quality or level of educational resources to pro-

59. *Id.*, at 17; *Montoy v. State*, No. 92032 (S. Ct. Kan. July 28, 2006), at 7.
60. *Campbell I,* at 1279.
61. *Id.*
62. *Campbell II,* at 538.
63. *Id.*
64. *Quality Counts 2006.*

vide. It effectively guarantees that anything the legislature enacts will be subject to second-guessing by the plaintiffs. Plaintiffs need only argue there is a "better" or more "visionary" education somewhere else that has not yet been made available to Wyoming students. Surprisingly, the latest Wyoming trial court to apply the *Campbell* decisions disregarded this language in finding that the current system of education complies in many respects with constitutional requirements. But whether its decision will be upheld in light of the Wyoming Supreme Court's earlier pronouncements remains to be seen.[65]

To many these decisions sound reasonable. Almost everyone would agree that providing the "best" education possible or having an educational system in which all students achieve at high levels and the achievement gap is closed are worthy goals. And, of course, they are right. The "goal" of any education system should be to educate all children so that they learn at high levels regardless of whether they are poor or wealthy, black or white. But this is a far cry from ruling that a state's educational funding system is unconstitutional unless it actually reaches these aspirational goals. The unfortunate reality is that a significant achievement gap exists in every state. There is not a state or school district of any size in the United States, no matter how good it is or how much money it spends, that has closed the achievement gap between black and white students or between poor and middle-class students (Jencks and Phillips 1998). Ipso facto, under the rationale used by the Kansas trial court, there is not one state in the country that provides an adequate education. The inevitable result of such a standard is to guarantee court supervision for years and even decades as plaintiffs seek even more money, returning to court repeatedly arguing that the unrealistic goals first set by the court have not yet been reached.

65. *Campbell County School District, et al v. State of Wyoming, et al*, Docket No. 129-59 (1st Jud. Dist., Wyo., Jan. 31, 2006) (hereinafter "*Campbell 2006*").

Moreover, state academic standards are not the same as the constitutional standard. If that were so, then the legislature or the state boards of education could amend the state constitutions at will by changing the state academic standards. The New York Court of Appeals recognized the inherent conflict in giving constitutional status to legislatively or administratively created academic standards, but, as discussed, the *CFE* trial court nevertheless used a cost study designed to meet such state academic standards as the constitutional measure of adequacy.

Plaintiffs argue that outcome standards are set by the states themselves and that they are therefore reasonable measures of adequacy. However, while states should encourage all children to learn by setting high standards, holding a state financially liable for the failure of their students to achieve at such levels puts the state in an untenable position. It can either adopt lower expectations for children or run the serious risk that, if it has set the standards too high, it will be held liable for untold hundreds of millions or even billions of dollars. No Child Left Behind (NCLB) has also set lofty goals, but these are not state or constitutional requirements. They are a condition precedent to receiving federal funds. Indeed, NCLB provides that a state is not required to incur costs to comply with any of its requirements that are not covered by federal funding.[66]

For these reasons, court decisions setting unrealistically high outcome requirements ensure a court veto over everything the legislature does. Even if ample inputs are provided, no one can honestly give any assurance that the required outcome standards will be satisfied by all or nearly all children. For example, the consultants in the costing out study relied on in *CFE* to justify another $5.63 billion a year for a "sound basic education" in New York City qualified their conclusions as follows:

66. 20 USC § 7907.

It must be recognized that the success of schools also depends on other individuals and institutions to provide the health, intellectual stimulus, and family support upon which the public school systems can build. Schools cannot and do not perform their role in a vacuum, and this is an important qualification of conclusions reached in any study of adequacy in education.[67]

The Elimination of Proof of Causation

The courts in some states have further ensured their domination over issues of education policy and funding by effectively rendering meaningless plaintiffs' burden to prove causation. The *CFE* case perhaps best illustrates this development. Before trial, the New York Court of Appeals in *CFE I* ruled that plaintiffs had the burden to prove both (1) that there had been a failure to provide a "sound basic education" in the New York City public schools and (2) that such failures were "caused" by the state financing system.[68] The court further cautioned the trial judge to "carefully scrutinize" outcomes such as standardized test scores because such outcomes were influenced by a "myriad of factors."[69] Thus, in accord with precedent and with common sense, plaintiffs had to prove that any inadequacies in the New York City schools were caused by the state financing system in order to hold the state legally liable. Moreover, because there were many other factors besides the state funding system that influenced achievement, outcomes were not to play a major role in the trial court's decision on whether the education offered was adequate.

However, when it revisited the case after trial in *CFE II*, the same court eviscerated its earlier holding that causation had to be established. First, the court disregarded substantial evidence

67. AIR/MAP Study, at f.n.12, p. 3.
68. *CFE I,* at 318.
69. *Id.*

that alleged funding shortages were caused by mismanagement, waste, and fraud in the New York City School District, and not the state funding system. It avoided examining these difficult, but obviously relevant, issues by ruling, as a matter of law, that the state was legally responsible for the shortcomings of the local district.[70]

Second, it held that factors outside the schools, such as student poverty, were not the cause of substandard achievement by many of the district's "at-risk" pupils, relying largely on a policy adopted by the New York Board of Regents that, "all children can learn given appropriate instructional, social and health services."[71] It scornfully rejected extensive scientific evidence showing the issue was much more complicated than the Board of Regents' simple statement suggested, stating simply "we cannot accept the premise that children come to the New York City schools ineducable, unfit to learn."[72] That, of course, was not the state's position. No one disputed that every child can learn, but it is equally true that because of their differing backgrounds, children start out at different levels, may learn at different rates, may not be similarly motivated, and may face many difficulties and obstacles that schools have not caused and that schools may not be able to solve. These real world problems were never addressed by the court. The court also failed to discuss how a constitutional provision requiring "free common schools" carries with it the constitutional obligation of the state to provide the "social and health services" needed, according to the policy statement relied on by the court, for "all children to learn." However, the court, having the last say on the matter, was under no obligation to explain this gap in its reasoning.

Strangely, the same day it was holding the state liable for

70. *CFE II,* at 922–23.
71. *CFE II,* at 915, 920–21.
72. *CFE II,* at 919.

failing to overcome adverse socio-economic influences in New York City, the court was doing the exact opposite in another adequacy case involving the Rochester, New York, schools. This time, after quoting the words of *CFE I* about the need to exercise "caution" in judging outcomes because of the "myriad of factors" influencing them, it ruled for the state, holding that the claims asserted in the Rochester case did not rest on a lack of funding but "on the failure to mitigate demographics."[73] That, of course, is the very same thing the court was holding the state liable for in the *CFE* case—the failure to mitigate the demographics of New York City's large impoverished public school population.

Because of its rulings, the *CFE II* court effectively eliminated the consideration of evidence of any causes of low student achievement, other than a lack of funding. Other problems having an adverse effect on learning, both inside and outside the schools, were ignored. The practical result was to largely remove the element of causation from the case and hold the state strictly liable for poor test scores and other substandard conditions in the city's schools, regardless of the complicity of others, including the local district, in causing such circumstances.

Part of the court's opinion purports to address causation, but its reasoning is less than persuasive. It concludes that plaintiffs proved causation based on evidence that (1) some of the resource shortcomings plaintiffs alleged could be resolved, for example, large class sizes, if the state funding system provided the school district more money, and (2) such added resources would yield better student performance.[74] There is no doubt that more money could buy more things, but that should never have been the issue. The relevant issue was whether the $10-billion-plus budget then available to the New York City School District was

73. *Paynter v. State of New York*, 100 N.Y.2d 434 (2003), at 3, 6.
74. *CFE II*, at 914–919.

enough for it to provide a "sound basic education," the constitutional standard laid down in *CFE I, assuming the money was
not wasted*. That issue was never addressed or decided. The
only evidence offered on the issue, a cost study offered by the
state showing that existing funding was sufficient to provide a
sound basic education if used effectively, was rejected by the
trial court on hearsay grounds, even though the same court later
accepted a cost study offered by plaintiffs during hearings on
remedy that relied on exactly the same methodology.[75] Under
the rationale employed in *CFE II*, the New York City Board of
Education could have been wasting half its budget, and plaintiffs
could still have established the necessary causal link by showing
that more money from the state would have allowed it to purchase the education resources its schools were lacking because
of the board's waste.

The *CFE II* court further ignored the cautionary note in *CFE
I* about outcome evidence. It not only relied on test scores and
other outcome evidence in reaching its decision but declined to
consider the "myriad of factors" that affect student achievement,
such as student poverty."[76] In Kansas, the court applied similar
reasoning and relied mainly on the evidence of substandard performance of poor and minority students in holding the state li-

---

75. During subsequent remedial proceedings, CFE retained two of the state's
trial experts to conduct a cost study to determine how much an adequate education should cost in New York City. Relying on the same professional judgment approach they used when working for the state, the same experts, working with another group of consultants, conducted another cost study, using as
the standard of adequacy the Regents Learning Standards. This time the trial
court overlooked the hearsay problems that it had cited in rejecting the study
tendered by the state at trial, and relied on the plaintiffs' study in ordering an
additional $5.63 billion a year in funding for the New York City public schools.
Tr. 18386-18415 (Smith testimony) and DX19415, *CFE* trial record; *CFE* (Orders
dated Feb. 14, 2005 and March 22, 2005).

76. *CFE II*, at 915, 919–923.

able, while paying lip service to possible causes of such low performance, besides a lack of funding.[77]

This treatment of the essential element of causation is unprecedented. In earlier federal court school finance litigation, both states and school districts have been held liable and ordered to correct deficiencies that they had caused and that they had the power to correct. However, the courts drew the line at holding them responsible for problems they did not cause. In *Freeman v. Pitts*, the Supreme Court declined to hold school districts liable for eliminating one-race schools caused by demographic forces.[78] In *Milliken I*, the Court refused to extend its remedy to suburban school districts in order to further integrate the schools in a metropolitan area unless it could be shown that such school districts had played a role in causing the segregated schools.[79] In *Jenkins III*, the Court held that the state of Missouri and the Kansas City School District could not be held liable for the low achievement of black children unless it was shown that their actions had caused such low achievement.[80] In the state court equity cases, the states had it in their exclusive power to correct inequities in their school funding laws. There was never a question of the state being held liable to correct problems it had not created and that were beyond its power to remedy.

This critical analysis of the courts' treatment of the element of causation is not just legal nitpicking. By disregarding evidence of waste of existing funds by local school districts and other nonfinancial factors inside and outside of the schools leading to substandard student performance, the courts are traveling down a road of no return that has serious consequences for the legislature, students, taxpayers, educators, and courts themselves.

77. *Montoy v. State*, No. 92032 (S. Ct. Kan., June 3, 2005).
78. *Freeman v. Pitts*, 503 U.S. 467, 491 (1992).
79. *Milliken v. Bradley,* 418 U.S. 717, 744 (1974).
80. *Jenkins III*, 515 U.S. at 101.

Remedies are unlikely to be effective if they disregard the actual causes of the problems. Perhaps the thought is that the real problems can be papered over with enough money. However, that premise is dubious as demonstrated in later chapters of this book.

Since the courts have ruled that all children can learn if only more resources are provided, there is enormous pressure on the legislature to appropriate more money for such things as more teachers, higher teacher pay, smaller class sizes, before- and after-school programs, preschool programs, and other special programs. Other means of educational reform that do not depend on more money but may ultimately be more effective at raising achievement are pushed to the back burner or off the legislative agenda. These include, for example, stronger accountability programs designed to motivate both students and schools to do better, expanded choice options that introduce healthy competition into public education, alternative methods of paying teachers based on merit and their success at improving student performance, and most important, steps to ensure that local districts are effectively using their current funding. They might also include more state spending on programs outside the schools to deal with societal ills faced by at-risk students, such as poverty, crime, and dysfunctional families. Nonschool programs that directly attack the root of the problem may be more effective at improving student achievement than more money spent inside the schools (Rothstein 2004; Armor 2005). However, by ruling that low achievement is caused by insufficient resources, the courts have essentially closed the door on other forms of educational reform.

Substantial spending increases in the past on K–12 education have had little or no effect on improving student performance. Statistics compiled by the National Center for Education Statistics show that from 1960 to 1996, inflation-adjusted spending on public schools more than tripled. Despite this huge three-fold increase in resources, reading and science scores on the National Assessment of Educational Progress (NAEP) showed little or no improvement from 1969 to 1999, while math scores showed only slight improvement (Peterson and West 2004; Burtless 1996). Moreover, the academic research is mixed, at best, over whether increased funding and resources are likely to lead to significantly improved achievement. See Hanushek (1989, 1994), Odden and Picus (1992, 277–281), and Hedges (1994). This suggests that increased spending under an adequacy order is no more likely to improve achievement in the future than it has in the past, unless there are fundamental changes in the way such money is spent. Yet in another twist of irony, adequacy plaintiffs and their supporters in the public school establishment and the teacher's unions strongly oppose fundamental changes in the way education monies are spent (Lindseth 2004).

New Jersey is a good example of the problems inherent in such remedies. It has been in continuous litigation over its school finance system for more than thirty years.[81] At first the litigation focused on equity issues. In 1998, however, the court began to concentrate on the adequacy of the education being offered in thirty "special needs districts."[82] After a dozen trips to the legislature, followed by return trips to the courts in which the courts have ordered billions of dollars in additional resources, New Jersey now spends more per student on education than any other state in the country does.[83] Moreover, the thirty special needs districts are funded at a level about $3,000 per

81. *See* history of New Jersey school funding litigation from 1973 through 1998 in *Abbott v. Burke*, 710 A.2d 450, 455–456. The litigation continues to the present. *See, also Abbott*, 798 A.2d 602 (N.J. 2002), clearing the way for further claims and appeals.

82. *Abbott v. Burke*, 710 A.2d 450 (N.J. 1998) (history of case through 1998).

83. *Quality Counts 2006*.

student higher than even the "wealthy" school districts in the state.[84] As expected, this financial effort has led to more resources and programs for the schools but has done little to bring about higher achievement.[85]

Although many state constitutions use the word "efficient" to describe the education system required, the critical question of whether waste, mismanagement, and inefficiency at the local district level are the reasons for the lack of critical resources or of acceptable outcomes is seldom addressed in the court decisions. The courts sidestep this important issue by ruling that *if* such problems are present at the local level, the state is also liable for them. For example, in the *CFE* case, extensive evidence was introduced at trial of waste, fraud, corruption, and mismanagement in the New York City public schools that cost hundreds of millions of dollars a year. Even though the court of appeals found such evidence "disturbing," it did not rule on the extent of such problems or on whether they constituted a significant cause of the inadequacies found by the court in the city's public schools. Instead, the court ruled that to the extent such problems exist, the state is also responsible for seeing to it that they are corrected.[86] It concludes, without any significant analysis, that elimination of waste will not "obviate the need for changes to the funding system" and that the remedy it favors is increased funding.[87]

---

84. Center for Government Services, Rutgers, *New Jersey's Public Schools: A Biennial Report for the People of New Jersey 2002–2003 Edition*, Appendix A.4, www.policy.rutgers.edu/cgs/PDF/NJPS02.pdf.

85. A recent report states that third grade test scores in New Jersey have improved in the last three years; however, there has been little or no improvement in achievement in other grades. Long and Goertz (2004). After more than thirty years of litigation and at least ten years of huge funding increases for the thirty special needs districts, such results are, to say the least, disappointing. *See also* Guthrie (2004).

86. *CFE II,* at 921–923.

87. *CFE II*, at 929.

Wyoming's constitution requires, among other things, an "efficient" system of education. However, aside from one sentence in the supreme court's opinions suggesting that "efficient" means "productive without waste," there is no further discussion about requiring the efficient or cost-effective use of funds.[88] Indeed, the court's order that the "best education" and an education "visionary and unsurpassed" be provided indicates that efficiency was not a significant concern to the court.[89] In Kansas, the trial court evinced the same attitude: "Addressing problems of management and accountability is *also* Defendants' responsibility."[90]

Courts are empowered to make determinations about the effects of waste and mismanagement at the local level and about what part of the problem calls for a nonfinancial remedy. Such a finding would notify the legislature that funding is only part of the solution, and perhaps not even the principal solution, and allow it to concentrate on cutting out waste and inefficiency, instead of solely on appropriating more money. Suitable legislation could then be enacted instead of simply throwing money at the problem. Unfortunately, because all other causes of low achievement are given only lip service by the courts in finding liability, the primary and often sole focus of the court orders, and thus of the legislative response, has been on increasing funding for education. Nary a word is said about reform at the local district

88. *Campbell County School District v. State*, 907 P.2d 1238,1258-1259 (Wyo. 1995); *State v. Campbell County School District*, 19 P.2d 518, 538 (Wyo. 2001).

89. Yet in contrast to the state supreme court decisions, the latest Wyoming trial court to rule on adequacy issues relied on the words "productive without waste" in judging recent legislative efforts, without ever mentioning the supreme court's direction that the education provided be the "best." *Campbell 2006*, at 127. How the Wyoming Supreme Court will view this fundamental change in emphasis remains to be seen.

90. *Montoy v. State*, Case No. 99-C-1738 (Dist. Ct. Shawnee County, Kan., Dec. 2, 2003) at 79.

level or about alternative measures of educational reform that might hold out more hope for success.[91]

3. The Efficacy of Court-Ordered Remedies

The intrusion of the courts into what have traditionally been political matters reserved to the executive and legislative branches of government has put a tremendous strain on the relations among the three branches of government in many states. This is most apparent during the remedial phase of adequacy litigation as the court tries to impose its will on recalcitrant legislators who believe that they, and not the courts, are endowed under the constitution to make education policy and to decide how much of the state's public treasury should be spent on education. In New York and other states, the situation has been exacerbated by the court's extraordinary financial demands, which ignore the political and financial realities facing a state and its legislature. The result has been a showdown between the courts and the legislature, leading in some instances to suggestions that the legislature simply refuse to obey the court order. In his column in *Newsweek* magazine, George Will, the well-respected conservative writer, had this to say to the New York legislature about how it should treat the court order in that state which dictated a $23 billion increase in funding for the New York City public schools over the next five years: "New York's Supreme Court can neither tax nor spend. The state legislature is not a party to the suit, so it cannot be held in contempt. Perhaps it should just ignore the court's ruling as noise not relevant to the rule of law. Which happens to be the case."[92]

---

91. There are other strong reasons why the courts are not suited to decide what are essentially policy and funding issues, but a full treatment of these problems is beyond the scope of this chapter.

92. George Will, *Judges and "Soft Rights," Newsweek*, Feb. 28, 2005.

To date, only one court has been faced with the direct refusal of the legislature to obey its order. Either the courts have backed down, as happened in Ohio and Alabama, where after years of litigation the courts finally dismissed adequacy cases, belatedly acknowledging that educational funding was for the legislature to decide,[93] or the legislature of the state has increased funding for education enough to satisfy the court, at least for the time being. However, the issue has come to a head in both New York and Kansas where the courts expressly ordered the state legislatures to raise K–12 education spending by specific amounts. This places the burden of complying with the court order directly in the lap of the state legislature, which more than likely has not even been a party to the litigation, but is handed the bill after the state's liability has been established.

If a legislature refuses to comply with a court order to increase funding, the courts have two mechanisms to force compliance—enjoining school funding and the power of contempt. Both are problematic in the context of an adequacy case for several reasons.

The clearest power the court possesses is its authority to enjoin any further spending on schools under the education funding statutes of the state until the legislature adopts reforms that will, in the eyes of the court, cure the constitutional defects in the educational funding system. Cutting off education funding and closing the schools is obviously a step any court would be extremely reluctant to take. Implementing such a remedy would hurt the very children that an adequacy remedy is supposed to help. Therefore, it is not a remedial measure but a blunt weapon the courts use to bludgeon the legislature into doing its bidding.

93. *State ex rel. State v. Lewis*, 789 N.E.2d 195 (Ohio 2003), *cert. denied*, 124 S.Ct. 432 (2003); *Alabama Coalition for Equity v. Fob James, et al.* (Case Nos. 1950030, 1950031, 1950240, 1950241, 195040, 1950409, S.Ct. Ala. May 31, 2002).

The courts of only two states have thus far flirted with this enforcement tool. In 1976, the New Jersey courts enjoined any funding of the schools until the legislature appropriated the additional education funding ordered by the court. After eight days, the governor and the legislature blinked first, passed the state's first income tax, and appropriated the court-ordered increase.[94] In 2003 a Kansas trial judge enjoined all further spending on the state's public schools until the legislature acted to pass remedial legislation.[95] It caused a furor in the state, and within a week the Kansas Supreme Court stayed the order.[96] However, in 2005 the Kansas Supreme Court threatened similar action when it upheld the trial court's decision and the Kansas legislature at first failed to comply with its order. In the closing moments of a special session called to address the court order and over the objections of its leaders, the legislature approved the required first installment of $285 million in additional funding ordered by the courts, thereby narrowly averting, for at least the next year, an impasse between it and the courts.[97] Only the appropriation of an additional $466 million increase in 2006 ended the crisis, at least until another suit is filed challenging the new funding system.

Closing the schools is the "nuclear option" and how the courts or legislative bodies would react if the schools were actually closed is unknown. Whether any court ever resorts to this measure, other than during the summer break, most likely depends on the court convincing itself that legislators will not let the public schools close under any circumstances and will "cave in" to the courts' directives.

94. Education Law Center, *History of Abbott*, http://edlawcenter.org/ELCPublic/AbbottvBurke/AbbottHistory.htm.

95. *See* footnote 57.

96. *Montoy v. State*, No. 92032 (Kan. S. Ct., May 19, 2004).

97. Steve Painter, *$148 Million More*, Wichita Eagle, July 7, 2005.

The second measure a court has to enforce an adequacy order lies in its power to hold in contempt the state, its institutions, and the state officials who refuse to comply with the court's order, and either to fine them, or in the case of officials, possibly to put them in jail until they obey the order. However, the legality and the practicality of using the contempt power are uncertain, to say the least. First, there is a serious question about whether a court can order a legislature to appropriate a specific amount for education. Most state constitutions expressly provide that the power of appropriation is vested exclusively in the legislature.[98] Moreover, in most cases, neither the legislature nor its members are even parties to the adequacy case, and the authority of the court to hold nonparties in contempt is limited in most states. Most states require that a nonparty must not only have knowledge or notice of the court order but must also either be in privity with the party named in the injunction, or act in collusion with the named party.[99]

Even if the court has the jurisdiction to hold state officials in contempt, there is the question of exactly who the court should penalize. No single legislator has the power to bind the state or to pass legislation, and therefore the ability to purge himself or herself of contempt. Theoretically, the court could hold all legislators in contempt or perhaps only those who vote against a funding bill. However, such a blanket contempt citation would enmesh the court right into the heart of the legislative process

---

98. *E.g.*, N.Y. Const., Art. VII, §7; Fla. Const., Art. VII, §c. ("No money shall be drawn from the treasury except in pursuance of appropriation made by law.") Kan. Const., Art. 2, § 24 ("No money shall be drawn from the treasury except in pursuance of a specific appropriation made by law."); Kan. Const., Art. 11, § 5 ("No tax shall be levied except in pursuance of a law, which shall distinctly state the object of the same; to which object only such that shall be applied").

99. *See e.g., Frey v. Willey*, 166 P.2d 659, 662 (Kan. 1946*); State Univ. of N.Y. v. Denton*, 316 N.Y.S.2d 297, 299 (N.Y. App. Div. 1970).

by requiring a "yes" vote on legislation that there might be a hundred reasons for a legislator to oppose. Besides, does anyone seriously believe a court would put the entire legislature in jail, and if it did, who would carry out such an order?

A more likely target of a contempt citation would be the state itself. The "state" could not be imprisoned, but it could be fined. That is the enforcement mechanism plaintiffs are relying on in the *CFE* case, where they are seeking to have the state fined $4 million for each day it fails to comply with the court order. In 2004 the trial court denied plaintiffs' contempt motion because no unequivocal order had yet been entered requiring the state to increase funding by a specific amount.[100] A specific order has now been issued, but it has been stayed during the pendency of the appeal.[101] If the orders of the trial court or appellate division are affirmed, it remains to be seen what action the court will take if the legislature fails to appropriate the sums ordered, but plaintiffs will almost certainly seek large fines.[102] But suppose the state is fined and the legislature refuses to appropriate money to pay the fines, as would be likely if it had already re-fused to appropriate money to satisfy the courts' spending or-der? It is possible that the governor, as the chief executive officer of the state, could be fined or jailed for contempt, but that is unlikely. No governor has it within his or her power to appro-priate state money, no matter how much he or she might favor such an appropriation. Moreover, who would enforce an order to jail the governor for contempt? A contempt order against the state education department, state superintendent of education, and state board of education, would be equally unavailing be-cause they have no power or financial wherewithal to raise

---

100. *CFE*, Index No. 111070/93 (Sup. Ct. New York County, Feb. 14, 2005).
101. *See* footnote 2.
102. *See* footnote 100.

spending without additional appropriations from the state legislature.

Because of these inherent legal and practical problems, in the end the power of the courts to enforce their remedies seems to lie in the reasonableness and persuasiveness of their orders. If the voting public believes that the courts are right, and that spending increases in the range ordered by the courts, and the tax increases to support them, are warranted, a legislature is likely to comply with the court orders enough to satisfy the court without the court having to resort to such drastic remedies. However, if legislators are not convinced the public will support such spending and tax increases, the courts are unlikely, as a practical matter, to be able to force their will on a reluctant legislature. The result will be a constitutional crisis that will serve to weaken and diminish respect for both the judicial system and for other branches of government without benefiting children.

4. A New Direction

Until 2005 plaintiffs had won almost every adequacy case that had survived a motion to dismiss on separation of powers grounds and been taken to trial. However, beginning in 2005 this winning streak came to an end, when the highest courts in Texas and Massachusetts ruled for the state defendants. Although the trial courts, reflecting the trends discussed above, had found the educational financing systems in both states unconstitutional, the supreme court of each state soundly reversed. In both cases, the high courts took a fundamentally different view of the state's constitutional obligations than had previously been the case. Picking up on the themes expressed in this chapter, both courts recognized that perfection in the form of all or most students meeting high state academic standards was not demanded by the constitution, that the choices made by the legislature in establishing the state's educational system should be afforded deference by the court, and that evidence that more money was the answer to achievement problems was not to be trusted.

Massachusetts

Of the two decisions, Massachusetts should have been the least surprising, except that its highest court is reputed to be one of the most liberal in the country. The commonwealth had previously been held liable in an adequacy case in *McDuffy v. Secretary, Executive Office of Education*. However, in the decade following that decision, its legislature had not only tripled spending on education from roughly $3 billion to $10 billion a year but had made other important reforms, all to satisfy a vague constitutional command to "cherish education."[103] Because of this enormous effort, if the defense could not win in Massachusetts, it was unlikely to prevail in any state. The main significance of the decision lies in its recognition that attainment by all or most children of academic standards purposely set high to challenge them should not be the measure of whether a state's educational system is constitutional or not. State legislatures have choices to make, the court said, and if those choices are reasonable and are having a positive effect, such choices are entitled to deference by the court.[104] Other courts had not previously given effect to these seemingly simple and obvious principles.

Texas

Texas was a more difficult case for the state. Although it could make claims similar to Massachusetts' of improving student

103. *Hancock,* at 1139.
104. *Hancock,* at 1139, 1156.

achievement, for example, the "Texas Miracle" and the establishment of strong accountability measures, that was where the similarities ended. While Massachusetts was the fourth highest spending state in the country in 2002–2003, Texas was the thirty-fourth highest, spending almost a thousand dollars per pupil below the national average.[105] For money-oriented plaintiffs, this is a critical distinction.

The background of the case is complex in that it involved not only issues of educational adequacy but of whether the state system of financing public schools was a "state property tax" prohibited by the state constitution. Plaintiffs prevailed on the latter issue; however, in the same decision, the court rejected adequacy claims by less affluent intervenor school districts.[106] Thus, although the Texas legislature will still have to wrestle with redoing its state tax system to replace the illegal "state property tax," it is under no duty to increase funding for schools in order to provide an "adequate" education.

In reversing the trial court, the Texas Supreme Court gave substance to the principle that courts should give deference to legislative choices. While it refused to dismiss the case on separation of powers grounds, it heeded long-standing precedent that judicial intrusion be minimized. It expressly recognized that its role was not to make policy but only to decide if the education being provided satisfied the constitution.

> [W]e must decide only whether public education is achieving the general diffusion of knowledge the Constitution requires. Whether public education is achieving all it should—that is, whether public education is a sufficient and fitting preparation of Texas children for the future—involves political and policy considerations properly directed to the Legislature.[107]

105. *Quality Counts 2006.*
106. *West Orange Cove.*
107. *Id.*, at 7.

Therefore, the court held it would not remedy "deficiencies and disparities in public education" in Texas that fell "short of a constitutional violation."[108] Those problems, the court ruled, would have to be remedied "through the political processes of legislation and elections." It acknowledged evidence of "wide gaps in performance" between disadvantaged students and other students, high dropout and noncompletion rates and a low rate of college preparedness but refused to condemn Texas's system because of low achievement, holding that "they [low performance outcomes] cannot be used to fault a public education system that is working to meet their stated goals merely because it has not yet succeeded in doing so."[109] Instead, it focused on the positive—that standardized test scores were improving, even as the tests themselves were being made more difficult, that NAEP scores in Texas had improved relative to those in other states,[110] and that the necessary elements of a system of education had been provided, that is, "a state curriculum, a standardized test to measure how well the curriculum is being taught, accreditation standards to hold schools accountable for their performance, and sanction and remedial measures for students, schools, and districts to ensure that accreditation standards are met."[111]

On the more-money argument crucial in other cases, the court recognized that the "end-product of a public education and resources" are related, but that "the relationship is neither simple nor direct."[112] It flatly rejected the notion that more money was either the solution or the only solution, holding that "more

108. *Id.*, at 8.
109. *Id.*, at 90.
110. *Id.*, at 90.
111. *Id.*, at 35.
112. *Id.*, at 88–89.

money does not guarantee better schools or more educated students."[113]

Showing due deference to its coequal branches of government, the court ruled that the constitution allowed the legislature "much latitude in choosing among any number of alternatives that can reasonably be considered adequate, efficient, and suitable." It therefore held that "[i]f the legislature's choices are informed by guiding rules and principles properly related to public education—that is, if the choices are not arbitrary—then the system does not violate the constitutional provision."[114]

Moreover, it emphasized that "arbitrary" did not mean "a mere difference of opinion [between judges and legislators], where reasonable minds could differ . . ." and that the courts "must not substitute their policy choices for the Legislature's."[115] Based on its examination of the record and applying the previously mentioned principles, the court rejected plaintiffs-intervenors' adequacy claims.[116]

In summary, based on a set of rules that did not preordain the outcome, both states were able to convince the courts that their education systems, while far from perfect, nevertheless satisfied the minimum constitutional standards of their respective states and that control over such systems should therefore properly remain in the legislature.

Conclusions

In conclusion, adequacy cases are increasing in number and intensity. In many states, the courts have made themselves not only the final arbiter of educational policy and of funding deci-

113. *Id.*, at 89.
114. *Id.*, at 81.
115. *Id.*, at 81.
116. *Id.*, at 91.

sions, but have done so in a way that maximizes, and not minimizes, judicial interference with the legislative process. Through their rulings, the courts have adopted definitions of adequacy that are extremely difficult for state legislatures to meet, no matter how much the state spends on education. This ensures court domination for decades as legislatures struggle to meet court orders that ignore political and financial realities.

Several recent court decisions suggest that the courts themselves realize that some of the earlier court decisions have gone too far. The 2005 decision of the Texas Supreme Court, in particular, avoids the "presumption" of unconstitutionality discussed in this chapter and preserves the traditional balance of power between the courts and the legislature. It provides for court review to ensure that minimum constitutional guarantees are satisfied, while at the same time recognizing that the courts' role is a limited one and that substantial discretion should be left in the legislature to decide matters of educational policy and appropriations.

The stakes in adequacy litigation are huge for children, educational reform, and representative government, but only the future will tell which of these radically different paths the courts in other states will take.

References

Armor, David J. 2005. "Can NCLB Close the Achievement Gap?" presented at the American Sociological Association special session on No Child Left Behind, Philadelphia, PA, August.

Burtless, Gary. 1996. *Does Money Matter? The Effect of School Resources on Student Achievement and Adult Success.* Washington, DC: Brookings Institution Press.

Dunn, Joshua and Martha Derthick. 2005. "Who Should Govern? Adequacy Litigation and the Separation of Powers," presented at conference entitled "Adequacy Lawsuits: Their Growing Impact on American Education," Kennedy School of Government, Harvard University, October 13–14.

Fischel, William. 2004. "Did John Serrano Vote for Proposition 13? A Reply to Start and Zasloff's 'Tiebout and Tax Revolts: Did Serrano Really Cause Proposition 13?,'" a paper delivered at the 2004 American Education Finance Association meeting in Salt Lake City, March 10–13.

Gorman, Siobhan. 2001. "Can't Beat 'em? Join 'em! What Liberal Lawyers Love about Bush's Education Plan." *Washington Monthly*, December.

Guthrie, James W. 2004. "Serrano's Education Finance Successors: Have Policy System Aspirations Outstripped Social Science Answers?," a paper presented to the American Education Research Association at its annual meeting in San Diego, California, April 15.

Hanushek, Eric A. 1989. "The Impact of Differential Expenditures on School Performance." *Education Researcher* 18, no. 4:45.

Hanushek, Eric A., Charles S. Benson, Richard B. Freeman, Dean T. Jameson, Henry M. Levin, Rebecca A. Maynard, Richard J. Murname, et al. 1994. *Making Schools Work: Improving Performance and Controlling Costs*. Washington, DC: Brookings Institution Press.

Hanushek, Eric A. 2005. "The Alchemy of 'Costing Out' and Adequate Education," presented at conference entitled "Adequacy Lawsuits: Their Growing Impact on American Education," Kennedy School of Government, Harvard University, October 13–14.

Hedges, Larry V., et al. 1994. "Does Money Matter? A Meta-Analysis of Studies of the Effects of Differential School Inputs on Student Outcomes." *Education Researcher* 23, no. 3:5.

Heise, Michael. 2002. "Educational Jujitsu; How School Finance Lawyers Learned to Turn Standards and Accountability into Dollar." *Education Next* (Fall).

Jencks and Phillips, eds. 1998. *The Black-White Test Score Gap*. Washington, DC: Brookings Institution Press.

Lindseth, Alfred A. 2004. "Educational Adequacy Lawsuits: The Rest of the Story," presented at conference entitled "50 Years after Brown: What Has Been Accomplished and What Remains to Be Done?" Kennedy School of Government, Harvard University, April 23–24.

Long, David and Peg Goertz. 2004. "Linking Funding Adequacy to Educational Improvement," a paper presented at conference entitled "Education Finance in a Time of Fiscal Stress," 29th annual conference of the American Educational Finance Association, Salt Lake City, Utah, March 11.

Murray, S. E., W. N. Evans, and R. M. Schwab. 1998. "Education Finance Reform and the Distribution of Education Resources." *American Economic Review* 88(4).

Odden, Allan R. and Lawrence Picus. 1992. *School Finance: A Policy Perspective.* New York: McGraw-Hill.

Peterson, Paul E. and Martin R. West. 2004. "Money Has Not Been Left Behind." *Education Week.* March 17.

Rebell, Michael J. 2001. "Educational Adequacy, Democracy, and the Courts." In *Achieving High Educational Standards For All,* ed. Timothy Ready, Christopher Edley, Jr., and Catherine E. Snow. Washington, DC: National Research Council.

Rothstein, Richard. 2004. *Class and Schools, Using Social, Economic, and Educational Reform to Close the Black-White Achievement Gap.* New York: Economic Policy Institute, Columbia University Teachers College.

Shrag, Peter. 2003. *Final Test: The Battle for Adequacy in America's Schools.* New York: New Press.

3

High-Poverty, High-Performance Schools, Districts, and States

Herbert J. Walberg

THE CENTRAL CONTENTION of plaintiffs in financial adequacy cases is that schools, particularly high-poverty schools, can achieve more only with higher spending. It is true that poverty has consistent and substantial effects on achievement, but many studies show little consistent effect of the amount spent on K–12 schools (Hanushek 1997). State legislators are justifiably concerned about spending more on education: not only are they pressed against raising taxes, but they are increasingly aware of the facts about the futility of additional spending. National comparisons show the United States has been and is a top spender on schools; yet American students fall further behind students in other countries, the longer they are in school (Walberg 2001). Ever larger expenditures, moreover, in the last several decades have not resulted in higher achievement.

Even so, the surveys of schools, districts, and states reviewed in this chapter show that some are able to make outstanding progress in overcoming the effects of poverty; without necessarily spending more money, they produce much higher levels of achievement than their peers. These surveys not only identify such high performers (also called "outliers") but reveal the reasons for their success.

The chapter begins with a more detailed explanation of high-poverty, high-performance outliers. To set this research in a legal context, the chapter next turns to evidentiary material from an adequacy litigation case in South Carolina that suggests the causes of high performance, including evidence-based legislation described in appendix 3.1. It is followed by a summary of large-scale national studies of schools, showing that high-performance outlier schools can be found throughout the nation.

The next section summarizes field studies in New York City and Texas that identify outlier schools and confirm a pattern of outlier performance. The last section shows that outlying school districts and states use on a larger scale the features that make schools high performers. Thus, research reviewed in this chapter shows the prevalence and causes of high-poverty, high-performance schools, districts, and states that are unrelated to spending.

Understanding High Performance

Poverty and factors related to it usually impair learning; they overwhelm the impact of school and neighborhood factors. A recent study, for example, showed that poverty and related socioeconomic and demographic factors accounted for 93 percent of the variance in students' twelfth-grade mathematics scores in a large national sample (Hoxby 2001).

Figure 3.1 illustrates the relationship between poverty and achievement proficiency in South Carolina school districts: the higher the percentage of students in poverty in the district, the

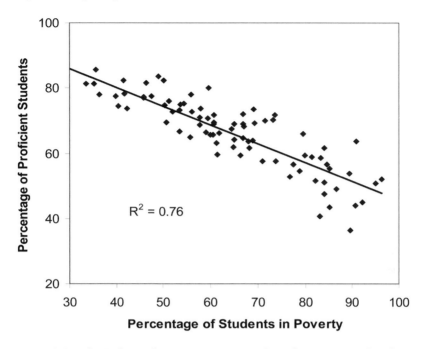

Figure 3.1   The Relation between Poverty and Proficiency in Eighty-five South Carolina School Districts

lower the percentage of proficient students. There are, however, important exceptions. The degree of exception can be taken as the vertical distance above and below the (regression) line, which indicates the general or average relation between poverty and proficiency. Districts below the line can be called "underachievers"; those above the line, "overachievers." Those far above the line are highly efficient districts whose students achieve far more than those in districts that are comparable in poverty.

As illustrated in the right-hand portion of figure 3.1 (the same district as in the last row of table 3.1), the clearest such high-poverty, high performer has 91 percent of its students in poverty, though 64 percent of its students scored proficient on the state tests, which placed them far ahead of their peers of similar poverty levels. The right-hand portion of figure 3.1

Table 3.1   Poverty and Proficiency Levels of South Carolina Plaintiff
Districts and a High-poverty, High-performance Nonplaintiff District

District Category	Percent Proficient	Percent in Poverty	Expenditure per Student
Plaintiff A	57	85	$6,108
Plaintiff B	54	89	$7,895
Plaintiff C	49	87	$8,211
Plaintiff D	44	91	$8,031
Plaintiff E	41	83	$7,365
Plaintiff F	45	92	$10,536
Plaintiff G	36	90	$8,404
Nonplaintiff	64	91	$7,176

shows that only 38 percent of the students in another district
with the same level of poverty were proficient, a colossal difference of 26 percent.

In fact, the high-performing district had poverty levels equal
to or higher than all but one of the seven plaintiff districts that
brought a lawsuit against the state of South Carolina. Even so,
as shown in table 3.1, the high-performing district had a substantially higher proficiency level and spent less money per student than all but one of the plaintiff districts. This chapter shows
that many such high-poverty, high-performance schools, districts, and states can be identified, and the reasons for their su-
periority can be found.

A Case Study of a Successful, Allegedly Inadequate State

It seems ironic that South Carolina was taken to court in an
adequacy lawsuit since it is among the top states in its standards
and accountability system, and the districts, including those of
the plaintiffs, have made excellent progress on the rigorous state
tests (Finn and Kanstoroom 2001 and further evidence below).
Table 3.2 shows that South Carolina is one of five states given

Table 3.2   States Classified by Quality of Standards and Accountability

	Solid Standards A or B	Mediocre Standards C	Inferior Standards D or F
Strong Accountability	The Honor Roll: Alabama, California, North Carolina, South Carolina, Texas	Shaky Foundations: Florida, Illinois, Indiana, Kansas, Maryland, Nevada, New York, Oklahoma, Virginia, West Virginia	Trouble Ahead: Kentucky, New Mexico
Weak Accountability	Unrealized Potential: Arizona, Massachusetts, South Dakota	Going through the Motions: Delaware, Georgia, Louisiana, Mississippi, Nebraska, New Hampshire, Ohio, Utah, Wisconsin	Irresponsible States: Alaska, Arkansas, Colorado, Connecticut, Hawaii, Idaho, Iowa, Maine, Michigan, Minnesota, Missouri, Montana, New Jersey, North Dakota, Oregon, Pennsylvania, Rhode Island, Tennessee, Vermont, Washington, Wyoming

Source: Finn and Kanstoroom, 2001.

an "A" or "B" for its standards and a "strong" designation for its accountability system. South Carolina ranks in the upper 10 percent of states in the nation because it has clear, measurable, comprehensive, and rigorous standards, and because it uses report cards and ratings of schools, rewards successful schools,

Table 3.3   South Carolina's Testing and Accountability Program
Report Card

Criteria	Grade
Academic Alignment: High-stakes tests are aligned with academic content knowledge and skills as specified by the states' curriculum standards.	B−
Test Quality: The tests can determine that those curriculum standards have been met.	B+
Sunshine: The policies and procedures surrounding the tests are open to public scrutiny and to continuing improvement.	B−
Policy: The accountability systems affect education in a way consistent with the goals of the state.	A−

has authority to reconstitute or make major changes to failing schools, and exercises such authority.

In Table 3.3, South Carolina is also ranked in the upper range for its testing and accountability program (Princeton Review 2003). Independent organizations unassociated with the litigation carried out both the ranking studies.

Besides a highly ranked standards and accountability system, the South Carolina legislature enacted a series of laws reflecting considerable control-group research by psychologists and other research evidence by social scientists accumulated during the past few decades (Walberg 2006). The high points of the legislation are shown in the appendix together with evaluative comments on supporting evidence. As the comments indicate, most of the legislation embodies principles that promote student achievement.

Accumulating evidence suggests that standards, accountability, and evidence-based programs cost effectively raise achievement (Walberg 2005). A recent analysis, for example, showed that state achievement gains on the National Assessment of Educational Progress (NAEP) were related to the quality and features of their accountability systems, including extensive testing, school report cards, high school exit examinations, and consequences for school staff. High levels of accountability led to higher NAEP score gains, particularly for African American and Hispanic students (Carnoy and Loeb 2002). Accountability for meeting common standards not only provides information for rational decision making but also increases the likelihood that students, particularly at-risk students, will not miss crucial knowledge and skills they need for subsequent learning and, we can hope, for life beyond school.

As Caroline Hoxby (2002) points out, test and other accountability costs are surprisingly small and represent a tiny percentage of K–12 costs. For twenty-five states with available information, accountability costs of about twenty dollars per student were only about 0.3 percent of the average costs of around $7,250 per student.

Did the South Carolina accountability system and evidence-based legislation pay off? Reflecting general state trends from 1999 to 2002, the plaintiff districts in nearly all years had rising percentages of students at the required level of proficiency. The average percentage of those meeting state requirements in the plaintiff districts rose from 22 to 43 percent, nearly doubling in three years.

How did the schools attain such results? Deposition testimony from a principal in one of the plaintiff districts concretely reveals how she had achieved outstanding success in line with the standards and testing system. Her testimony may have harmed plaintiffs' case because her school had no more money than other schools. Despite the high rate of poverty in her school, more than 90 percent of her students scored above the required proficiency level. Her school won an exemplary learning award from Clemson University and was one of the top twenty-three Title 1 (the federal education program for students in poverty) schools in the nation. How did she and her staff accomplish these feats?

The principal had long lived in the neighborhood of the school, and she and her staff were dedicated and worked long hours. She kept up with research literature on effective teaching and, according to what she learned, closely guided her staff, especially newcomers. She required weekly lesson plans of all teaching staff and visited classrooms every day. She and the staff carried out weekly testing on material similar to that required by the state standards and collaborated after school to identify strengths and weaknesses and to make plans for improving the instructional program.

Such leadership activities are straightforward and commonsensical. These and similar results-oriented techniques are prevalent themes in the surveys and case studies of high-poverty, high-performance schools shown in later sections of this chapter.

National and State Surveys of Schools

A 2001 Education Trust study (Jerald 2001) showed that of the roughly 89,000 elementary and secondary schools in the nation, 4,577 were high-performance outliers.[1] They served well more

1. As this book was going to press, a study (Harris 2006) was released that estimates there are fewer high-poverty, high-performing schools than estimated in the Education Trust study. This finding, however, corroborates the main point of the Education Trust study and the extensive research of other investigators reviewed in this chapter: some schools, districts, and states substantially reduce the adverse consequences of poverty on students' learning. The Harris study also concludes that the adverse effects of poverty are often underestimated. The studies reviewed here vary in their estimates of the poverty effect, partly because poverty is measured in various ways; the purpose of the studies, however, is not to measure poverty effects but to discover what can reduce their adverse consequences, whatever the degree of poverty and however large its

than a million poor students and more than a partly overlapping group of a million minority students in the top one-third of schools in their states. These schools often outperformed predominantly white schools in advantaged communities. What are the common features of such schools?

An earlier, less formal, and less explicitly described study by the Education Trust (1999) profiled 366 schools in twenty-one states with greater than 50 percent poverty levels, schools that had been identified as high performing or making substantial improvements. Their common features include

- State standards used extensively to design curriculum and instruction, assess student work, and evaluate teachers.

- Increased instructional time in reading and math to help students meet standards.

- A larger proportion of funds devoted to support professional development focused on changing instructional practice.

- Comprehensive systems put in effect to monitor individual student progress and to provide extra support to students as soon as needed.

- Focused efforts to involve parents in helping students meet standards.

- State or district accountability systems in place that have real consequences for adults in the schools.

A similar but smaller study of twenty-one high-performing, high-poverty schools around the country (Carter 2000) spon-

---

usual effect. Harris principally recommends that policymakers focus on student outcomes attributable to schools, extend their efforts to homes and communities, and recognize that both homes and schools affect student learning—points that the studies reviewed in this chapter also have made. The studies in this chapter also point to other constructive policies to reduce poverty effects.

sored by the Heritage Foundation showed the following common features:

- Principals' autonomy in hiring and budgeting.

- Measurable goals to establish a culture of achievement.

- Parents encouraged to make their homes centers of learning.

- Master teachers helping the other faculty.

- Regular testing to guide the improvement of student achievement.

- Student self-discipline promoted to help concentration on learning.

- Belief that effort creates ability.

It might be argued that outlier performance is evanescent: high-poverty schools may perform well one year but fail the next. The consistent pattern of their features, however, dispels this argument. In addition, a longitudinal study of 257 high-poverty California schools involving some 257 principals and 5,500 teachers (Williams and others 2005) showed that high-performing schools identified the first year tended to perform well in the following years of the study. The research team from the American Institutes of Research, EdSource, Stanford University, and the University of California at Berkeley found that the identified high-performing schools

- Prioritized student achievement,

- Implemented a coherent, standards-based curriculum and instructional program,

- Used assessment data to improve student achievement and instruction,

- Ensured availability of instructional resources,

- Had principals that effectively managed an accountability-based school improvement process, and

- Were located in districts that focused on accountability and student achievement.

Catholic and Public Schools

Groups of schools controlled by a single organization such as a school district or religious organization can be high performers on average. Because they are the most numerous among private schools, Catholic schools have been most often studied. Well-controlled survey analyses by economists and sociologists show that Catholic schools generally outperform public schools (Bryk 1993).

Valerie Lee (1997) summarized the reasons that Catholic schools do well in general: They follow a delimited core curriculum followed by nearly all students, regardless of their family background, academic preparation, or future educational plans. They engender a strong sense of community exemplified by frequent opportunities for face-to-face interactions and shared experiences among adults and students; school events such as athletics, drama, and music shared by most adults and students; and teachers who see their responsibilities beyond classroom subject matter extending into hallways, school grounds, neighborhood, and homes. Finally, Catholic schools are decentralized: funds are concentrated and decisions are made at the school level.

For my testimony in adequacy litigation in New York City, Paul Peterson and I (2002) found that Catholic schools are also cost effective and especially suited to diminish poverty effects. We investigated several hundred Catholic and public schools in three New York City boroughs—Brooklyn, Manhattan, and the Bronx.

To make the figures comparable, we subtracted the costs of government-funded special programs from each public school's expenditures, including compensatory programs for children in poverty, bilingual education for children with limited proficiency in English and for non-English speakers, and special programs for children with various categories of special needs such as learning disabilities and mental retardation. The costs of transportation and food services were also subtracted from public school outlays. We deducted the public school costs of the central office and of the thirty-two community school boards that oversee and regulate public schools.

With these adjustments, Catholic schools' per-student costs were 46.8 percent of those of public schools. Even so, Catholic school achievement in reading and mathematics exceeded achievement in public schools in the three boroughs among students in high, middle, and low ranges of poverty. Most striking, however, was that the adverse poverty effect was substantially diminished in Catholic schools. In other words, the differences between schools of middle-class and poor children were far smaller in Catholic than in public schools.

My visits to Catholic schools showed why they excelled in both effectiveness and efficiency: they had to compete for their (often black Protestant) customers, that is, parents and students. My visits and interviews with principals revealed that in public schools, procedures and practices were largely instituted from the central office, the thirty-two community boards, and the U.S. Department of Education—entities that fund and regulate the public schools and their complicated categorical programs. The public schools faced frequently replaced administrators and "policy churn" from constantly changing regulatory mandates from above. Grade levels and attendance boundaries were altered without parental or staff consultation. In public school classrooms, many students were inattentive, lacked books, and failed to complete assignments. Children were often resting, chatting, and walking around the classroom.

In contrast, interviews and observations in Catholic schools revealed an atmosphere of courtesy, fairness, and respect. The schools had strong principal leadership with a clear mission for learning. Most decisions were made at the school site. An academic curriculum was taught well to large classes. Students kept notebooks of assignments and notes for each subject, and their homework was completed and graded every day. Parents and teachers were in close contact in the school and by telephone. Finally, the central office and schools had few administrative and support staff such as program developers, consultants, vice principals, and teacher aides.

African American Private Schools

Besides Catholic schools, other nonsectarian southern and northern private schools appear to have well served low-income African Americans, some of whom have risen to distinguished positions. Thomas Sowell (1974) reported case studies of schools that have produced outstanding members of the African American elite. Of the schools he studied, four (located in Atlanta, Baltimore, New Orleans, and Washington) educated a long list of graduates who have made important breakthroughs, including the first African American state superintendent of schools, Supreme Court Justice, and military general, as well as the discoverer of blood plasma, a Nobel Prize winner, and the first black U.S. senator in this century.

Sowell attributed the outstanding success of these schools and of other successful schools he studied neither to random events nor to the students' natural abilities but to the social order of the schools and to their concerted, persevering educational efforts: "Each of these schools currently maintaining high standards was a very quiet and orderly school, whether located in a middle-class suburb of Atlanta or in the heart of a deteriorating ghetto in Brooklyn" (p. 54). Strong principals concentrated on achievement and discipline.

> 'Respect' was the word most used by those interviewed to describe the attitudes of students and parents toward these schools. 'The teacher was *always* right' was a phrase that was used again and again to describe the attitude of the black parents of a generation or more ago. . . . Even today, in those few instances where schools have the confidence of black parents, a wise student maintains a discrete silence at home about his difficulties with teachers, and hopes that the teachers do the same. (p. 54)

Public School Case Studies

Other case studies of high-performance public schools show the critical role of results-oriented principals and staff in high-poverty schools. An investigation of eleven high-poverty, high-performance successful public schools in New York City (New York City Department of Education 2001) showed strong leadership of the staff by principals. Observations and interviews in schools in Harlem; Pittsburgh; Wichita, Kansas; Clay, West Virginia; Mission City, Texas; and Ajax, Ontario, Canada (Cawelti, 1999) showed the following common features:

- Strong principal leadership.
- A focus on clear standards and on improving results.
- Teamwork to ensure accountability.
- Teachers committed to helping all students achieve.
- Multiple changes made to improve the instructional life of students.
- These efforts sustained in concert.

Similar themes were uncovered in twenty-six Texas high-achieving schools with over 60 percent of students in poverty (Lein, Johnson, and Ragland 1996):

- Focus on the academic success of each student.

- No-excuse attitude that all children should learn.

- Experimentation to discover the best teaching methods.

- All adults included in fostering student learning.

- Humane, almost familial, treatment of students.

Studies of School Districts and States

Except for the South Carolina example, the research reviewed above concerns schools, but districts and states can "scale up" accountability and evidence-based practices to increase the effectiveness of high-poverty schools within their purview. Two examples are instructive.

An investigation of school districts with large percentages of poor children who made substantial achievement gains included Brazosport Independent School District, Clute, Texas; Twin Falls, Idaho, School District; Ysleta Independent School District, El Paso, Texas; and Barbour County School District, Philippi, West Virginia (Cawelti and Protheroe 2001). Their common features remind us of those found in high-performance schools:

- High expectations and focus on achievement results.

- Decentralized budgeting and management at the school level.

- Aligned curricula and instruction to state standards and tests.

- Sustained evidence-based practices.

- Frequent testing, practice, and reteaching for students in need of it.

Similarly, a large-scale RAND study (Grissmer and Flanagan 1998) commissioned by the National Educational Goals Panel showed that North Carolina and Texas, the two states that made the biggest recent gains on the National Assessment of Educational Progress, were distinctive in employing

- Grade-by-grade standards with aligned curricula and textbooks,
- Expectations that all students would meet the standards,
- Statewide assessments linked to the standards,
- Accountability for results with rewards and sanctions for performance,
- Deregulation and increased flexibility in ways the standards could be met, and
- Computerized feedback systems and achievement data for continuous improvement.

Echoing many previous studies, the research showed the major cost factors made no difference in state performance. These included per-pupil spending, pupil-teacher ratios, proportion of teachers with advanced degrees, and teacher experience.

Conclusions

Despite plaintiffs' adequacy lawsuits, money is not the answer to poor school performance. Ever greater infusions of money have a bad record of improving learning. Because achievement levels have remained low and spending has risen substantially, the productivity of American schools fell by more than 50 percent from 1970 to 2000. If schools were as productive in the year 2000 as they were in 1970, the *average* seventeen-year-old would score at the level that fewer than 5 percent of seventeen-year-olds attained in 1970 (Hoxby, forthcoming).

Even so, the research reviewed above documents the prevalence of high-poverty, high-performance schools in more than a dozen independent investigations. Of course, this conclusion might be inescapable since most distributions of human and group phenomena show the normal distribution of a large middling group and few high and low outliers. Even so, the fact that some schools, districts, and states can beat the poverty odds to achieve well suggests that others also can. The new federal No Child Left Behind act may induce more schools to rise to the challenge since it allows students in failing schools to seek supplementary educational services and, in cases of repeated failure, allows students to transfer to successful schools. The new achievement information required by the act should provide a better basis for parent choice.

The studies described in this chapter identify the factors that make for outstanding success. Although the research rigor and findings vary from study to study, the common success themes are clearly identified, rigorous content goals; results-oriented management; staff teamwork oriented toward student success; curriculum and instruction aligned with state standards; frequent testing and use of information about student performance to guide teaching and learning; and a humane, goal-directed atmosphere in the school. Remarkably, the school-level findings about the constructive role of standards, accountability, testing, and instructional alignment are echoed at the district and state levels.

References

Bryk, Anthony. 1993. *Catholic Schools and the Common Good.* Cambridge, MA: Harvard University Press.

Carnoy, Martin and Susanna Loeb. 2002. "Does External Accountability Affect Student Outcomes? A Cross-State Analysis." *Educational Evaluation and Policy Analysis,* no. 4 (Winter): 305–331.

Carter, Samuel Casey. 2000. *No Excuses: Lessons from 21 High-Performing, High-Poverty Schools.* Washington, DC: Heritage Foundation.

Cawelti, Gordon. 1999. "Portraits of Six Benchmark Schools." Arlington, VA: Educational Research Service; also see http://www.ers.org/reports.htm; January 29, 2005.

Cawelti, Gordon and Nancy Protheroe. 2001. *High Student Achievement: How Six School Districts Changed into High-performance Systems.* Arlington, VA.: Educational Research Service.

Education Trust. 1999. *Dispelling the Myth: High Poverty Schools Exceeding Expectations.* Washington, DC: Education Trust.

Finn, Chester E. and Marci Kanstoroom. 2001. "State Academic Standards." In *Brookings Papers on Education Policy,* ed. Diane Ravitch, 131–180. Washington, DC: Brookings Institution.

Grissmer, David and Ann Flanagan. 1998. *Exploring Rapid Achievement Gains in North Carolina and Texas.* Washington, DC: National Educational Goals Panel.

Hanushek, Erik A. 1997. "Assessing the Effects of School Resources on Student Performance: An Update." *Educational Evaluation and Policy Analysis* 19, no. 2:141–164.

Harris, Douglas N. 2006. "Ending the Blame Game on Educational Inequity: A Study of 'High Flying' Schools." Tempe, AZ: Arizona State University Educational Policy Studies Unit, March.

Hoxby, Caroline M. 2001. "If Families Matter Most, Where Do Schools Come In?" In *A Primer on America's Schools,* ed. Terry Moe, 89–126. Stanford, CA: Hoover Institution Press.

Hoxby, Caroline M. 2002. "The Cost of Accountability." In *School*

Accountability, ed. Williamson Evers and Herbert J. Walberg. Stanford, CA: Hoover Institution Press.

Hoxby, Caroline M. Forthcoming. "School Choice and School Productivity, or Could School Choice Be a Tide that Lifts All Boats?" In *Economics of School Choice,* ed. Caroline Hoxby. Chicago, IL: University of Chicago Press for the National Bureau of Economic Research.

Jerald, Craig D. 2001. *Dispelling the Myth Revisited.* Washington, DC: The Education Trust.

Lee, Valerie. 1997. "Catholic Lessons for Public Schools." In *New Schools for a New Century*, ed. Diane Ravitch, 147–163. New Haven, CT: Yale University Press.

Lein, Laura, Joseph F. Johnson Jr., and Mary Ragland. 1996. *Successful Texas School-wide Programs.* Austin, TX: University of Texas, Charles A Dana Center.

New York City Department of Education. 2001. *Debunking the Myth.* New York City Department of Education.

Peterson, Paul and Herbert J. Walberg. 2005. "Catholic Schools Excel." *School Reform News* (July): 4; see also Internet version, http://www.heartland.org/Article.cfm?artId 88, January 29.

Princeton Review. 2003. *Testing the Testers 2003: An Annual Ranking of State Accountability Systems.* New York, NY: Princeton Review.

Sowell, Thomas. 1974. "Black Excellence: The Case of Dunbar High School." *Public Interest* 35 (Spring): 1–21.

Sowell, Thomas. 1976. "Patterns of Black Excellence." *Public Interest* 43 (Spring): 26–58.

Walberg, Herbert J. 2001. "Achievement in American Schools." In *A Primer on American Schools: An Assessment by the Koret Task Force on K–12 Education,* ed. Terry Moe, 43–68. Stanford, CA: Hoover Institution Press.

Walberg, Herbert J. 2005. "Standards, Testing, and Accountability." In *Within Our Reach: How America Can Educate Every Child,* ed. John Chubb. Stanford, CA: Hoover Institution Press.

Walberg, Herbert J. 2006. "Improving Educational Productivity: An Assessment of Extant Research." In *The Scientific Basis of Edu-*

cational Productivity, ed. Rena Subotnik and Herbert J. Walberg. Greenwich, CT. Information Age Press, in press.

Williams, Trish, Mary Perry, Carol Studier, Noli Brazil, Michael Kirst, Edward Haertel, Sean Reardon, et al. 2005. *Similar Students, Different Results: Why Do Some Schools Do Better?* Mountain View, CA: EdSource.

Appendix 3.1
Analysis of South Carolina's Education Legislation, 1977–2000

Legislation	Features	Evaluation
The Education Finance Act of 1977	Guaranteed each student the availability of at least a minimum education appropriate to individual needs and equal to similar students, notwithstanding geographic and economic factors; created student weighting formulas, instituted tax-paying index.	Within a normal range, the amount of educational spending is a highly inconsistent influence on achievement but fair allotments seem reasonable.
	Funded half-day kindergarten program for five-year-olds.	*Academic* kindergartens can improve achievement.
Basic Skills Assessment Program of 1978	Established statewide K–12 educational objectives in the basic skills of mathematics, reading, and writing for K–12 and minimum standards in mathematics, reading, and writing in several grades.	Objectives, standards, and testing improve achievement.
Educator Improvement Act of 1979	Intended to provide a fair and comprehensive program for the training, certification, initial employment, and evaluation of public educators.	The usual teacher qualifications such as education levels and experience are weak, inconsistent influences on achievement.
	Provided entrance examination for selective admission into teacher education programs.	Verbal and subject mastery are linked to student achievement.

Legislation	Features	Evaluation
Education Improvement Act of 1984	General: Included the following goals: raise student performance, teach and test basic skills, evaluate the teaching profession, improve leadership, implement quality controls, reward productivity, create more effective partnerships, and provide school buildings.	Goal setting, emphasis on identified skills, quality controls, rewards for performance, and parental partnerships can improve achievement.
	Specific: Increased graduation requirements, began child development programs for four-year olds, instituted Advanced Placement courses and examinations, supported gifted and talent programs, funded statewide testing programs.	Evidence supports the achievement efficacy of these elements.
	Specific: Began school incentives reward program and evaluation of the quality of student performance.	Rewards and accountability tend to improve achievement.
Target 2000 School Reform of 1989	Created "flexibility through deregulation" and local innovation funds.	Operational control at the local district level accords with policies in highly achieving states and nations.
	Supported parental education programs.	Evidence supports parent involvement.
Early Childhood Development and Academic Assistance Act of 1993	Early childhood development and academic assistance initiatives including parent programs; accelerated children in grades K–3; academic assistance for children needy children aged 4–12.	Evidence supports parent involvement and childhood programs to give children a good start in schooling.

Legislation	Features	Evaluation
Education Account-ability Act of 1998	Standards required in math, English/language arts, social studies and science, with a high school exit exam; assessments required in grades 3–8; end of course assessments in benchmark courses in grades 9–12; readiness tests for grades 1 and 2 to be developed; tests administered to all tenth grades to guide curriculums and counsel students; norm-referenced tests adminis-tered to random samples for evaluating the system.	Evidence supports testing and accountability.
	For failing students in grades 3–8, a conference must be held of the student, parents, and school person-nel to develop an academic plan for improvement; for repeated failure, student must be retained in grade or attend summer school.	Incentives, parent involvement, and summer school improve achieve-ment.
	Required annual report-ing on status of and improvement in achieve-ment must be advertised, reported to parents and on accreditation forms; dis-tricts must develop strategic plans on accountability sys-tems.	Reporting and local plan-ning probably have positive effects.
	Established Palmetto Gold and Silver Awards for high performance and rapid improvement; schools that fail must report, with their districts, improvement plans; the State Superinten-dent may replace principals and manage schools.	Rewards and sanctions matter in human affairs, and evidence supports their use in education.

Legislation	Features	Evaluation
	Created the Education and Oversight Committee to monitor and evaluate the act; has gubernatorial representative, six legislators, five business people, and five education representatives.	Such a group can uncover possible flaws and recommend remedies.
	Programs begun for failing schools including grant programs for retraining staff, teacher specialists, principal specialists, principal mentors, professional and school improvement activities, and grant programs for homework centers.	Such assistance would seem likely to help; homework can have large effects on learning.
First Steps to Readiness Act of 1999	Provided preschool preparation and readiness for school through prenatal and maternity care, nutrition, health awareness, scholarships for day care, half- to full-day kindergarten.	Well-designed early childhood programs constructively influence students' success in school and life.
Alternative Schools Act of 1999	Provided special programs for roughly 5 percent of disruptive students or consortia of alternative schools.	Safe and orderly schools are conducive to learning; reduced disruption means more learning time and concentration.
Parent Involvement in Their Children's Education Act of 2000	Delineated responsibilities of governor, state superintendent, state board, local boards, superintendents, principals, teachers, and parents to increase parent involvement; identified educationally constructive parental activities.	Parent involvement in their children's learning increases achievement.

4

High-Spending, Low-Performing School Districts

Williamson M. Evers and Paul Clopton

PROPONENTS OF "ADEQUACY" argue in court and in other fo-
rums that substantially more money needs to be spent on the
existing school system in order to provide an adequate education
for children. A premise of the adequacy campaigns is that it is
easy to quantitatively measure and objectively determine the
cost of providing an adequate public education to all children.[1]
Once adequacy proponents come up with their cost figures, they
demand the resources from the political system, usually through

The authors wish to acknowledge research assistance from Matt Rojansky, Kate
Feinstein, Andrew Dawson, and Ze'ev Wurman. The authors also wish to thank
Eric Hanushek, Derrell Bradford, Casey Lartigue, and Neal McCluskey for read-
ing drafts of this chapter and making suggestions for improvement.

1. For a discussion of problems with determining how much government
spending in some domain is enough, see Buchanan (1965), especially chapter 18.

the courts.[2] But if provided, would such money be effectively used?[3] After all, one should not judge a foreign aid program simply on the amount spent, nor should one review a Hollywood motion picture based on its budget.[4]

Do school districts, as presently constituted, have the capacity to succeed academically with low-performing students? Are school districts organized in a way that ensures they are making productive use of the money they now receive from taxpayers or of the additional money they would receive if adequacy campaigns prevailed? The goal of this chapter is to look at the politics and organization of school districts to see if they are likely to be productive enough that their schools can effectively teach low-performing students. Unless school districts as currently constituted have the needed capacity for productivity, channeling large amounts of additional money to those districts will not succeed in boosting student achievement.

Adequacy campaigns and adequacy lawsuits maintain that infusing large amounts of money into poorly performing districts will bring about student academic success. Yet money and other added resources have not in the past brought about successful schools (Hanushek 1986, 1989, 1997). In the case of Kentucky, the first state to which an adequacy verdict applied, George Cunningham writes that despite the "enormous commitment in resources" (almost a billion dollars in the first eight years) and putting in place the "most expensive testing system of any state"

---

2. To the extent that the lawyers for the plaintiffs are paid for or reimbursed with tax money, this is an instance of what Daniel Patrick Moynihan calls an "autogamous mode" of government growth: "big government ordering itself to become bigger" (Moynihan 1972, 70).

3. As one set of researchers put it: "[W]hile equal funding across schools and school districts might be desirable, it does not assure that funds would be directed productively toward the goal of academic achievement. . . ." (Ladd, Chalk, and Hansen 1999, 2)

4. The authors owe the film-reviewing analogy to Postrel (2006).

(on a per-pupil basis), there is "scant evidence" of any success in improving student academic performance (Cunningham 2004, 297, 299).[5]

Many proponents of adequacy efforts would, in a sense, agree with those who question the efficacy of merely adding funds and other resources. These adequacy proponents would say: "We agree with you that money should be spent wisely and spent on things that foster academic success."[6] But critics of adequacy campaigns ask: Will the school districts that receive all this money be blinded by fads and fashions? Will politics, ideologies, or the institutional structure of districts (including susceptibility to corruption) tend to divert money into paths and projects that do not advance student achievement? In other words, even if considerable sums of money are forthcoming from taxpayers, are there incentives in place in local school systems that will encourage, on a regular basis, effective efforts that lead to academic success?

Previous studies have compared school district spending and performance, for example, in the states of Colorado, Idaho, and Minnesota (Mitchell and Morson 2006; Wenders 2005b; Yecke 2005).[7] But here we will put five school districts under the microscope: Kansas City, Missouri; Washington, D.C.; Cambridge, Massachusetts; Newark, New Jersey; and Sausalito, California. Though these districts are high-spending (figure 4.1), they are also low-performing. Scrutiny of such districts can help to identify some of the reasons why adequacy funding might fail to

5. On Kentucky, see also Innes (2006).

6. For example, the court in *Abbott II* said: "[The research] does not show that money makes no difference. What it strongly suggests is that money can be used more effectively." *Abbott v. Burke*, 119 N.J. 287, 575 A. 2d (1990), 375. See also Schrag (2005, 115, 117–18, 243) ("if money is well spent, it can have a major impact"); Murnane and Levy (1996, 96).

7. Such comparisons were also done in the 1970s, during an earlier wave of school finance reform. For Michigan, see Murphy and Cohen (1974).

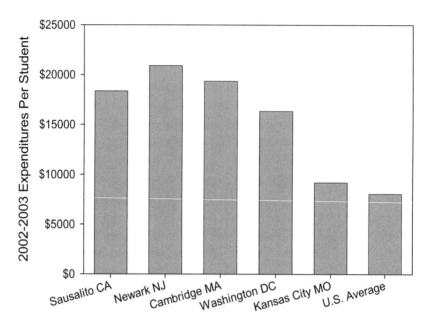

Figure 4.1   Expenditures per Student for 2002–2003 for Five Selected
Districts and the U.S. Average

Note: This chart of 2002–2003 expenditures does not show the level of spending
in Kansas City during its 1984–1997 desegregation plan. The peak of Kansas City
school district spending came in 1991–1992, when the district was spending over
$11,700 per pupil per year. This would be over $15,400 in 2002–2003 dollars.

Sources: Data from Ciotti 2001, 329; U.S. Department of Education, National
Center for Education Statistics (NCES) Common Core of Data, http://nces.ed.gov/
ccd/districtsearch/.

produce effective schooling. After looking at the five districts one
at a time, we will compare what they did, and we will analyze
the politics and operations of school districts in general to evaluate the prospects for adequate spending as a route to student
academic success.

Case Studies

Kansas City, Missouri

Kansas City, Missouri, is a "low-key, sleepy" metropolis, at least as compared with New York, Los Angeles or Chicago, which are often the focus of discussions of urban school performance (Ciotti 2001, 310).[8] Yet a major, court-ordered experiment in high spending took place in the schools of Kansas City from 1984 through 1997, with effects that continue to the present. Despite continued spending on Kansas City's public schools to the tune of almost twelve thousand dollars per student (compared with an average of almost five thousand dollars per student at the state level at the time), the performance of the district's public schoolchildren would not qualify today as even mediocre.[9] This is not surprising in light of the district's long history of spectacular mismanagement.

In April 1984, Federal District Judge Russell G. Clark found the state of Missouri and Kansas City, Missouri, School District (KCMSD) liable for the abysmal conditions of the city's schools that he said amounted to de facto segregation. Judge Clark believed that a rejuvenated school system would attract white students from the surrounding suburbs to return to the city. To achieve this revitalization, Judge Clark ordered the plaintiffs (who represented schoolchildren) to propose a list of ideal im-

8. This case study relies heavily on the research of Morantz (1996) and Ciotti (2001).

9. According to Ciotti (2001, 329), who cites the Desegregation Division of the Missouri Department of Elementary and Secondary Education, at the peak of KCMSD's desegregation-plan spending in 1991–1992, the district was spending over $11,700 per pupil per year. According to Morantz (1996), from 1985 (before the court order took effect) to 1992, total KCMSD expenditures per enrolled student increased from $3,464 to $11,513, while the state average increased from $3,030 to $4,723.

provements for their schools.[10] With the judge's backing and a guarantee of state financing compelled by the court, the plaintiffs dreamed up a bold plan to reinvent Kansas City schools. By 1997, when Judge Clark finally recused himself from the litigation, the plan had ballooned to a total cost of over $2 billion (Ciotti 2001; Gewertz 2000).

Much of the revitalization money went not to personnel costs but to lavish (and often wasteful) infrastructure projects. Fifteen new schools were built, and fifty-four others renovated, including the construction of an Olympic-sized swimming pool (which district officials called a "natatorium") with underwater viewing room, a robotics lab, a planetarium, an arboretum, a zoo and twenty-five-acre wildlife refuge, an elaborate moot-court layout, and a model United Nations chamber (with simultaneous translation facilities). As if such paradisiacal facilities would not promote themselves by word of mouth, the district also allocated almost $1 million for broadcast and print media advertising to attract suburban students back to the city's schools. The students could be brought by bus or taxi, to be paid for by the district, to schools where they would enjoy student-teacher ratios of 12 or 13 to 1, the lowest of any major school district in the United States (Morantz 1996; Ciotti 2001; Lindseth, this volume, chapter 2).

Worse than these outlandish and wasteful projects was the gross, even criminal, mismanagement of the flood of state funding. Employees stole hundreds of thousands of dollars worth of equipment every year, finance officers wrote checks directly to themselves, and insiders described the atmosphere as that of a "third world country" suddenly endowed with "unlimited

10. In this case the plaintiffs (who represented schoolchildren) and the defendant (the school district) had cooperated to keep the case going during the trial and the appeals. They also worked together to create the revitalization plan (Morantz 1996; Ciotti 2001).

wealth." Nearly half the state's education budget was flowing to the KCMSD and St. Louis schools, which together had less than 10 percent of the state's students.[11] Even though the KCMSD maintained an administrative staff three to five times larger than that of any comparably sized school district, administrators in the district's central office were so overwhelmed by this lavish spending that they simply threw up their hands and allowed fiscal management to go into meltdown. Equipment and materials were arriving before building and remodeling projects were prepared to make use of them, and construction costs were pork-barreled up to three or four times what they would have cost in any other district (Ciotti 2001).

The district hired teachers with little weight being given to merit. Knowledgeable observers concluded that during the revitalization effort somewhere from 20 to 50 percent of teachers in the district were "totally incompetent" at their jobs. The district was so rapidly swamped with cash that it raised teacher salaries almost 50 percent in one year (Ciotti 2001). Yet when it came to salary hikes, the state of Missouri contended that the 1990 hike that was part of the revitalization effort had "virtually no effect on increasing the quality of new hires or decreasing the quality of staff who left the District" (Morantz 1996, 254). During the revitalization effort, class sizes shrank from the thirties to the low twenties (Gewertz 2000).

By 1991, even with the huge amounts of money being funneled from the state to improve the KCMSD educational offerings as part of the desegregation effort, the district was facing a multimillion-dollar deficit in its regular budget. Despite Judge Clark's doubling of Kansas City property tax rates to fund his school revitalization effort, the district could not come up with

11. The St. Louis school district had its own court-ordered finance plan that brought it extra money, but not at the scale ordered for Kansas City.

the financial wherewithal to service its debts, and thus flirted with bankruptcy and state receivership (Ciotti 2001).

As one might predict, the measurable academic results of the revitalization effort were as disappointing as the corruption, inefficiency, and mismanagement. Test scores failed to improve over the course of the program. For example, on the statewide criterion-referenced Missouri Mastery and Achievement Tests, for each year (1990–1993) and for each of the four grade levels tested, the KCMSD continued to be 10 to 20 points below the state average. The revitalization program also did not narrow the gap between the district and state averages (Morantz 1996). Likewise, the black-white gap remained substantial, with African American twelfth-graders scoring at levels roughly three years behind those of white students in the same grade. By the mid-1990s few white students remained in the district, and as a result, nonwhite enrollment was above 90 percent in many schools (Ciotti 2001; Armor 2002).

In the end, even most of the basic educational infrastructure that the district had built (leaving aside the lavish extracurricular investments) went unused, since the KCMSD's thirty-seven thousand students simply could not fill seats for fifty-four thousand. The inevitable finally happened in 1997, when the school board voted to shut down two high schools and a middle school, and Judge Clark finally recused himself from the case after twenty years of guidance from the bench (Ciotti 2001).

The KCMSD desegregation and revitalization plan, under the sponsorship of Judge Clark, suffered from two basic fallacies. The first was that the mere presence of whites is the key to African American achievement. In fact, this rigid policy simply meant that the pressing needs of urban African Americans were ignored, while millions of dollars were invested in educating white suburban students who hadn't needed extra help in the first place.[12] The second fallacy was that simply throwing money at a problem like underperforming schools would solve the problem. The KCMSD did the usual things that advocates of more funding for public education propose, including boosting spending per student, raising teacher salaries, reducing teacher workloads and class sizes, and investing in facilities and resources. These are the inputs commonly suggested by the educational establishment as sure ways to enhance student performance.

Yet student test scores, the only impartial measure of academic success, had an almost inverse correlation to all these "improvements" in the educational system. The KCMSD students routinely scored lower than students outside Kansas City, where schools spent about half as much per pupil, and than Kansas City parochial school students, for whom the per-pupil cost was less than a third as much (Ciotti 2001).

After the final settlement of the desegregation case in 2003, the KCMSD situation began to stabilize somewhat. Nonetheless, the district still maintains only provisional accreditation from the state board of education and is surviving largely on the largesse of a four-year, $6.1 million grant from the Bill and Melinda Gates Foundation. As shown in figure 4.2, the district's troubles with low student achievement have not subsided. Most of the seventh grade students still have unsatisfactory reading achievement, meaning that these students "lack the basic reading skills needed to meet typical grade-level expectations." Most tenth grade students are scoring at the "step 1" level in mathematics, meaning that they "demonstrate only a minimal understanding of fundamental concepts and little or no ability to apply that knowledge."

12. A telling illustration of this phenomenon was the district's policy in the early 1990s of indifference toward 50-to-70 percent drop-out rates among African American males in high school, because lowering black attendance was an easier way of bringing the black-white ratio closer to the prescribed 60-to-40 than attracting white suburban students (Ciotti 2001).

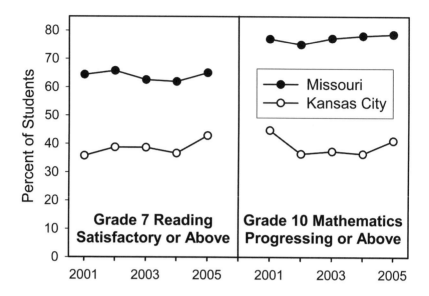

Figure 4.2   Achievement in Kansas City versus the Missouri State Average

Sources: Missouri Dept. of Elementary and Secondary Education, Missouri School Improvement Program (MSIP), Reading Score, http://dese.mo.gov/schooldata/four/048078/map7none.html.

Missouri Dept. of Elementary and Secondary Education, Missouri Assessment Program (MAP), table posted August 19, 2005.

Annual Report of School Data, http://dese.mo.gov/schooldata/four/048078/mapmnone.html.

Missouri Dept. of Elementary and Secondary Education, Missouri Assessment Program (MAP), table posted August 19, 2005.

The court provided the Kansas City district with, as Alison Morantz put it, "what most educators can only dream of," namely, "vast economic resources" with which to take on "the challenge of improving achievement" and of attracting white suburban students (Morantz 1996, 242). Unfortunately for Kansas City's children, and for those advocates with no better prescriptions for failing schools than high spending, the city's schools may have been among the best funded in the country, but they remain among the worst performing to this day.[13] As

13. In 2000 the district flunked every one of eleven performance measures

the Kansas City School Board treasurer commented in 2000, "we're not any better off than we were 23 years ago" (Gewertz, 2000).

It is apparent in retrospect (as it was to many observers at the time) that Kansas City and Missouri's investment in the KCMSD focused too much on glitzy inputs and not enough on internal effectiveness and outputs (Morantz 1996; Gewertz 2000). "We did all the easy but expensive things," commented the attorney for the plaintiffs, who was also a chief architect of the revitalization plan. District managers built new buildings, added new equipment, and created transportation programs. But they did not do "the inexpensive, dauntingly difficult things," like creating a curriculum, overseeing teaching practices, putting incentives in place, and hiring able teachers and principals and firing ineffective ones (Ciotti 2001, 320).[14] The court almost entirely declined to emphasize more effective teaching. The district neglected teacher quality, effective on-the-job teacher training, tenure reform, merit pay, empowerment of principals, charter schools, solid textbooks, and proven lesson plans. When Judge Clark repeatedly asked the district to come up with a core curriculum, it failed to do so (Ciotti 2001). Likewise, the monitoring committee pushed for greater concentration on curriculum and testing, but to no avail (Gerwertz 2000). But why should district officials have done the things that would have been effective, when they had no incentive to do so? In the words of the Missouri Board of Education president, Betty Preston, "you don't have a formula for success when you just throw money at a problem" (Gewertz 2000).

---

for accreditation, which it lost, further jeopardizing its funding situation (Gewertz 2000).

14. Compare the comments of this attorney, Arthur A. Benson II, in Gewertz (2000).

Washington, D.C.

Under the sponsorship of President Thomas Jefferson, the District of Columbia's city council in 1804 established "a permanent institution for the education of youth in the city of Washington."[15] The Board of Trustees, to which Jefferson was appointed, declared that "in these schools poor children shall be taught reading, writing, grammar, arithmetic, and such branches of the mathematics as may qualify them for the professions they are intended to follow" (Lartigue 2004, 69). Today, more than two centuries after the school system's founding, all too few of the schoolchildren of the District of Columbia Public Schools (DCPS) can read, write, and calculate, and its schools are in crisis, despite huge spending on public education.

In part, the crisis in Washington, D.C.'s schools stems from financial mismanagement, which Congress and President Bill Clinton sought to remedy through the formation of the District of Columbia Financial Responsibility and Management Assistance Authority (the "Control Board") in 1995. The Control Board concluded that "for each additional year that students stay in DCPS, the less likely they are to succeed, not because they are unable to succeed, but because the system does not prepare them to succeed" (Lartigue 2004, 70). Because of this, the Control Board restricted the Board of Education's management authority for five years (until 2000), after which the elected board resumed full authority.

Such dramatic failure, however, is not a new phenomenon for the DCPS but rather dates back almost a century. In 1920 a U.S. senator said "a crisis ha[d] been reached" for DCPS schools and their sixty thousand pupils, while in 1939, the DCPS super-

15. The authors are indebted to the work of Casey Lartigue (2004) and of the Council of the Great City Schools (2004).

intendent reported that police were called in to protect school principals from "youthful hoodlums" (Lartigue 2004, 69–70). Just eight years later, the school district's new superintendent described his domain as "one of the sorriest school systems in the country" (Lartigue 2004, 70). Journalist Peter Schrag calls the DCPS "perhaps the nation's most famously dysfunctional district" (Schrag 2005, 226).

One notable exception to the DCPS's history of consistent underperformance is the story of Dunbar High School during the late nineteenth and early twentieth centuries. Dunbar was an African American high school whose students' standardized test scores in 1899 averaged higher than those of most white high school students in the district. The school was composed overwhelmingly of urban black students from poor households and had an all-black staff, including the principal, Mary Jane Patterson, who in 1862 became the first African American woman to earn a college degree. Principal Patterson's influence, along with that of other well-educated African American teachers, resulted in Dunbar graduates who outperformed the national averages consistently for some eighty-five years. From 1870 to 1955 most of Dunbar's graduates went on to higher education, many to Harvard and other elite institutions. The accomplishments of the school's alumni have been admirable. These alumni include the first African American graduate of Annapolis, the first African American woman to receive a Ph.D. in America, the first African American federal judge, the first African American general, the first African American cabinet member, and the first African American U.S. senator since Reconstruction (Sowell 2005).

The example of Dunbar shows that heroic individuals can build a culture of achievement. Such heroes can provide—with meager resources—a high-quality education in public schools, even for students from the poorest households.

Sadly, Dunbar's culture of achievement was destroyed in the

mid-1950s. After *Brown vs. Board of Education*, the DCPS ended Dunbar's status as what today would be called a magnet school and made it a neighborhood school. Enough of these neighborhood students were so highly disruptive and inadequately motivated that Dunbar's ethos of excellence was soon under siege. When district administrators and Washington, D.C., politicians declined to defend that ethos, Dunbar's all-star teaching staff retired or moved away, and its motto ("Perseverance is . . . king") was replaced by self-serving excuses. Today, although Dunbar has better facilities and funding than it ever had during its eighty-five-year reign as a jewel of student achievement, Dunbar is a failing ghetto school (Lartigue 2004; Sowell 2005).

For the past half-century, standardized test results have shown that both black and white students' achievement in Washington, D.C., fall significantly below the national average. In Spring 2003 DCPS students, on average, scored lower on the National Assessment of Education Progress (NAEP) in mathematics and reading in fourth and eighth grades than did students in nine other comparable big city districts (State Education Office 2004).[16] The DCPS performance on the NAEP has been consistently dismal as shown in table 4.1. This is particularly true in mathematics, where DCPS eighth graders only outscored U.S. fourth graders by a margin of 9 points in 2003.

Underperformance is the norm today in the DCPS. Fully 85 percent of DCPS graduates who enter the University of the District of Columbia require remedial education for up to two years. In 1994 the bulk of DCPS students who took the Armed Forces Qualification Test after they had graduated from the District's schools failed it. For the past four decades, almost half of students enrolling in the eighth grade have failed to graduate from

---

16. The sole exception was eighth grade reading, where DCPS students, on average, outscored those in Los Angeles. But DCPS eighth grade readers did not outscore the students in the seven other cities.

Table 4.1   National Average and Washington, D.C., Average
NAEP Scale Scores

	US	DC	DC Rank
Grade 4 Reading			
1998	213	179	Last
2002	217	191	Last
2003	216	188	Last
Grade 8 Reading			
1998	261	236	Last
2002	263	240	Last
2003	261	239	Last
Grade 4 Math			
1992	219	193	Last
2000	224	192	Last
2003	234	205	Last
Grade 8 Math			
1990	262	231	Last
1992	267	235	Last
1996	271	233	Last
2000	272	235	Last
2003	275	243	Last

Rank is for Washington, D.C., and all participating states in each test.
Source: U.S. Department of Education, Digest of Education Statistics, Washington,
D.C.: National Center for Education Statistics, 2004.

high school (Lartigue 2004). In 2005 DCPS students who took
the College Board SAT test had scores that were on average 210
points below the national average of 1028 (Office of Accountability 2006). The historical achievement record of the DCPS on
the College Board SAT is shown in table 4.2, along with funding
information and Stanford-9 composite scores. Washington, D.C.,
students are not catching up with the rest of the country despite
funding levels at 50 percent, 60 percent, and even 70 percent
above the national average.

Much of the DCPS's failure can be attributed to poor admin-

Table 4.2 Washington, D.C., Public School Expenditures and Standardized Test Outcomes

| Year | Spending ($ per ADA) | | | | College Board SAT Mean Scores | | | | | | Stanford-9 Scores Proficient or Above | |
| | US | DC | DC as a % of US | Rank | Verbal | | | Mathematics | | | Reading (%) | Math (%) |
					US	DC	Difference	US	DC	Difference		
88–89	5,092	8,204	161	3								
89–90	5,527	9,596	174	1								
90–91	5,856	10,109	173	1	422	405	−17	474	435	−39		
91–92	6,052	10,334	171	1	423	405	−18	476	437	−39		
92–93	6,252	10,063	161	2	424	405	−19	478	441	−37		
93–94	6,473	10,589	164	1	499	479	−20	504	468	−36		
94–95	6,715	9,847	147	4	504	485	−19	506	471	−35		
95–96	6,922	9,990	144	4	505	489	−16	508	473	−35		
96–97	7,244	9,784	135	4	505	490	−15	511	475	−36		
97–98	7,633	10,127	133	3	505	488	−17	512	476	−36		
98–99	8,047	11,309	141	3	505	494	−11	511	478	−33		10
99–00	8,505	13,302	156	1	505	494	−11	514	486	−28	12	11
00–01	9,086	16,319	180	1	506	482	−24	514	474	−40	15	11
01–02	9,520	18,277	192	1	504	480	−24	516	473	−43	15	11
02–03	9,834	18,088	184		507	484	−23	519	474	−45	12	11
03–04					508	489	−19	518	476	−42	13	10

Notes: From 1993–1994 the College Board SAT results are in recentered values. Throughout this period DCPS College Board SAT scores were typically either the lowest in the nation, or the second lowest. Spending rank is compared to states.

Sources: Spending per average daily attendance (ADA) data are from NCES Common Core of Data based on total expenditures and ADA for fifty states and the District of Columbia, http://nces.ed.gov/ccd/bat/index.asp.
College Board SAT scores from NCES Digest of Education Statistics, 2004, table 131.
Stanford-9 scores from Office of Accountability (2006).

istration, and even corrupt or deceptive practices, but certainly cannot be attributed to a lack of funds or personnel. Today the DCPS has a ratio of one employee for every six students. In 1997, to support its continuing employee bloat, the school district took $1.6 million meant for teaching underprivileged students and diverted it to salaries, causing the federal government to revoke $20 million in targeted grants. Similarly, the school district falsified its records and over-reported enrollment figures to increase its budget and support-staff salaries and benefits. DCPS school administrators have employed ghost workers (who never came to work) and kept two sets of accounting books. The DCPS employed 511 central-office staffers in 1979, when it served 113,000 students, but by 1992–1993, despite the loss of 33,000 students, the DCPS's central office staff almost doubled to 967 employees (Lartigue 2004). Again in 1992–1993, the DCPS had 16 teachers for every administrator, whereas the national average for public school districts was 42:1 and Washington, D.C., Catholic schools had 255:1 (Shokraii et al. 1997).

Together with inadequate financial controls and dishonest spending, the DCPS has simply not paid attention to academics. An investigative team from the Council of the Great City Schools found that "the district hasn't done anything to improve achievement" (Council of the Great City Schools 2004, 10). This team found that the DCPS's academic content standards were not rigorous and that on-the-job teacher training ("professional development") was unconnected to what was being taught.

What the Great City Schools investigative team discovered was a school district without a coherent curriculum, with each school venturing off on its own. Schools either had a hodgepodge of conflicting academic programs or adhered to a "whole school reform" scheme that was not effective.[17] Teachers and staff (but

17. For example, the whole-school interventions in elementary schools have

not parents) "throughout the district's schools" had low expectations of students (Council of the Great City Schools 2004, 29). Children were overclassified as learning disabled, in large measure because the district was doing an ineffective job of teaching reading.[18] Children of Latino background were actively discouraged from exiting from mostly-Spanish instruction.

When it comes to teacher quality and to student, teacher, and administrator accountability, there are problems as well. Out of the twenty-two states and Washington, D.C., that use the Praxis teacher-readiness test, the DCPS is one of five that accepts the lowest minimum passing score for reading and one of four that accepts the lowest minimum score for writing (State Education Office 2004). The DCPS had no districtwide high school end-of-course exams or exit exam.[19] "[N]o one in the central office" was held accountable for student achievement, and teacher evaluations had "no meaningful tie" to it as well. Principals were considered responsible for achievement, but their evaluations were "weighted heavily towards items that are more procedural and operational than academic" (Council of the Great

---

followed the model created by the National Center on Education and the Economy. It is a content-oriented Progressive Education approach, featuring discovery learning, performance-based standards and assessment, portfolio assessment, and "real world" problem-solving. See National Center on Education and the Economy (2002). Academic results have been decidedly mixed. See Academic Performance Database System (2005).

18. The "ineffective district reading program" contributes to "the over-identification of students as disabled" (Council of the Great City Schools 2004, 40). On the "pattern" of "uncontained" spending on certain aspects of education for learning-disabled students ("special education"), see State Education Office (2004, 61–62).

19. Before switching to the Stanford-9 in 1997, the DCPS used the Comprehensive Test of Basic Skills. Here is the testimony of Bruce K. MacLaury, chairman, Emergency Transitional Education Board of Trustees, DCPS: "For 13 years, the CTBS, the Comprehensive Test of Basic Skills, was used, and I am told that exactly the same exam was given year after year after year, so that it was compromised, and, from my point of view, useless" (Committee on Governmental Affairs 1997, 36). On such testing practices, see Cannell (2006).

City Schools 2004, 34). The District of Columbia State Education Office (2004, 62) summed up the accountability problem, saying that, first, there "are not clear, publicly embraced goals" for public education in the District of Columbia, and, second, there "is not the kind of accountability system needed" to measure progress toward and attainment of such goals.

Besides their corrupt and inefficient financial practices and lack of attention to academics and accountability, DCPS officials show a routine indifference to their students' failing performance on standardized tests, and they continue to move students forward through primary and secondary education, even when they are clearly unqualified for promotion.[20] In 1997, at two high schools, every student was "Below Basic" in mathematics achievement (Committee on Governmental Affairs 1998). Ninety percent of students at fourteen of the DCPS's nineteen high schools are unable to do math at grade level (according to the Stanford-9 exam). These poor math competency scores are complemented by failing reading and writing scores (one quarter testing at the failing "Below Basic" level on the Stanford-9). Yet despite such scores, 86.5 percent of DCPS high school students were promoted to higher grades or graduated in 2002 (Division of Educational Accountability 2002; Lartigue 2004).

Although the DCPS spends more than fifteen thousand dollars per student annually, the system is also losing students every year.[21] The result of the DCPS's unacceptably poor performance has been a dramatic decline in enrollment in Washington, D.C.'s public schools, as families leave the city and as the remaining students who can afford to do so switch to private education. In 1969 the DCPS enrollment was at a high of 149,000, but by 2006, audited regular-school enrollment had

20. In theory the DCPS abolished social promotion in 1985 (Committee on Government Reform and Oversight 1998, 13).

21. On the DCPS per-pupil spending, see Lartigue (2004, table 5-11, 94).

dropped to 58,394, its lowest level in seven decades (*Washington Post* 2006).[22] In contrast, despite a decrease in the number of school-age children living in the district, private school enrollment figures have remained consistent at around 20,000 for the past half-century (Lartigue 2004). Mayor Anthony Williams, despite his record of increasing the DCPS funding 39 percent since taking office in 1998, is correct to question why the DCPS should receive any further money when it is so obviously underperforming, asking "how can you justify increasing funds for a school system that is losing students?" (Bhatti 2001).

The DCPS is yet another case in which huge spending by local and federal taxpayers has yielded only waste and underperformance. Despite resources above the national average, students continue to fail on national standardized tests, yet are still promoted through the system by an overstaffed administration.

Cambridge, Massachusetts

Cambridge, Massachusetts, is a "town and gown" community outside Boston, where the academic gowns are worn at Harvard University and the Massachusetts Institute of Technology (MIT).[23] The presence of these great universities in Cambridge is palpable. Harvard's domes and bell towers dominate the town skyline, and experimental alternative-fuel vehicles frequently appear on the town streets around MIT. Most Cantabrigians have a college degree. Though most of the town's children attend public schools, a larger than normal proportion go to private schools. The public school system must balance between children from well-educated households, some of whom are often

22. When charter school students are included, enrollment is 71,969 (*Washington Post* 2006).
23. We are indebted to the work of the Education Management Accountability Board (2000).

non-English-speaking foreigners arriving in the United States for the first time, and other local students, whose parents are less educated and work in blue-collar service jobs. Yet for a municipality so overflowing with academic brilliance, Cambridge's public schools consistently disappoint.

Cambridge Public Schools as a district serves roughly sixty-five hundred students and spends an average of $17,239 per pupil to provide for public education—almost twice the state average per student.[24] This spending costs taxpayers an average of two thousand dollars per taxpayer per year, which is substantially higher than the amount paid by property owners in any neighboring communities (Schlichtman 2003). Per-pupil expenditures by the district, the state, and the nation are illustrated in figure 4.3. Cambridge's property values are about double the state average, yielding much higher property tax revenues than elsewhere in Massachusetts.[25] The student-teacher ratio is low (11:1) compared with the state average, class sizes are comparatively small (on average fifteen students or fewer in core academic subjects), and teacher salaries are comparatively high (Education Management Accountability Board 2000).

Despite this substantial expenditure per student, the district consistently performs below both the state and national averages for grade-level reading and math proficiency. Besides Cambridge's 6,500 public school students, 1,218 students attend private and parochial schools, and 367 attend public schools outside the Cambridge district (*Boston Globe*). These relatively high numbers of students outside the Cambridge Public Schools system attest both to the failure of public schools in serving student needs and to the preference of many parents for the more rigorous education in private schools.

24. Figures from 2004 and 2003, respectively (SchoolMatters).
25. Figures from 2005 (SchoolMatters).

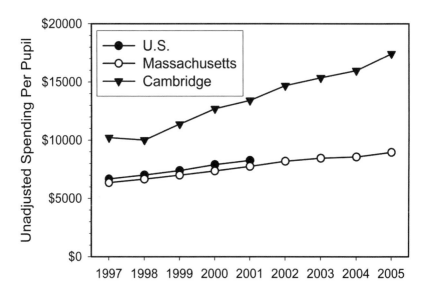

Figure 4.3   Per-Pupil Expenditures in Cambridge, Massachusetts, and Nationwide

Sources: U.S. Data: Table 168: Current Expenditure per Pupil in Average Daily Attendance in Public Elementary and Secondary Schools, by State or Jurisdiction: Selected years, 1959–1960 to 2001–2002, U.S. Department of Education, National Center for Education Statistics, Statistics of State School Systems, 1959–1960 and 1969–1970; Revenues and Expenditures for Public Elementary and Secondary Schools, 1979–1980 and 1980–1981; and The NCES Common Core of Data (CCD), "National Public Education Financial Survey," 1989–1990 through 2001–2002,. http://nces.ed.gov/programs/digest/d04/tables/dt04   168.asp. (This table was prepared April 2005.)

Massachusetts and Cambridge Data: Massachusetts Department of Education, Chapter 70 Trends, FY97 through FY06, http://finance1.doe.mass.edu/schfin/Chapter70/profile.aspx?.

As of 2005, despite an increase in reading and math achievement, Cambridge tenth graders' tests at the proficient or advanced level haven't shown nearly the gains that the Massachusetts average has shown. In fact, the performance gap between Cambridge and the rest of the state has increased from about 2 percent in 1998 to 21 percent in 2005.[26] In 1998 the percentage

26. See table 4.3.

of Cambridge students failing standardized tests in the fourth, eighth, and tenth grades was roughly equal to the state average, while by 2005 the percentage of Cambridge students failing was nearly double the state average, despite a decrease in the numbers of students failing (Massachusetts Department of Education). In other words, Cambridge has consistently trailed improvements in the rest of the state despite much higher spending per pupil, volunteer work by students from Harvard, MIT, and elsewhere, and improvement programs that follow the ideas of professors at Harvard and other universities (Solo 1992).[27] This phenomenon is illustrated in figure 4.4 where value added by the district is plotted against spending. Note that Cambridge stands out in spending but does not show any benefit as a result.

Cambridge's school district has enjoyed increased revenues from school adequacy lawsuits and responsive legislation in the 1990s. The 1993 adequacy case of *McDuffy v. Secretary of Education* resulted in a victory for the plaintiffs and the passage of the Education Reform Act three days later. This act decreased reliance on property taxes for school funding, in order to equalize funding across districts, and established a set of state standards and accountability measures known as the Massachusetts Comprehensive Assessment System (MCAS) (Ward 2005). The MCAS required student assessments at three grade levels in five subject areas (English, math, history, science, and foreign languages), leading to increased standardized requirements for high school graduation across the state. But Cambridge is a stronghold of Progressive Education (see discussion of Progressive Education under Teaching Practices: Counterproductive Ideology, later in this chapter), and many Cambridge teachers, parents, and students oppose these tests because the tests alleg-

27. Other colleges and universities include Wheelock College and Lesley University.

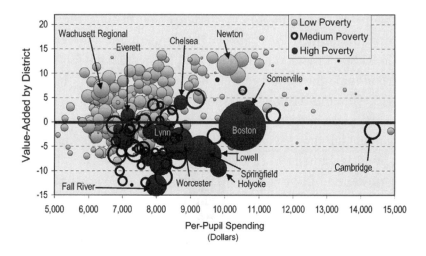

Figure 4.4   Value Added versus Per-Pupil Spending for Selected
Massachusetts Districts by Poverty Level of District (<20% Low, >40%
High)

Source: The testimony of Ed Mostovitch of Cape Ann Economics in the
Commonwealth of Massachusetts case *Julie Hancock and others v. David P.
Driscoll and others,* Superior Court Civil Action No. 02-2978 and Supreme Judicial
Court No. SJ-1990-0128, Nov. 3, 2003, exhibit 5378.
Notes:
    All the students were classified by the following demographic characteristics:
sex, race or ethnicity (white, Asian, Native American, black, Latino, mixed, other),
limited English proficiency, poor (defined by eligibility for free or reduced price
lunch), and not poor. Expected scores were calculated for each group.
    The left axis is "value added," which is the difference between the Proficiency
Index (0–100) used by the state and an estimated Proficiency index based on what
would be expected if each student scored at the average score of his or her
demographic group. Thus, a positive number indicates performance higher than
expected based on demographics. The bubble size represents the district size
based on examination counts.
    The bubble design indicates economic status based on percentage of students
eligible for free or reduced price lunch.
    Proficiency is from the 2001–2002 MCAS.

edly encourage teachers to concentrate narrowly on the subject
matter listed in the state's academic content standards. Some
Cambridge teachers spoke out against the tests, and some Cambridge students boycotted them (White 1999; Gehring 2000).
Moreover, the local school board in 2002 approved a resolution

Table 4.3   Percentage of Students Scoring Proficient or Above on MCAS Exams for Massachusetts and for Cambridge

| Year | MCAS English Language Arts | | | MCAS Mathematics | | |
	Mass.	Cambridge	Difference	Mass.	Cambridge	Difference
1998	38	37	−1	24	22	−2
1999	34	24	−10	24	21	−3
2000	36	15	−21	33	15	−18
2001	50	37	−13	45	36	−9
2002	59	40	−19	44	30	−14
2003	61	48	−13	51	43	−8
2004	62	47	−15	57	46	−11
2005	65	44	−21	62	41	−21

Source: Massachusetts Department of Education, Massachusetts Comprehensive Assessment System (MCAS) Directory Profiles, http://www.doe.mass.edu/mcas/results.html.

that said that the test was not conducive to testing different learning styles and that the district would, in defiance of state policy, award diplomas to students who hadn't passed the MCAS (Gehring 2002). The MCAS data for Cambridge are displayed in table 4.3 and show a continued progressive decline from 1998 through 2005.

Cambridge's academic failures are ironic when one considers that researchers at Harvard's Graduate School of Education, and others, have put in place school-improvement programs throughout the city's schools. The nearby availability of these schools and students has been of use to researchers. For example, Graham and Parks Alternative Public School takes a "developmental approach." Its premise is that children should develop "their intellectual, social, and moral capacities through their own self-selected activity rather than through formal instruction." In other words, the students themselves decide what they will study (Clinchy 1997, 28). For a long time, the now-defunct Pilot School, a school-within-a-school at the high school, was "the oldest progressive alternative public school . . . in the United States" (Grady 1994, 14).[28] King Open School proclaims that its teachers "engage in open conversation with the students," rather than in expository teaching.[29] In addition, "Different Ways of Knowing," which supposedly follows Harvard educational psychologist Howard Gardner's theory of multiple intelligences (Gardner 1983), has taken hold in the classes of dozens of Cambridge elementary school teachers. At Harrington Elementary School, for example, students come together to perform visual arts and mental association exercises. The Gardner-style approach claims to organize instruction to mesh with the different learning styles of students (Viadero 1994). At the high school the Harvard-based "Teaching for Understanding Project" has been directly under the guidance of Gardner himself (Grady 1994).

Over the years Cambridge has been renowned for letting each of its fifteen schools "do its own thing" in both content and teaching practices.[30] Cambridge has had (and in many cases still has), in addition to the formats already described,

- multicultural schools,

- self-esteem programs,

- a school-sponsored, student-led effort at curriculum reform,

- authentic, portfolio and project-based assessment,

- schools with multidisciplinary classes (e.g., a ninth-grade history-literature-math class on the theme "location"),

- a school without report cards or grade levels,

28. The Pilot School was founded as a clinical site for the Harvard Graduate School of Education.

29. See Cambridge Public Schools (2006).

30. In 1998 developments in statewide accountability reined in Cambridge's decentralized practices to some extent.

- mostly-Spanish programs,

- project-based learning,

- cooperative learning,

- learning through community service,

- radical, constructivist discovery learning K–8 math (e.g., Connected Mathematics Project, TERC's *Investigations*[31]),

- "real world," discovery-learning algebra,

- mathematics-light physics, and

- outdoor adventure learning (including ropes courses).[32]

Yet the test scores for Cambridge indicate that these site-based improvement efforts did not result in academic gains.[33] These Cambridge schools offer an illustration of the reason why the American Federation of Teachers president, Albert Shanker, disdained "all those alternative schools of the 1960s." Without testing and accountability, Shanker said, alternative schools were irrelevant and "useless" (Shanker 1994).

Cambridge Superintendent Bobbie D'Alessandro acknowledged that the district's curriculum "wasn't aligned to state standards." In other words, Cambridge schools haven't differed from one another only in the way they provide education; they have differed from one another and from the rest of the state in the subject matter they teach. Furthermore, a state audit of the district's operations found that the district had no districtwide professional development plan, no in-depth principal evaluations,

31. TERC was formerly the Technical Education Research Center.
32. Compare Cambridge Public Schools (2005). See also Grady (1994); Cambridge Public Schools (2006).
33. The district superintendent acknowledged that a barrier to education reform in the district was a "lack of systematic process" for evaluating academic programs in terms of their effect on student achievement (Education Management Accountability Board 2000: Appendix F).

and scanty teacher evaluations (Education Management Accountability Board 2000; Richard 2000).[34]

While in some ways the Cambridge Public Schools' story has much in common with other high-spending, low-performing districts, it is unusual in three respects. First, while many other high-spending, low-performing districts have been plagued by corruption, Cambridge has had considerable funds, spent them for educational purposes without corruption, and still not succeeded academically. In fact, a plurality of Cambridge teachers have come to believe that in their district increased spending does not lead to improved schooling.[35] Second, Cambridge has defied the maxim that "a rising tide lifts all boats." Since the 1990s, Massachusetts public schools' performance has improved dramatically as measured by statewide and national standardized tests, yet these improvements have largely left Cambridge behind. This underperformance is especially striking in light of the third feature of the Cambridge school district, namely, its elite academic setting, with its many highly educated parents and unique access to university researchers. Since Cambridge lacks neither financial resources nor improvement proposals and is not more challenged by socioeconomic conditions than are comparable cities elsewhere, one would have to consider whether it is these improvement plans themselves, together with recent local resistance to the state's accountability efforts, that have held the district back in the past two decades (Evers 2001; Alexakis 2001).

34. The Report of the Education Management Accountability Board (2000, 2) said: "There were no clear lines of accountability or reporting for curriculum, professional development, or testing."

35. When asked "Have you perceived an increase in school funding tied directly to improvements in education in your district?," 17 percent said "Yes"; 42 percent said "No"; and 41 percent said "Not Sure" (Education Management Accountability Board 2000, Appendix E).

Newark, New Jersey, and *Abbott* Districts

New Jersey is number one—the highest spending state on K–12 public education in the nation.[36] That makes it an important case study in evaluating the extent to which "money matters." The state has been the top spender nearly every year since 1990. Indeed, since the 1960s the three highest spending states have consistently been Alaska, New York, and New Jersey (U.S. Department of Education 2004).

Although New Jersey has been a long-term leader in K–12 spending, its big-city politicians and special interest groups have sought for decades to boost the funding of the urban school districts (Badessa 2004). Their efforts have been greatly facilitated by the courts. As a follow-on to previous lawsuits on school finance, a class action suit (*Abbott v. Burke*) was brought on behalf of students from low-wealth school districts, now known as *Abbott* districts. When the court handed down its initial decision in this case in 1990, it held that twenty-eight low-income districts were not providing a "thorough and efficient" education (a phrase out of the state's constitution). As evidence of inefficiency and lack of thoroughness, the court cited the scores of ninth graders from the low-income districts on the state's high school proficiency test. In *Abbott* districts, less than half the students passed the separate reading, mathematics, and writing tests while in well-to-do districts, more than 90 percent passed each test. The court pointed out that school spending in well-to-do districts averaged $4,029 per student (1984–1985), 40 percent more than the $2,880 average in the low-income districts. These figures did not include considerable federal aid that was (and

36. The authors are indebted to the treatments by Wilbur Rich (1996) and Peter Schrag (2005) and to Derrell Bradford of Excellent Education for Everyone (in Newark) for assembling background materials on the *Abbott* districts.

still is) targeted on the poorer districts (Coate and VanderHoff 1999).

Ultimately, the court ordered the state to give the *Abbott* districts as much money per student as the average per-student spending of the well-to-do suburban districts and to provide supplemental programs that would (it was thought) improve education. In 1999, in one of the *Abbott* cases, the state supreme court outlined the supplementary support the state was to provide in these districts. The court ordered the state to put into effect whole-school reform, provide full-day nursery school and kindergarten for all three- and four-year-olds, launch a state-managed building program, provide advanced technology, and provide additional vocational education, summer school, and after-school programs (Schrag, 2005).[37] The funding increase and the supplementary plans were, according to long-time education journalist Peter Schrag, one of the "best plans" ever devised for consciously providing an adequate education (Schrag 2005, 239).

Rather than focusing directly on improved student achievement, the court and the state commissioner of education focused on plans for whole-school reform. But the favored version of whole-school reform did not succeed. One critic says it was too monolithic and inflexible and not aligned to New Jersey's curriculum and testing.[38] Other critics say it concentrated on reading to the neglect of other subjects. Many schools using the favored reform did not bring student achievement up to the state average (Walberg and Greenberg 1998; Pogrow 2003). Not sur-

37. The building program amounted to $10–12 billion, of which over half would go to the *Abbott* districts (Schrag 2005).

38. Gordon A. MacInnes, the assistant state commissioner of education for the *Abbott* districts, testified that whole-school reform in the *Abbott* districts had prevented teachers there from teaching what was in the state curriculum. Asked by a state senator how this had happened, MacInnes said that he didn't know and could not explain it (Bradford 2005).

prisingly, in light of what modern bureaucracy theory would predict that officials would avoid doing—but "most perplexing" to Peter Schrag—the state (despite years of high adequacy-based spending) had "no effective mechanism" for assessing student performance until 2003 (Schrag 2005, 121).[39]

Today, statewide current-operations spending for K–12 education in New Jersey comes to about $12,000 per student per year on average. Spending in many *Abbott* districts exceeds $15,000 per student. In certain *Abbott* districts (such as Asbury Park and Camden), it is as high as $18,000 per student. In comparison with the *Abbott* districts, suburban districts spend less, about $10,000 to $11,000 per student (Denton 2002; Schrag 2005).

Yet despite more than $3 billion in additional funds, there has been no improvement across the *Abbott* districts. Student achievement in New Jersey's lowest-income school districts is persistently far worse than that in other school districts in the state. As Peter Denton—founder and chairman of Excellent Education for Everyone (E3)—says, the "horrible reality" is that over the several decades in which New Jersey has tripled spending on its low-income urban schools, their performance has "steadily declined," as measured by college attendance rates, standardized test scores, K–12 attendance rates, and high school graduation rates (Denton, 2002).

Likewise, Douglas Coate and James VanderHoff, economics professors at Rutgers University, analyzed in 1999 the effect of the state's school-finance system on student achievement. According to their findings, increased spending per student had no positive effect on achievement in the state. Moreover, when they looked specifically at the *Abbott* districts, they once again found

39. New Jersey's lengthy evasion of a workable accountability-oriented testing system calls into question Schrag's thesis that adequate funding will lead directly to increased accountability (Schrag 2005, 240–241).

no positive effect (Coate and VanderHoff 1999). Nonetheless, the law professor who initiated the *Abbott* suits claims that the results have been "an enormous success" (Schrag 2005, 125).

Among the *Abbott* districts is Newark, which has had public schools since 1666 (Rich 1996). One promotional statement describes the city as one of the Garden State's brightest flowers:

> As the third oldest city in America, Newark is home to generations of Americans drawn by economic opportunity, cultural offerings, quality of life, and a superior location. Today, more than three centuries after a band of Puritan settlers arrived at its shores eager to build a new life in 1666, the 275,000 people who now hang their hats in Newark are breathing new life into this vibrant urban center, and every day, more people are calling Newark their home. (Renaissance Newark Foundation 2006)

An alternative appraisal has been given by Steven Malanga, an editor of *City Journal*, who has said that for decades Newark has been one of the "most crime-ridden, inhospitable" cities in the country, a depopulated city of vacant lots and empty buildings (Malanga 2005).

Cory Booker, elected mayor of Newark in 2006, suggested a few years previously that there are six themes to political life in that city:

> First, . . . by every means necessary, protect your turf. Second, resist change. Third, expand one's sphere of control, always hoping to control more and more resources and authority. Fourth, enlarge the number of subordinates underneath you because having subordinates means having power, having election workers, and keeping yourself in office. Next, protect programs and projects regardless of whether they are effective or not. Finally, maintain the ability to distribute the greatest amounts of wealth from taxpayers to people and organizations of your own choosing. (Booker 2001)

Some of the crime Stephen Malanga alluded to has included corruption in the Newark school system. Under district leaders from a variety of ethnic groups over the years, there have been tales of new cars, fancy meals, trips to tropical places, ghost students, ghost teachers, contractor kickbacks, and selling jobs. The school system makes a tempting target, for it hands out more jobs and contracts than the city of Newark does (Rich 1996; Segal 2004). Wilbur Rich writes: "The [Newark] school system retains its reputation as being one of the most corrupt in the nation" (Rich 1996, 123). Peter Schrag says that in light of the pervasive corruption, there were "serious questions" about whether Newark and the other *Abbott* districts had the capacity to spend their adequacy money well (Schrag 2005, 124).[40]

Newark has a strong teachers' union, which has dominated school board politics since 1983. From the late 1970s through the mid-1980s, Kenneth A. Gibson, Newark's pioneering African American mayor, attempted several performance-oriented reforms. For example, in 1978 Gibson proposed evaluating teacher performance and requiring less teacher absenteeism. The union filed an unfair labor practice suit against the district over the absenteeism-reduction effort. The union built its reputation and legitimacy on its opposition to this effort, while it also sought a union say on textbook selection and exclusively-union classroom evaluations of teachers (Rich 1996). After he was no longer mayor, Gibson told an interviewer:

> The union just spends all its time fighting for the interest of the teachers, 'If we were better paid, morale would be better.' They opposed any kind of merit system. Everybody gets paid the same. An outstanding teacher cannot be given more. There is no incentive to be a teacher outside the love of children. (Rich 1996, 122)

40. Schrag (2005) emphasizes the corruption problem in another *Abbott* district, Camden.

Newark's social problems have attracted the attentions of the poverty-alleviation industry, including urban-renewal contractors who have torn down entire once-thriving neighborhoods (Malanga 2005). The schools are part of the poverty-alleviation effort and have sought their share of the money. In 2004–2005 Newark had 41,710 students and spent $21,978 per student, the student-teacher ratio was twelve to one, and the average teacher salary was $77,000 (Newark Public Schools 2005, 2006; Rone 2005). After this infusion of funds and supplemental programs, Newark's graduation rates have improved slightly, and its test scores have gone up.[41] But achievement in Newark still lags far behind that of the state as a whole. Figure 4.5 shows the state of achievement in Newark on the 2004 New Jersey Assessment of Knowledge and Skills (New Jersey Department of Education 2005).

Booker said in 2000.

> If you look at the entire school system in Newark, you have to find it repugnant. The graduation rate in public schools is down to 45 percent. Over 75 percent of eighth graders fail math proficiency tests, and nearly 50 percent fail in the language arts. . . . [T]oo many grade schools, especially in the area I represent which is the poorest ward in the city, have failure rates that range upwards into the 90th percentile. (Booker 2001)

Currently, most of Newark's freshman high school students cannot read at grade level. In 2005 Newark school board member Dana Rone provided specific numbers:

> Of Barringer's 459 incoming freshmen, 324 of them read at or below a sixth grade level. At Shabazz, 303 of 385 freshmen

---

41. Both New Jersey and Newark scores are going up, Newark's at a slightly faster rate. See Grade 4 New Jersey Assessment of Knowledge and Skills and Grade 8 Proficiency Assessment, 1999–2004 (New Jersey Department of Education 2005).

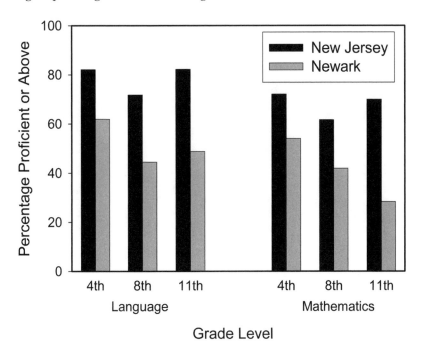

Figure 4.5   Results of the 2004 New Jersey Assessment of Knowledge and Skills

Source: New Jersey Department of Education, 2005 New Jersey Department of Education Statewide Assessment Reports, http://www.state.nj.us/njded/schools/achievement/2005/njask4/.

> read at or below a sixth grade level. And at Weequahic High, once considered one of the nation's finest high schools, 253 of 346 incoming freshmen read at or below a sixth grade level. In effect, many of our middle schools are, annually, generating only nine students who can read on grade level. (Rone 2005)

Some might suggest that given how dismal the record has been in Newark, why not have the state take over the operation of the district? It has already happened. Newark does not have local control of its schools, which have been run by the state since 1995. But students in state-takeover districts—that is, Newark, Paterson (run by the state since 1991), and Jersey City (since

Figure 4.6   Jeff Stahler, *The Cincinnati Post*, May 9, 1998 [reproduced with permission]

1989)—have long had and continue to have among the lowest test scores in New Jersey (Kvasager 2005).

The state of New Jersey requires that students demonstrate proficiency in knowledge of academic subject matter in order to graduate. Ordinarily, students satisfy this requirement by passing the High School Proficiency Assessment. But for those who fail three times, there is an alternative test, the "Special Review Assessment," which is widely recognized as much less rigorous. In a July 25, 2005, *Star Ledger* opinion column, Dana Rone wrote that the New Jersey State Board of Education should drop the alternative test, which she called an "academic charade," because it permits many students to "dodge" the state's regular high school exit examination. She contends that there is a lot of evidence that the students who obtained diplomas through the alternative process had not learned the material (Rone 2005).

In testimony before the budget committee of the New Jersey assembly, Rone laid out Newark's school problems and tore the veil off what is hidden by Special Review Assessment. She noted the startling results if one combined the data from Newark and Camden, two of the state's most troubled *Abbott* school districts, which are also northern and southern New Jersey's largest school districts. Their combined budget in 2004 was about $1 billion dollars. If one throws out the academically substandard students who graduate through the alternative-test process, the cost per academically qualified high school graduate in these two districts was nearly $1 million (Rone 2004).

This estimate of $1 million in spending per successful pupil sounds "outside the ballpark," but shouldn't if it is properly understood. Of course, most of the budgets in Newark and Camden are spent on students who will not pass the state high school exams. But as a measure of productivity, this million-dollar figure is a valid statistical indicator. This is what it actually costs these districts to produce an academically successful student.

Does money matter (figure 4.6)? Based on Newark and the *Abbott* districts, the answer is clearly "not much, if at all."

Sausalito, California

The town of Sausalito is, in the words of two public policy analysts, a "small, wealthy, politically liberal" suburb of San Francisco (Kirp and Leff 1979). The neighboring unincorporated area of Marin City is African American and low-income, with "moderately low" welfare dependency (Fiscal Crisis and Management Assistance Team 1997, 60). The Sausalito–Marin City K–8 district includes Sausalito and Marin City, and used to include nearby military bases until they closed in the early 1990s. The district itself in the 1960s called its policies and practices the embodiment of the "American Dream" (Freebairn-Smith 1968).

Black Power advocates took over the Sausalito schools in the late 1960s, with the initial help of white liberals.[42] In response, many bourgeois parents, both black and white, pulled their children out of the public schools and sent them to parochial or private day schools (Kirp and Leff 1979). The Black Power era came to an end when the white, liberal board members who supported it were ousted in a 1970 recall election. In 1997–1998 a grass-roots community group organized another recall campaign, aimed at improving student performance (Bertram 1997; Johnston 1997; *Education Week* 1998; Fimrite 1998; *San Francisco Examiner* 1998). It succeeded in recalling and replacing school board members, and the district superintendent and a school principal resigned under pressure.

After the equalization of school funding in California in the 1970s, Sausalito remained one of the state's few districts largely funded (because of its affluence) by local property taxes, which in Sausalito's case are heavily supplemented by state and federal aid. During the 2004–2005 school year, 263 students were enrolled in the district's two regular schools and its charter school—each of which had, as might be expected, small numbers of pupils. Almost half the district's children now attend a K–8 charter school that emphasizes the project-based learning favored by Progressive educators (Trotter 2006). One hundred percent of the teachers in the regular schools are fully credentialed.

Spending in Sausalito has been growing and far exceeds the state average (see figure 4.7). The district has modern, attractive facilities and $24,388 in revenue per student per year (com-

42. Young children were guided in giving the clenched-fist salute and chanting "Free Huey," a reference to Huey Newton, the jailed Black Panther Party leader. A Black Panther–sponsored breakfast program was set up in a school. A principal was hired whose book on Afrocentric curriculum included a photograph in which he is depicted pointing a rifle in the air, with a knife on his hip. Black Panther supporters carried steel staves to a school board meeting (Kirp and Leff 1979).

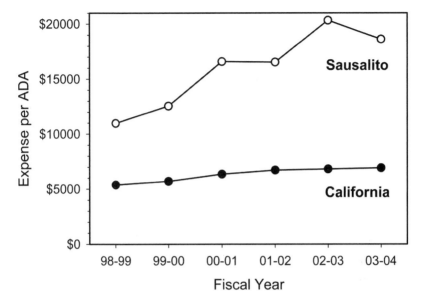

Figure 4.7   Per-Pupil Expenditures in Sausalito Compared with the State
Average
Source: California Department of Education, Current Expense of Education—
Financial, http://www.cde.ca.gov/ds/fd/ec/.

pared with a statewide average revenue per student for elementary districts of $6,996). Thus, Sausalito receives per student 3.5 times the average for California elementary districts—or about $17,400 more than the per-student average for elementary districts (Bova 2005b). An official 1997 California state fiscal audit said that "any failure of the district" to attain high academic performance "cannot be attributed to lack of revenue" (Fiscal Crisis and Management Assistance Team 1997, 6).

Class sizes are reasonably small, averaging twenty-four students per class in 2003–2004 (Education Data Partnership). As a 1997 curriculum (as opposed to fiscal) audit put it: "Class sizes are small; volunteers are plentiful; children receive personal and individual attention on an ongoing basis" (California Curriculum Management Audit Center 1997, 65). Teacher salaries are quite high, on a per-pupil basis. In 1997 average teacher salaries and clerical and blue-collar salaries in Sausalito were, on a per-pupil basis, double the averages in comparable California districts.[43] A *Los Angeles Times* reporter said a district school looked "like a ski resort sans snow." "The paint is fresh. The lawn is manicured. The playground equipment looks new"[44] (LaGanga 1997a).

Yet the district's performance is low. The *Los Angeles Times* reporter asked: "Why aren't children performing better in a district that wants for nothing money can buy?" (LaGanga 1997a). Out of 1,025 districts in California, Sausalito is ranked 724th, which is at the 29.4th percentile (California Department of Education 2004). The academic performance index (API) in California is shown as a function of expenditures per average daily attendance in figure 4.8 for all elementary school districts in the county. Note that Sausalito stands out as being well funded without showing corresponding achievement. According to 2004–2005 California test scores, 25 percent of Sausalito sixth grade students are proficient or advanced in English and 13 percent are proficient or advanced in mathematics (California Department of Education 2005). A notable difference between Sausalito and demographically similar districts is that, as one researcher put it,

> [H]alf of the comparable districts with half of the revenues have all of their schools score in the 6 to 10 [out of 10] rankings in the [California State Academic Performance Index (API)], while with its much greater funding, none of Sausalito/Marin City's

43. Fiscal Crisis and Management Assistance Team (1997, 14). Employee benefits are also double what they are in comparable districts.

44. An article in *Education Week* described that same school as sitting on "a 13-acre wooded site in picturesque Sausalito." "Its computer lab hums with new equipment. The library resembles a two-story chalet" (Johnston 1997).

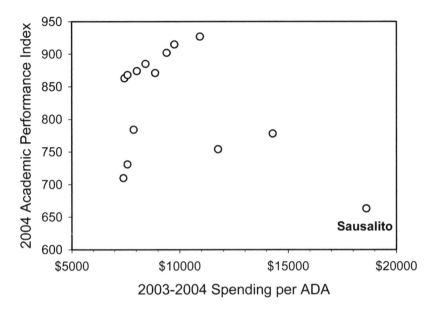

Figure 4.8   Per-Pupil Expenditures (Expense per ADA) versus Academic Performance Index Score for all Elementary Districts in Marin County, California, for 2003–2004

Sources: California Department of Education, Current Expense of Education—Financial, http://www.cde.ca.gov/ds/fd/ec/. California Department of Education, Academic Performance Index (API)—Data Files, http://api.cde.ca.gov/datafiles.asp.

schools are in the 6 to 10 rankings for the API. (Timar 2004, 15)

In the late 1990s, spending in Sausalito was running at $16,555 per pupil, well above the state average of $7,535 (Izumi and Coburn 2000). At that time, in 1999, Sausalito had substantial majorities reading and doing sums below the state average of performance for their grades.[45] Table 4.4 shows the achievement of the district against national norms. In the late 1990s the district's scores on California's Academic Performance Index

45. For Sausalito performance on the Cognitive Tests of Basic Skills, Fourth Edition, see California Curriculum Management Audit Center (1997, 104).

Table 4.4   Percent of Sausalito Students Scoring at or above the Fiftieth
Percentile on the 1999 Stanford-9 Test

Stanford-9	*Grade 2*	*Grade 6*
Reading	30%	38%
Math	36%	33%

Source: California Department of Education, Standardized Testing and Reporting
(STAR) Web site, http://star.cde.ca.gov/star99/reports.

were in the 600s (the scale ranges from 200 to 1000; the state
wants schools at 800, the federal government at 850).

In October 1996 the district was overclassifying students as
learning disabled, placing 145 students out of 248 (58 percent)
in special education programs for the learning disabled,
whereas the average district in the state had 10 to 12 percent
learning disabled.[46] One of the authors of this chapter inter-
viewed a central figure in the 1998 recall campaign, a recall
leader who had served in Sacramento as deputy state superintendent of schools, in San Francisco as director of the housing
authority, and later became board president of the Sausalito
school district. According to her, schools identified many African
American students in preschool as speech-impaired or devel-
opmentally delayed based on "preconceived notions." These
identifications became a self-fulfilling prophecy: the identifications were never revisited, and students were trapped in special
education classes in which they didn't belong (Thornton 2005).

The 1998 recall campaign leader told one of the authors that
Sausalito was paralyzed by a "lack of belief that these children
could learn." She said that this mindset about the African American children of the Sausalito district "permeated" southern Marin County, not just Sausalito. As a result, she said, the African
American parents in Marin City didn't believe in the Sausalito–

46. See California Curriculum Management Audit Center (1997, 76).

Marin City schools and didn't trust teachers and officials. These parents "saw no education going on" and were therefore alienated from the school system (Thornton 2005).

A top administrator in a neighboring school district says that, after decades of funding at the highest levels in California, Sausalito is perhaps "a quarter of the way" to solid academic achievement (Anonymous 2005a). Education professors at universities have been stumped by the Sausalito case and have offered no explanation. "It's a puzzle," said Michael Kirst, professor of education at Stanford University, who noted that Sausalito has been "high-spending for years" (LaGanga 1997a).

Nonetheless, it seems clear that years of curricular confusion, ineffective teaching practices, overemphasis on student self-esteem, low academic expectations, adult corruption, and violent student crime have trapped Sausalito in a high-dollar heaven that is at the same time a dysfunctional-district hell.

The curricular confusion was documented in a curriculum audit done by outsiders, which the school board commissioned in 1996–1997 (Johnston 1997). The audit found that

- the curriculum in any one classroom meshed neither with other classrooms in the same grade nor with curriculum in the next grade;[47]

- on-the-job training of teachers (professional development) was unconnected to curriculum and unevaluated for effectiveness;

- numerous and conflicting programs in support of curriculum were almost never evaluated for effectiveness, but the few

47. "[T]he lack of focus on articulation [from grade to grade] and coordination [within each grade] from the central office level creates a learning environment that is irrational and impedes the progress of students. . . . This breakdown in curriculum continuity is a serious obstacle to improving student performance. . . ." (California Curriculum Management Audit Center 1997, 87).

times when they were evaluated, ineffective programs were
neither modified nor ended;

- teachers had low expectations and "doubt[ed] the learning
  capabilities of their students";[48] and

- testing of students was uncoordinated with curriculum, and
  test results were neither analyzed nor used to drive instruction[49] (California Curriculum Management Audit Cente
  1997).

Students were assigned perhaps a half hour of homework a
night, most of which they were encouraged to complete in the
classroom.[50] In terms of scope and sequence, the curriculum
was unstructured and uncoordinated: "Every teacher was doing
his or her own thing." "Teachers were not looking at the tran-
sition from grade to grade." Students were working from "work
sheets and Xerox pages," rather than from textbooks. What was
deemed "acceptable work" from students was "embarrassing."
They were dropping out, even though they were not yet of high
school age (Thornton 2005).

Because the Sausalito school district did not properly prepare its students, those students who went on to high school
could not prosper and could not compete. Students from Sausalito were joined in high school by students from high-performing neighboring districts like Tiburon and Mill Valley, but Sausalito students were not prepared to work at the same level.[51]

48. California Curriculum Management Audit Center (1997, 52).

49. The curriculum audit team found that the district's approach to testing
was "chaotic" and that the testing process was "confused, unfocused, and irrational" (California Curriculum Management Audit Center 1997, 95).

50. Similarly, a parent told the curriculum audit team, "I took my child out
of North Bay [School] because the curriculum was not challenging. My child
could do a week's homework assignment in one afternoon" (California Curriculum Management Audit Center 1997, 19).

51. A staff member from the high school that receives the students from

An inspection of freshman grades in the fall of 1997 shows that 72 percent of Sausalito graduates were below a 2.0 grade point average, as compared with 18 percent for all freshmen at the public high school that serves Sausalito. That semester, no Sausalito freshman earned above a 3.0 (Johnston 1997).

At the same time that the district had "beautiful facilities" and was paying teachers high-end salaries compared with other districts in the state, the district was also beset with corruption. Although the district was flush with property taxes and extra state and federal money, an individual who was already a veteran teacher when he taught in the district in the 1980s told one of the authors that the district in those days was characterized by "blatant, despicable" misuse of public money. He described it as the "most unethical" conduct he had seen in a career of over thirty years in public education. "Deals were brokered and money pocketed." He said that top staff took rake-offs from contracts with the district. Top staff had new, fancy cars and took high-cost trips. Money was not getting to the classroom level, and the district had not put into effect needed remedial programs (Anonymous 2005b). The 1998 recall leader told one of the authors that the scene in the Sausalito district in the late 1990s was "poverty pimping at its worst," with "many people feeding at the trough" (Thornton 2005).[52]

The interviewee who had taught in Sausalito in the 1980s

Sausalito said in a newspaper interview: "[T]hose [Sausalito] children are a 'mixed bag' of considerable talent and unpreparedness. Overall their achievement lags far behind students from other districts." Quoted in California Curriculum Management Audit Center (1997, 58).

52. There may have been ghost workers on the Sausalito payroll. The curriculum audit team asked the district for "a list of persons on its payroll" and also for "a list of all staff members assigned to positions in the school district as well as a list of persons who have left the district during the last five years." "The auditors found discrepancies between the two lists and were unable to account for all employees even after they identified persons who had left the district." (California Curriculum Management Audit Center 1997, 42).

said that the "least qualified teachers" he had seen in his life made up the teaching staff, and any able teachers left within a short time.[53] There was no focus on children's learning; all the focus was on the interests of the adults employed by the school system. No administrator and no one who stayed on the Sausalito teaching staff was offering "hope [to the schoolchildren] or a sense that they would stand by them [the schoolchildren]" in adversity (Anonymous 2005b).

In 1997 the Marin County civil grand jury said violence in Sausalito schools had gotten out of hand—despite the fact that this was a K–8 district with no high-school students. The grand jury said that police were called to the schools fifty times during the 1996–1997 school year and that teachers "actually fear turning their backs on students" (Fimrite 1997).

A *Los Angeles Times* article reports that a student injured a school principal by assaulting her, but the district neither suspended nor expelled the student.[54] The principal said Sausalito had severe classroom discipline problems, low expectations for student achievement, and no consistency in its curriculum.[55] That principal moved to another low-income district. The article quotes a Marin City mother as saying that many of these problems had their source in fellow Marin City parents who didn't care about discipline or academics. The *Los Angeles Times* quoted departing Sausalito teacher Josephine Pearson: "It's the

53. Kirp and Leff (1979) point out that in 1973 "approximately 10 teachers, a sizeable number in a district with only 37 teachers altogether, were extremely weak in the classroom." Kirp and Leff point out that because California teacher tenure law protects teachers' jobs, the Sausalito district administration could not fire these weak teachers, if and when it wanted to.

54. Many student misdeeds were punished. There were 166 suspensions for bad behavior in 1996–1997 (Johnston 1997). For more data on suspensions, see California Curriculum Management Audit Center (1997, 81–84).

55. In a follow-up article, the reporter said that the district had used a "mishmash" of programs to address district problems and described the academic curriculum as uncoordinated and inconsistent (LaGanga 1997b).

biggest mess I've ever seen. It's so sad. All that money, and nothing for those kids" (LaGanga 1997a).

The 1997 curriculum auditors said that the Sausalito teachers "view the students as victims" and "do not hold them responsible" for disruptive or injurious behavior. Those whom the teachers believe should be held responsible are the parents and the administration. On the other hand, "neither the parents nor the administration" are willing to assume responsibility. Therefore, "conditions continue to worsen" (California Curriculum Management Audit Center 1997, 53).

The *Los Angeles Times* said a local nonprofit group saw low student self-esteem as a major cause of low achievement and disruptive behavior, and a follow-up article in the *Times* quoted Sausalito's vice mayor as saying that the district's program concentrated more on improving students' self-esteem than on academics (LaGanga 1997a, 1997b).

Since 1999, district leaders have improved performance, as compared with performance in past years. Nonetheless, current performance remains low in absolute terms and compared with other districts in the state. District leaders have adopted certain practices that have boosted achievement, but other current practices are still holding the district back. Although the district has more than ample funds, district leaders do not have enough of an incentive to eliminate practices that are counterproductive.

After insurgent-led voters recalled board members and the district superintendent and a school principal resigned in 1998, the new board hired a new superintendent. When she arrived, the new superintendent could see that Sausalito's problems "were not about money."[56] She saw a district with "a lack of a systematic approach." Bits and pieces of reading programs, for

---

56. Similarly, a community member told the curriculum audit team, "Money is channeled to the district; it is not the problem . . ." (California Curriculum Management Audit Center 1997, 17).

example, were scattered in the classrooms of different teachers. But no complete reading program was everywhere. There was no training of teachers in reading instruction (Roberson 2005).

The new superintendent adopted Open Court, a reading program she describes as having a strong emphasis on vocabulary development, "demanding" for students and requiring a "disciplined" effort on the part of teachers. She also made considerable efforts to connect K–8 academics to what a student would be expected to need for success in high school (Roberson 2005). By 2003–2004, Sausalito's rating on the state's academic performance index was 663, still a long way from 800 or 850, but an improvement from the rating in the low 600s when she arrived.[57]

In an important sense, the district is not, in fact, helped by Marin County institutions and the surrounding political and cultural milieu in its efforts to improve; indeed it is held back. Marin County is correctly seen as an affluent repository of the counterculture and left-liberalism of the 1960s. In the late 1960s the Sausalito superintendent believed that traditional schooling "favored the middle-class child" and "stifled" the socioeconomically "deprived child." So the superintendent sought to build student self-esteem and foster creativity and "non-verbal communication" (Freebairn-Smith 1968).[58]

The district participated in a project on teaching mathematics that was developed in 1963 by William F. Johntz, a Berkeley,

57. The district school board fired this superintendent in August 2005. Neither the board nor the fired superintendent offered an explanation (Bova 2005a, 2005b).

58. One reform of the 1960s that was radical in form, which might well be considered traditionalist in substance and tendency was the use in Sausalito schools of Sir James Pittmans's initial teaching alphabet (i.t.a.) (Freebairn-Smith 1968). Such a reform was radical form in that it resembled the invented-spelling movement of the 1990s. But it was traditional in substance because it was based on phonics. On the i.t.a., see Balmuth (1992).

California, high school math teacher. Math was supposed to be learned through student self-discovery. The teachers would teach almost entirely by asking "provocative questions" of the students. Lecturing was "practically eliminated." Marilyn Burns, a nationally famous proponent of the discovery method of teaching mathematics, formerly taught in the Sausalito schools. At report card time, Mrs. Burns would have her students grade the teacher (Freebairn-Smith 1968).

Countercultural and left-liberal attitudes among white Sausalito school administrators and community leaders at first encouraged the Black Power takeover in the school district in the 1960s, which led to a subsequent loss of culturally bourgeois school parents of both races. These attitudes fostered a breakaway Progressive Education school in the 1970s, which later was reabsorbed into the district.[59] The breakaway parents were, in fact, dismayed that the largely educationally traditionalist African American parents wanted an emphasis on educational basics (Kirp and Leff 1979). The district's "Vision Statement" emphasizes fostering students' "positive attitudes" and encouraging students to "accept themselves and others." As the 1997 curriculum audit team said, the Vision Statement "implicitly reinforces the social aspects of school life before the academic commitment" (California Curriculum Management Audit Center 1997, 52). School board policy explicitly required the district superintendent to lead in "developing *creative* curricular programs" but said nothing about leadership on curriculum effectiveness and student achievement (emphasis added, California Curriculum Management Audit Center 1997, 29).

In another guise, these countercultural attitudes are found today in the South Marin County Education Task Force, as well as in the Buck Trust and the Marin Community Foundation. Sau-

59. The current project-based charter school is to some extent a parallel.

salito and neighboring districts collaborate in the Education Task Force. As one of its functions, the task force produces tests used for diagnostic purposes, to guide instruction and to stimulate the creation of new teaching strategies.

The Buck Trust and the Marin Community Foundation are influential charities that pour money into the Sausalito schools. These influential charitable dollars often support Progressive Education. When these dollars arrive, they always bear with them the strictures of political correctness. As a result, according to a top administrator in a neighboring school district, the charities do not have the intestinal fortitude to require results from Sausalito. "They are giving money without requiring performance," because it might be deemed "racist" to hold Sausalito accountable (Anonymous 2005a).

According to the same administrator, the Educational Task Force "pooh-poohs" Sausalito's rigorous phonics-based Open Court reading program and fails to support Sausalito by training its teachers in Open Court. The task force also promotes and administers "superficial" tests that do not reflect Sausalito's curriculum (such as it is) or California standards (Anonymous 2005a).

Sausalito states that these tests are aligned with the California Academic Content Standards. However, after having looked at the publicly released test questions in reading and mathematics, the authors have found that the reading test questions neglect word-attack skills and word recognition.[60] The mathematics test questions are below grade level and poorly written.

To evaluate the task force tests further, the authors sought the views of a third party. An anonymous member of the California statewide testing system's mathematics Assessment Re-

60. On testing word-attack skills and accurate word recognition, see Chall and Popp (1996, chapter 7); Spear-Swerling and Sternberg (1996, chapter 7); Torgesen (1998).

view Panel reviewed the test questions for seventh grade mathematics. He found that the seventh grade math-test questions suffer from below-level expectations, sloppy and ill-posed problems, and incorrect grading and evaluation of the sample answers. Some questions are aimed at fourth grade math abilities, rather than seventh grade ones.[61] Many require assumptions that are not explicit in the problem statement. The suggested exemplary grading is subjective, incompetent, and likely to lead teachers to misapprehend students' actual achievement. Because of these limitations, such a test is likely to misguide classroom instruction and distract from focused attention on achieving the goals outlined in the California Standards (Anonymous 2005c).

How can a district spend so much money and have so little to show for it? Sausalito has or has had

- an ineffective and inconsistent curriculum,

- on-the-job training for teachers unconnected to curriculum,

- student lawlessness and absence of classroom discipline,

- adult theft and corruption,

- unproductive efforts to raise student self-esteem,

- parental alienation from the schools,

- parental indifference (perhaps related to the alienation) toward achievement,

- inadequate and misleading districtwide tests, and

- low expectations for students.

Yet Sausalito has three and a half times the revenue per student of the average California elementary school district. If

61. Grade levels are discussed here in terms of the grade-level expectations in California's Academic Content Standards.

money were all that matters or most of what matters, Sausalito (which had an abundance of money) should have been successful. But because the district did not impose classroom discipline, clean out corruption, raise academic expectations, hire and retain effective teachers, adopt good tests, adopt a research-based curriculum, and train teachers how to make the most of it, all that money didn't matter. The district didn't do these things— things that are challenging but not costly—or has only accomplished bits and pieces of them after decades. If the district had done what was needed, parents who cared would have been pleased with their children's accomplishments. Children would have earned a real improvement in self-esteem. Some parents who didn't care would have had a concrete reason to change their minds or might have been reached through adult education. Clearly, this is a case that raises questions about the extent to which money per se matters. The case of Sausalito shows that solid curriculum, productivity-oriented incentives, and a work-ethic culture are a requisite for schools to be effective and for spending to accomplish what it should.[62]

Comparative Analysis

Looking over these five high-spending, low-performing school districts (Kansas City; Washington, D.C.; Cambridge; Newark; and Sausalito), we find that they mishandled their large revenues in different ways, yet there are also many similarities. All of the districts were chosen for study because they have the essential characteristic called for by the educational establishment and by the proponents of adequate education: high spending per pupil. All of them mishandled the money in ways that were predictable, given what we know about organizational structure

---

62. On the power of a culture of achievement, see Mayer (1997).

and the politics of school districts. All had interest groups that blocked merit hires, merit pay, and adult accountability. All of the districts tried fashionable remedies prescribed by the education establishment and its affiliated experts.

Infrastructure and Class Size

Kansas City lavished its funds on infrastructure, in the apparent belief that beautiful buildings and fancy technology could substitute for good teaching and a culture of achievement. New Jersey's *Abbott* districts participated in an extensive building program. Sausalito with its beautiful school sites has made the same mistake on a smaller scale.[63] Kansas City and Sausalito also shared in experimenting with class size reduction, a reform that is so ubiquitous now that its curative powers should be manifest, yet they are not.

Neglect of Academic Content and School Effectiveness

We know that the most important components of academic success for students are high-quality teachers, effective teaching practices, a solid curriculum, and a culture of high academic expectations and accountability (Hanushek 2002; Walberg 2002). Yet Kansas City, Newark, and Sausalito neglected recruiting its teachers on merit, in favor of cronyism and racial preferences. Kansas City never formulated a core curriculum despite Judge Clark's several requests. Washington, D.C., and Cambridge had a different curriculum in every school, and Sausalito had a different curriculum in every classroom.

---

63. Picus et al. (2005) show that in Wyoming better facilities do not boost student achievement. They found "no relationship" between school facilities and student performance. This is significant in light of the 2001 adequacy case in Wyoming in which the court instructed the state to put more money into its construction budget.

Instead of using effective teaching practices and proven lesson plans, several of these districts indulged themselves in Progressive Education fads and fancies. For example, Cambridge created a school where students decided what they would study and turned other classrooms into laboratories for Howard Gardner's theory of different learning styles. Similarly, Sausalito, located in countercultural southern Marin County, has twice turned over a school to Progressive Education and remodeled its math program along Progressive lines. Sausalito has had a student discipline problem that probably is related to the permissiveness of Progressive Education and political correctness (Wenders 2005a). Low expectations for students were exemplified in light homework assignments. Critics described the Sausalito district as putting more energy into its self-esteem program than it did into its academics.

Dodging the Assessment Bullet

Several of these districts abandoned or never sought to foster a culture of setting high academic expectations and measuring outcomes. Cambridge schools have been crippled in part by an extramural culture in which the high academic expectations of a college town were in contradiction with the town's role as a center of opposition to testing—opposition that has been based on the doctrines of Progressive Education. Washington, D.C., and New Jersey evaded for years creating a testing system that could hold schools or students accountable. Some commentators have said that they expect that providing districts with great resources will directly and inexorably lead to accountability for the use of those resources. But the long-time evasion of accountability by Washington, D.C., and New Jersey calls such an expectation into question. Washington, D.C., turned its back on high-achieving Dunbar High School and went on to practice egregious policies of social promotion of students who were not ready for the next grade.[64] By congratulating itself on the test results from a deliberately watered-down test, New Jersey has made itself into a fool's paradise.

Corruption

Corruption was a prominent feature in four of the districts studied (Kansas City, Newark, Sausalito, and Washington, D.C.) and certainly contributed to district failures. The corruption manifested itself in embezzlement, self-dealing, rake-offs, overcharging, and ghost workers. But some observers might say, corruption is a problem that is peculiar to those particular districts. Yet there is no basis for presupposing that if adequate funding were poured into every school district, there would be a negligible amount of corruption.

According to several measures of honest government, the United States has a shabby record compared with other constitutional democracies. For instance, the 2003 Transparency International ranking on honest government indicates that, of the twenty-five nations in the survey with per-capita gross domestic product (GDP) of at least fifteen thousand dollars the United States is in eighteenth place. Likewise, in a World Bank evaluation of anti-corruption efforts, the United States was in sixteenth place, among twenty-four wealthy countries. Thus, we should not be surprised that corruption was rife in several of the districts examined in our case studies, and no one should assume that corruption will not be endemic if adequacy campaigns are successful and low-performing districts are flush with funds (Osborne 2005).

---

64. Social promotion is a policy of advancing students with their age group and not holding them back when they are not academically prepared for the next grade.

While there is a need for systemic reform to discourage corruption, we should remember that Cambridge has had severe academic deficiencies with no corruption in sight, and we should also beware of corruption charges as a diversion. In New Jersey, as Wilbur Rich reports, the educational establishment used corruption complaints not only to put a focus on corrupt individuals (which is reasonable) but also to divert "the public's attention away from school performance issues" (which is changing the subject) (Rich 1996, 120).

The Politics of School Districts

The seemingly simple suggestion of spending more money to get more output from public schools turns out to be not so simple. These schools are public agencies with all the efficiency and productivity problems inherent in public agencies.[65] Public agencies are governed by politics, and education agencies are not fundamentally different from other public agencies. School politics is a variant of regular politics.

The political context of public schooling will largely determine whether pouring more money into school districts will be enough to successfully educate low-performing students. The four elements of that context that are most important for the productivity of American school politics are

1. The "one best system" of organization that political scientists say has been captured by its bureaucratic denizens,[66]

65. For classic studies of bureaucracy, see Mises (1944), Tullock (1965), Downs (1967), Niskanan (1994), and Moe (1997). Martin (1962, 99) writes: "Through the two principal devices of isolating the public schools and maximizing professional influence, the educational bureaucracy has achieved notable success in driving the public school structure toward a monolith under oligarchic control. It is to be doubted, indeed, whether the bureaucracy plays so important a role in the governance of any other public undertaking in America."

66. On the "one best system" of the Municipal Reform–type administrative Progressives, see Tyack (1974).

2. The strength of the education interest groups who resist measures promoting effectiveness and accountability,

3. The dominant teaching practices whose adherents ideologically oppose focusing on academic content, and

4. The operational doctrine of school districts that discourages a long-term loyal opposition and that protects officials when they are ineffective or even corrupt.

Before we discuss interest groups, teaching practices, and district operations, it is important to get a sense of that "one best system," the organizational structure within which educational politics takes place.

Organizational Structure: Bureaucratic Capture

Public schools in this country are largely controlled at the local level. They are managed by a district superintendent, the superintendent answers to a locally elected board, and this board is elected by local voters, a small minority of whom usually turn out for school board and school finance elections (Ostrom 1961; Rich 1996; Nappi 1999).[67] A board member's power base rests, then, at the local level. But America's fifteen thousand school districts also exist within a federal system in which mandates and funds (but little day-to-day management) flow downward from the state and the national level. Add to that the fact that school districts receive most of their funding simply for having students in attendance, that their customers (parents) don't pay the full costs of operation, and the owners (citizen-taxpayers) cannot exercise ownership rights, and it is little wonder that economists and political scientists have said that—before the current accountability efforts—district decision makers faced

67. Political scientists have found that the educational establishment often deliberately encourages a low and selective turnout (Wirt and Kirst 1972).

few consequences (positive or negative) whether or not they succeeded in the job of educating their students (Alchian 1977; Chubb and Moe 1990).

Because school districts get their revenue from taxes determined by the political process, their costs tend to rise to meet the funds available. Before current accountability efforts, districts measured their gains by the resources they had been able to attract, rather than by productivity or effectiveness in securing student academic success. While spending had been going up, student performance had been flat or even dropping (Wenders 2005a).

Another feature of political life is that politicians and administrative officials know that the future is uncertain and that their successors may seek to undo what today's officials have done. Therefore, they seek to lock in programs through laws, rules, and bureaucratic procedures. They hope to leave a legacy of programs firmly in place, with a constituency to support it (Chubb and Moe 1990). But certain programs that sometimes are mandated and subsidized, like the antiphonics "whole language" way of teaching reading, can be ineffective and counterproductive (National Reading Pane 2000).

We must also remember that educating students has not been the sole focus of school districts. Like any public bureaucracy, local school districts want not only to hang onto their current budget and set of activities but to increase them as well.[68] Hence, districts are furnishing sports and recreation and dealing with various public health problems, the battle of the sexes, race relations, and adult illiteracy—as well as teaching academic subject matter to children (Homfeld 1959; Kirst 1984). School districts see nonacademic activities as categories for which they can

---

68. On the "functional imperialism" of public agencies, see Downs (1967, 12, 94, 109, 242, 246); Aranson (1981, 456–457).

seek funding and as alternative areas of accomplishment when academics are weak; but nonacademic endeavors are, in the end, a diversion from the school districts' academic mission.

This, then, is the organizational structure that will be called on to deliver if adequacy funding is put into place. School districts as presently constituted are somewhat ineffectual institutions with important inherent weaknesses. Yet they are the institutions that will use adequacy funds to deliver schooling to the nation's low-performing students.

Interest Groups: Resistance to Accountability

Having the internal dynamics described above, the school district is itself a political arena and also a part of state and national arenas.[69] In the arena of school politics, the political establishment consists of school district officials, principals, school clerical and physical-plant workers, PTAs, and teachers' unions.[70] This establishment, especially the teachers' unions, is one of the best-organized and most influential forces in American politics (Moe 2006). Also in the school-politics arena are those school reformers who stress academic achievement. They include parent organizations, business groups, think tanks, and proreform legislators and governors and are a more diffuse group than the education establishment.

The power of the educational establishment is an example of a common political phenomenon: small groups who can be readily organized and whose interests are concentrated have more leverage than the general public or larger groups with a

69. Iannaccone and Lutz (1967, 161) write: "The politics of education have been characteristically the politics of interest groups, as contrasted to those of party."

70. Iannaccone (1977, 281) contended that Parent-Teacher Associations are not independent but rather are "managed" by the district central office. On bureaucratic influence in PTAs, see Martin (1962, 99).

multiplicity of interests. Economist E. G. West points out that it is an established truth that "the suppliers of education" (his examples are local district officials, administrators, and unionized teachers) have a "disproportionate influence" as compared with that of the consumers of education. The customers, West says, have interests that are diffuse and "spread over many goods and services." The suppliers, who depend for their livelihood on the provision of education, can see the profit in assuming "the costs of pressure group politics" (West 1968, 31, 72).[71]

The most important instrument for encouraging student achievement has in recent years been state-level academic standards and accountability systems based on student test results. The powerful education establishment, of course, has little interest in being looked at or evaluated in this way (Murphy and Cohen 1974; Wildavsky 1979). The critics of standards and accountability come both from the education establishment and from advocates of Progressive Education, some (but not all) of whom are an influential part of the establishment. Some critics, for example, argue that statewide testing should be used only for diagnostic purposes, never for accountability (Association of California School Administrators 1997; Borja 1999; Gehring 2002). Other critics argue that it is wrong, in principle, to hold teachers accountable—claiming that once teachers are credentialed, they should not have to worry about being scrutinized as to their effectiveness (Ohanian 1999).

Of course, if arguments fail, one can always fall back on sheer political strength, which education interest groups have done in opposing any principal-accountability or teacher-accountability measures that have teeth. The states now have student-learning standards, testing of students, and rewards and sanctions for students based on test results. But by and large,

71. For further discussion of this topic, see Peltzman (1993).

they do not have systematic rewards and sanctions for district leaders, principals, or teachers.

Teaching Practices: Counterproductive Ideology

Researchers have good scientific evidence that certain teaching methods are more likely to boost student achievement and keep it at a high level. At the same time, other popular practices, often promoted by Progressive educators on ideological grounds, have little evidentiary basis or lack any such basis whatsoever. Progressive educators, who trace their roots to ideas propounded by John Dewey and others during the Progressive Era, are nonetheless highly influential from the district headquarters to the classroom. They also dominate other establishment institutions: the faculties of the schools of education at American universities, the early childhood groups, and the professional associations of subject matter specialists.[72]

Progressives believe in *discovery learning*. They contend that students truly learn only when they have "discovered" and applied knowledge and skills to solve problems.[73] Hence, Progressives often advocate project-based and "real world" learning, and, if there is to be testing, "authentic" or "performance-based" (project-based) testing. Progressives also believe in the doctrine of *developmental appropriateness*, which holds that each child goes at his or her own natural pace through a set of discrete learning stages that are biologically hard-wired into children.[74] Most Progressives take a child-centered approach to discovery learning, meaning that teachers should help their students, but the students' interests should guide the content and

72. For example, on Progressive Education and the mathematics subject matter group, see Loveless (2001).

73. Compare Tucker and Codding (1998, 78).

74. See Evers (1998, 15–17; Stone (1996); Hirsch (1996, 79–91).

direction of schoolwork.[75] Child-centered Progressives do not believe there is a culturally established body of knowledge that students need to learn (Hofstader 1963; Evers 1998; Ravitch 2000; Zoch 2004).[76]

Yet schooling itself presumes that there is a culturally established body of knowledge that students should learn. That body of knowledge needs to be in the curriculum, or students are unlikely to learn it (Hirsch 1996). Progressives favor a pure discovery approach to student learning, yet there is no evidence proving that reliance on pure discovery boosts students' achievement.[77] Indeed, the research evidence supports the efficacy of teacher-led instruction—whether explicit, expository instruction or guided discovery.[78] When teachers do use discovery methods, teacher-guided discovery (rather than pure discovery) is best. Teachers should focus lessons on clearly specified subject matter and encourage students to think about that subject matter (Mayer 2004).[79]

Progressives favor the whole-language approach for teaching

75. Throughout the history of Progressive Education, the child-centered Progressives have been more numerous than the intellectualist Progressives. The intellectualist minority calls for discovery learning but also believes that there is a culturally established body of knowledge that students need to learn. See Ravitch (2000, 16, 190, 463).

76. Clark University President Stanley Hall, a leading pioneer of child-centered Progressive Education in the late nineteenth and early twentieth centuries, said: "Alas for the teacher who does not learn more from his children than he can ever hope to teach them!" (Zoch 2004, 84) Hall also suggested that whatever learning went on should be through "play and games alone" and believed that "very few" children have a "taste or ability" for learning (Zoch 2004, 90, 95). On Hall, see also Ravitch (2000, 69–75).

77. Anderson et al. (1998, 240); Mayer (2004).

78. See Chall (2000); Hirsch (1996). An effective presentation by a teacher (expository teaching or reception-learning) is meaningful and much less time-consuming than discovery learning. See Ausubel (1961, 1964).

79. See, on mathematics: Geary (1994, 74, 125, 269); Anderson et al. (1998, 241, 249–50; Wu (1999); on science: Klahr and Nigam (2004); on written composition: Stotsky (1995); Graham and Harris (2000); Graham (2006).

reading. But researchers have found that systematic, explicit phonics is best for reading instruction (National Reading Panel 2000; Neuman and Dickinson 2001). Progressives want schools to directly foster children's self-esteem. But researchers have found that self-esteem does not encourage striving for academic success. Rather researchers have also found that greater empowerment comes indirectly, from self-esteem acquired through achievement and overcoming challenges (Lerner 1985; Damon 1995; Baumeister et al. 2005).

Progressives like the idea that students have different learning styles. But researchers have found that rather than tuning into the supposedly different learning styles of students, teachers should be tuning lesson plans to the form of presentation that is best suited to the subject matter (Traub 1998; Eberstadt 2001; Willingham 2005). Progressives want to teach generalized, abstract, mental training skills ("higher-order critical-thinking" skills or strategies for discovery) instead of, and detached from, academic content. But cognitive psychologists concur that such skills do not exist in the abstract and thus do not transfer from one subject matter domain to another.[80] Progressives do not like memorization, drills, and practice, but researchers have found that these are effective learning tools (Peladeau et al. 2003; Willingham 2004). Moreover, the Progressive doctrine of developmental appropriateness does not stand up under scrutiny. Psychological research shows that learning develops along a continuum over the years of a student's life, not in discrete stages.[81]

80. Hirsch (1985); Hirsch (1996, 135–43). David Ausubel (1964, 298) writes: "This principle has been confirmed by countless studies and is illustrated by the laughable errors of logic and judgment committed by distinguished scientists and scholars who wander outside their own disciplines."

81. See Brainerd, (1978); Siegler (1998, 5–7, 55–58); Anderson et al. (1998, 235, 251).

Educational research has accumulated a substantial body of evidence pointing us toward improved classroom teaching practices that could help millions of children, especially children from educationally weak households. Yet Progressive Education remains a roadblock that often prevents the adoption of these helpful practices.

Why has Progressive Education—despite its unscientific character—endured and remained politically attractive?[82] The answers are different for different groups.

For many teachers and administrators as individuals or as members of child development or subject matter groups, Progressive doctrines provide a ready excuse for ignoring evidence of students' academic failure and a ready rationale for evading or opposing holding teachers and district officials accountable (Evers 2001). To an extent, many Progressives seek to create a new kind of human being (or new society) through Progressive Education, and because the standards-and-accountability effort has more mundane academic goals, these Progressives are alienated from it (Wildavsky 1970; Zoch 2004; Osborne 2005). Because Progressives believe in the unfolding in natural stages of each person's capacity for learning, they oppose or are uncomfortable with standards and high-stakes testing organized on a grade-by-grade basis. Because child-centered Progressives oppose schooling that is oriented toward a set of content-based standards (rather than being oriented toward interests expressed by children), these Progressives oppose standards, testing, and accountability per se.

For professional development gurus, old Progressive ideas of discovery learning and child-centered classrooms can be endlessly recycled under different names as innovative reforms—

---

82. For a discussion of why public agency officials develop or adopt ideologies, see Downs (1967, chapter 19).

reforms that are innocuous from the point of view of the education establishment.[83] For education-school professors, Progressive doctrine makes them the secular high priests of a clerisy. Their best acolytes become the star superintendents, state bureaucrats and future professors. Education schools have, as a result, shaped a school system that has given short shrift to academic content.[84] The jargon of Progressivism has become the insider language and ideological glue that holds together much of the educational establishment.

Interestingly enough, the interests of teachers' unions are so clear that they do not need the ideological prop of Progressive doctrine, and the National Education Association pays comparatively little attention to it, while the American Federation of Teachers, at the national level, is hostile to Progressivism and supports evidence-based teaching practices. For federal and state court judges, school board members, and even many superintendents, Progressive doctrine also plays much less of a role. They are more influenced by Progressive doctrine's cousin, the doctrine of Municipal Reform, which offers them better guidance and a more suitable rationale for action.[85]

83. See Hirsch (1996, 2, 49, 132, 217); Finn (1997, 229); Ravitch (2000, 441).

84. Hirsch (1996, 50); Hirsch (2004).

85. Judges find the Municipal Reform doctrine useful because it provides a plausible rationale for delegating implementation of remedies (in cases like desegregation and adequate spending) to local district officials. Thus, a judge can in good conscience issue an order to desegregate or to spend more money, without feeling he or she should have to manage the operations of a school district, as Judge Arthur Garrity tried to do in Boston. See Ciotti (2001, 317); compare Hanushek (1996, 44).

District and School Board Operations:
Municipal Reform Doctrine as Protective Shield

Today, education researchers have considerable knowledge of
what makes for an effective school as well as an effective classroom. We know, for example, that effective schools need academic leadership from the principal, internalized goals of academic excellence, faculty teamwork, and focused classrooms.
Chubb and Moe (1990) contend that the current governance
structure of school systems (called by its original proponents the
"one best system") discourages effective schools, and, therefore,
Chubb and Moe, as well as other reformers, call for radical
structural changes.

The governance of the fifteen thousand local school districts
across America is almost uniformly the same. It is a product of
the Municipal Reform movement during the Progressive Era,
from 1890 to the First World War, the era that also gave birth
to Progressive Education.[86] Not only is district organization the
product of the Municipal Reform movement, but school board
elections and board deliberations and policymaking are still
strongly influenced by the ideology of that long-ago movement.
Laurence Iannoccone, a specialist on the politics of education,
has observed that the doctrines of Municipal Reform have become the "political myth" of education, "the ideology underlying
fundamental policy assumptions in education" (Iannoccone
1977, 277).

Iannoccone said that Municipal Reform ideology combined
"in a single package" a political and an administrative program.
Its organizational model was "hierarchically structured to produce highly centralized policy making and control." Program-

---

86. On the Municipal Reform Movement, see Banfield and Wilson (1963) and
Hays (1964). On the relation between Municipal Reform and local school systems, see Callahan (1975), Tyack (1974), and Tyack and Hansot (1982).

matically, the reformers called for "the concentration of power and professionalization of public services," with the provision of services "walled off from grass-root client and political influence." These centralized services were to be managed by professionals, who used the language and, they claimed, the methods of the social and behavioral sciences. These professionals were to be formally "accountable to small lay [boards], . . . elected by the short ballot, preferably in at-large nonpartisan elections." The timing of school board elections was to be distinct from that of other local elections, and boundary lines of school districts were intentionally "not coterminous with [those of] other local governments whenever possible." The reformers deliberately designed the school board so that it would not be a place for public debate of educational issues (Iannocconne 1982, 298, 300–301).[87] In particular, they sought to discourage school board debate and decision making on curriculum (Eliot 1959; Ostrom 1961).

The slogan of the Municipal Reformers when it came to schools was to "take education out of politics." But this is, in truth, impossible so long as there is a public school system. Since the schools are public, they cannot be above or outside politics. School districts are governed by people who are elected, spend money obtained through compulsory taxation, and rely on truancy laws to fill their classrooms with children (Peterson and Williams 1972; Peltzman 1993). School districts cannot and do not avoid politics, although politics in school districts is often, particularly in suburbia, conducted more quietly and less visibly and overtly than is usual in America. Nonpartisanship then and now inhibits the growth of a loyal opposition with an alternative platform for school improvement (Iannaccone and Lutz 1967;

87. See also Ostrom (1961), Martin (1962), Callahan (1975), and Evers and Clopton (2003).

Martin 1962; Iannaccone 1982). Off-year, nonpartisan elections hold down turnout, lessen competition, and protect incumbents (Zeigler et al. 1974).

The reality is that "taking education out of politics" in practice usually meant during the Progressive Era, as Michael W. Kirst puts it, taking school districts "away from decentralized control by certain lay people."[88] Political issues were rhetorically transformed by the Municipal Reformers into nonpolitical ones that were to be handled by professional administrators wielding wide discretionary power (Kirst 2004, 20). This reduced the district's accountability to its clients: the parents and taxpayers (Ostrom, 1961; Iannoccone 1977, 1982). Vincent Ostrom speaks of the isolation of school board members from "public scrutiny and debate" (Ostrom 1961, 34). The Municipal Reform doctrine of the Progressive Era assigned most district decision making to the professional administrators because of their purported expertise. Since the advent of the "one best system," various interest groups (including teachers' unions, early childhood education groups, and subject matter groups) have operated within the system's ideological framework. They have pointed to their own supposed expertise and endeavored to shoehorn themselves into the command posts of the school system, in the hope of sharing power with, or overshadowing, the professional administrators (Iannaccone 1977).

The Municipal Reform doctrine as applied to the school districts has created a rigid system of red tape and bureaucratic overspecificity, policed by top-down controls (called compliance

---

88. Ellwood P. Cubberley, later the dean of the Stanford School of Education, wrote disparagingly of Progressive Era immigrants: "Illiterate, docile, often lacking in initiative, and almost wholly without Anglo-Saxon conceptions of righteousness, liberty, law, order, public decency, and government, their coming has served to dilute tremendously our national stock, and to corrupt our civic life." Quoted in Ravitch (2000, 96).

accountability). The natural response of people who want to get things done is to work around these procedural rules. Employees adopt the practice: You scratch my back, and I'll scratch yours. They look for a helpful friend in high places. But an educational culture that must of necessity permit such rule-bending is not far from a culture that permits theft and other self-serving corruption. Although the Progressive Era proponents of city government reform and related school reform crusaded against corruption, the machine bosses of the twentieth century had no difficulty working within Municipal Reform–type city governments and school boards.[89] Likewise, present-day corrupt school district officials have taken advantage of habitual rule-bending and the protections offered them by deference to professionals, consensus seeking, and taking education out of politics (Segal 2004).

Bureaucratic structures, interest group pressures, Progressive pedagogic ideology, and the absence of a loyal opposition have all proven useful tools in avoiding accountability for poor performance and low productivity. No doubt, it has been easier to avoid accountability than to produce substantial gains in achievement. Here are some of the ways districts have endeavored to avoid accountability:

- Failing to establish clear, measurable objectives—if objectives are undefined or if they are vaporous and cannot be measured, then the school system cannot be held accountable for failing to meet the objectives.

- Elevating values unrelated to measurable academic achieve-

---

89. On the use of reformed city-governance structures by Mayor Hague (Jersey City) and Boss Pendergast (Kansas City), see Banfield and Wilson (1963, 149). On the use of reformed school boards by Mayor James Curley (Boston) and Mayor Richard J. Daley (Chicago in the 1950s and 1960s), see Tyack (1974, 168); and Peterson (1976).

ment—if nonacademic goals, such as building self-esteem, are valued above academic achievement, then the school system may not be held accountable for low academic achievement.

- Rejecting objective measures as antithetical to "critical thinking" or "higher-order learning"—if standardized testing can be shunned, then there will be no objectively measured results that can be used to hold a school system accountable.

- Failing to align between tests and what is taught—if tests can be shown to be unrelated to the instructional curriculum, then it can be argued that the school system should not be held accountable for test results.

- Adopting student-performance measures based on judgments of the district personnel being held accountable—if achievement is not evaluated by third parties and if in-house measures can be established as valid outcome indicators, then school personnel may well be tempted to evaluate the outcomes as successful.

- Establishing performance criteria that are too low—if low achievement is simply defined as high achievement, then school systems may claim credit for success that isn't real.

School districts may opt for the path of least resistance when faced with accountability pressures. Rather than undertake the difficult task of boosting student achievement, districts may take one or more of the many paths of avoiding accountability.

There have been modifications in the school system and in the relative strength of various participants in the years since the Progressive Era. Increasingly after 1960, the year of the New York City teachers' strike, teachers' unions have become a formidable force in American politics (Peltzman 1993; Moe 2006). Also, today, the schools receive tax money from new funding streams, and the proportions of funds from state and federal taxes have increased since the mid-1960s (Kirst 1984).[90] The teachers' unions now overshadow the district administration, especially in urban districts. In big cities school board campaigns occasionally get rambunctious. There has been some complexity added by the state and federal governments and their efforts to promote racial integration, by the Sputnik-era push for science and math, and by current accountability efforts. But the operating code of school districts and their boards remains largely that of the Municipal Reform movement: the district administration proposes policy initiatives, and boards offer advice and consent (Eliot 1959; Martin 1962; Zeigler et al. 1974: Lutz 1975; Tyack 1969; Tyack and Hansot 1982; Tyack 1993; California School Boards Association 2005).

School district bureaucracies as presently constituted and in the existing political context might well be poor prospects to successfully use huge amounts of additional resources to educate low-performing students. The existing institution is hemmed in by interest groups that shun accountability. The institution is hobbled by hundred-year-old ideologies that discourage research-based practices and provide excuses for nonperformance and buck-passing.

90. For a discussion of why spending on and regulation of schools has moved increasingly from the local to the state level, see Toma (1981, 1983, 1986) and Peltzman (1993). Toma contends that "the real reason the school system has lost its incentive and ability to produce a quality product is that localities and families have lost control over educational decision-making" (Toma 1980, 203).

Conclusion

Heroic Accomplishment

The politics and organization of school districts are potentially so counterproductive that it is astonishing when, in low-performing districts, some teachers succeed in teaching and some children succeed in learning. We contend that everyone should pay tribute to the heroic efforts of school boards, superintendents, principals, teachers, parents, and students themselves, when these students in low-performing districts triumph over adversity or when such schools and districts turn themselves around. We call these efforts heroic because these teachers and students and others who work with them have succeeded in the midst of poorly designed institutions, perverse incentives, political obfuscation, and the dominance of unscientific teaching practices.[91]

Social scientists have often commented on the perverse incentives, which include pay unrelated to productivity. Nobel Laureate economist James M. Buchanan once wrote that since teachers' pay is "not related in any way to the final output that they produce," which, he says, "should be measurable in student achievement," teachers have "no personal incentive" to teach effectively. "They are not so much bad teachers, as they are teachers who have no reason to be good" (Buchanan 1977, 16).

---

91. James Gordon Ward (1990, 244–245) uses a circulation-of-elites analysis to explain the persistence of these perverse incentives following the school finance reform movement of the 1960s and 1970s: "The Ford Foundation, the university scholars, the national organizations, and the lawyers involved were all representatives of the economic and political elite of the society, and as well intentioned as they may have been, they ended up enhancing their own power, not that of their stated clientele [the least educationally favored]. . . . [The school finance reform movement] did not attempt to alter . . . institutional structures to improve the school performance of those who were disadvantaged and not performing up to desired standards."

We have not concentrated our efforts in this chapter in discussing how good teachers and other schoolhouse heroes have succeeded in the face of such odds. Clearly, this success stems from solid curriculum, effective teaching practices, and creating a culture that does the extra functional work that normal incentives and healthy institutions ought to be doing to foster academic success (Rutter et al. 1979; Coleman and Hoffer 1982; Lee 1997; Sowell 2005; Walberg 2002 and this volume, chapter 3). These heroes with their makeshift cultural life vests have to swim against the tide in school politics, administration, or the classroom. Others have written about such success, though more work needs to be done on this topic (Education Trust 1999; Carter 2000; Izumi et al. 2002; Walberg, this volume, chapter 3).

The Role of the Courts

Only some of the five high-spending districts that we have looked at came by their revenues by way of the courts. Two (the *Abbott* districts and Cambridge) received funds from adequacy suits. One (Kansas City) got its money from a desegregation suit. (Sausalito and Washington, D.C., receive their high revenues because of political rather than judicial decisions.) Looking at all the problems of these districts, one might perhaps think that the problems could have been solved by more specific judicial decrees. But making demands from the bench did not work in these districts. The court in Kansas City demanded a curriculum, and the court in New Jersey demanded a testing and accountability system. The judges did not get what they asked for. The courts, in the specificity of their decrees, almost transformed themselves into school boards in these cases. The problems (corruption, poor incentives, weak teaching staff, no culture of achievement) are deep seated. There is no reason to believe that judges would be successful if in adequacy suits they took the next step and transformed themselves into superintendents running school districts on a day-to-day basis.

Missed Opportunity

The five districts that we have scrutinized in our case studies had a better chance of success, in one important sense, than the districts that may in the future receive large boosts in funds for adequacy, because these five districts had considerable extra money when other districts did not. Therefore, if the five districts chose to, they were in a position to bid away from other districts (and from elsewhere) high-quality teachers, principals, and administrators. The five districts neglected this opportunity, and some are still neglecting it, because they had little incentive to take advantage of the opportunity. But it is an opportunity that low-performing districts will not have if funding for adequacy arrives, because then all districts will be awash in money, and these five weak districts will have missed a unique chance.

Adequate Spending, Incentives, and Wise Use

The opponents of vastly increased spending often focus on wise use of current spending or a better incentive structure to accompany current spending or any increased spending. Those on the other side, the advocates of adequate spending, likewise acknowledge the need for wise use.[92] But usually the adequacy advocates neither locate an incentive for wise use in the current

---

92. Schrag (2005, 240–241) acknowledges the need for flexibility in assignment of teachers and differential teacher pay, but then retreats by saying that "when powerful interests are threatened," such change will be politically impossible. Thus, Schrag thinks that interest groups will not allow putting effectiveness measures in first, before putting in large amounts of additional money. But he is "certain" that if large amounts of money are added, effectiveness measures will follow. Compare Murnane and Levy (1996).

governance of schools nor propose new incentives for school officials and teachers. Adequacy advocates neglect to scrutinize the likely effects of increased budgets on bureaucratic behavior.[93]

Economist John T. Wenders goes too far when he writes:

> Public school expenditure is . . . driven by the ability of the public education industry to extract revenues from the taxpayers. . . . Expenditures are built from the top down, not the bottom up. Public school expenditures now average about $9,500 per student. If the various public treasures were to give this industry $12,000 per student, it would spend $12,000 per student. . . . And since *there is no connection* between public school spending and student achievement, . . . student achievement [would not] change. (Wenders 2005a, 221; emphasis added)

In fact, Wenders exaggerates when he says "there is no connection." In reality, truly massive additional amounts of money would probably lead to slight improvements. But the increase in funds required is quite steep for only a small improvement in student achievement.[94] In the particular hypothetical case that Wenders proposes, an increase to twelve thousand dollars per pupil would, by itself, be unlikely to cause a noticeable improvement in achievement. With current spending or the increases envisioned in adequacy efforts, there are simply not enough incentives in place to encourage steady and sustained academic improvement in low-performing districts. As Eric Hanushek has said, "how the money is spent is much more important than how much or adding more" (Schrag 2005, 211).

Yet proponents of adequacy are not focused on incentives that will encourage effective teaching and successful learning.

93. Compare Toma (1979, 675).
94. See Picus (1997, 30); Schrag (2005, 210); Hanushek (this volume, chapter 7).

When adequacy proponents speak of "effectiveness and efficiency," they are speaking not of productivity in learning but of the "effectiveness and efficiency" of "school funding delivery mechanisms," that is, administrative formulas for sending money to schools and districts (Perry 2006).

Nor are adequacy proponents concentrating directly on the most important output of schools: student achievement. As Paul Minorini and Stephen Sugarman point out, attaining adequacy, according to its supporters, "does not appear to be ultimately judged" by such achievement. Compliance with adequacy requirements is in the final analysis, "a matter of inputs" (Minorini and Sugarman 1999, 189).

Shortly after the 1970 California court decision in *Serrano v. Priest* on equity in school spending, policy analyst Aaron Wildavsky astutely observed that, when student achievement comes to public attention, politicians and officials respond by changing the subject: "Just define the input as the output, and by definition objectives are met" (Wildavsky 1979, 316). He was speaking in the context of the 1970s, but his observations are just as true today.

Wildavsky thought that as public attention came to focus on student achievement, it was "not purely fortuitous" that politicians wanted to shift that focus and to substitute measures of inputs (like spending) for measures of outputs (like achievement). Wildavsky (1979, 316–317) wittily recognized that such a shift was the consummate fulfillment of an old bureaucratic folk saying: "Now that we have lost sight of our objectives, we must redouble our efforts."

References

Academic Performance Database System. 2005. District of Columbia Public Schools (Spring). http://silicon.k12.dc.us/apds/APDS SummaryReports.asp.

Alchian, Armen A. 1977. The Economic and Social Impact of Free Tuition. In his *Economic Forces at Work: Selected Works*, 203–226. Indianapolis, IN: Liberty Press.

Alexakis, Georgia N. 2001. Test Prep: What Bush Can Learn from a Tryout of School Reform in Massachusetts. *Washington Monthly* (March): 29–36.

Anderson, John R., Lynne M. Reder, and Herbert A. Simon. 1998. Radical Constructivism and Cognitive Psychology. In *Brookings Papers on Educational Policy, 1998*, ed. Diane Ravitch, 227–255. Washington, DC: Brookings Institution Press, 1998.

Anonymous. 2005a. Interview with Williamson M. Evers. Marin County, CA, September 2.

———. 2005b. Interview with Williamson M. Evers. Marin County, CA, September 2.

———. 2005c. Communication with Williamson M. Evers. California. September 4.

Aranson, Peter H. 1981. *American Government: Strategy and Choice*. Cambridge, MA: Winthrop Publishers.

Armor, David J. 2002. Desegregation and Academic Achievement. In *School Desegregation in the 21st Century*, ed. Christine H. Rossell, Armor, and Herbert J. Walberg, 147–187. Westport, CT: Praeger.

Association of California School Administrators. 1997. *Special Report on Continuous Improvement Accountability System,* by Task Force on Student Performance and School Accountability. Sacramento: Association of California School Administrators. http://222.acsa.org/publications/.

Ausubel, David P. 1961. In Defense of Verbal Learning. *Educational Theory* 11:15–25.

———. 1964. Some Psychological and Educational Limitations of Learning by Discovery. *The Arithmetic Teacher* 11:290–302.

Badessa, Frank, 2004. The Inequitability of the Abbott Districts' Funding Law in New Jersey. http://www.newfoundations.com/ETHICPROP/Badessa718F04.html.

Balmuth, Miriam. 1992. *The Roots of Phonics: A Historical Introduction*. 1982. Reprt: Baltimore: York Press.

Banfield, Edward C., and James Q. Wilson. 1963. *City Politics.* Cambridge, MA: Harvard University Press.

Baumeister, Roy F., Jennifer D. Campbell, Joachim I. Krueger, and Kathleen D. Vohs. 2005. Exploding the Self-Esteem Myth. *Scientific America,* (January): 84–91.

Bertram, Charlotte. 1997. Exodus from Sausalito Schools. Letter to the Editor. *Coastal Post,* May. http://www.coastalpost.com/97/5/23.htm.

Bhatti, Jabeen. 2001. Williams Says Schools Should Get Private Aid; Suggests Edison as Viable Option. *Washington Times,* March 15: A1.

Booker, Cory A. 2001. School Choice and Government Reform: Pillars of an Urban Renaissance. *Civic Bulletin* (Manhattan Institute): 25. http://www.manhattan-institute.org/html/cb_25.htm.

Borja, Rhea. 1999. From Diagnosis Then to Treatment Now. *Richmond Times-Dispatch.* March 7.

Boston Globe. The State of Education. *Boston Globe* Web site. http://www.boston.com/news/special/inside_our_schools/districts_list.htm.

Bova, Carla. 2005a. Sausalito School Shake-Up. San Rafael (CA) *Marin Independent Journal.* August 25.

———. 2005b. Ex-Trustee Blames Personality Clash for Change at Top. San Rafael (CA) *Marin Independent Journal.* August 26.

Bradford, Derrell. 2005. N.J. Parents: No Trust in "Education Machine." Letter to the Editor. *Education Week.* June 15.

Brainerd, Charles J. 1978. The Stage Question in Cognitive-Developmental Theory. *The Behavioral and Brain Sciences* 1:173–182.

Buchanan, James M. 1965. *The Public Finances*, 2nd ed.. Homewood, IL: Richard D. Irwin.

———. 1977. Why Does Government Grow? In *Budgets and Bureaucrats: The Sources of Government Growth*, ed. Thomas E. Borcherding, 3–18. Durham, NC: Duke University Press.

California Curriculum Management Audit Center. 1997. *A Curriculum Management Audit of the Sausalito Elementary School District.* N.p.: California Curriculum Management Audit Center.

California Department of Education. 2004. Academic Performance Index (API). Reports and Data Files. http://api.cde.ca.gov/.

————. 2005. Standardized Testing and Reporting (STAR) Results, STAR 2005 Test Results. http://star.cde.ca.gov/.

California School Boards Association. 2005. Institute for New and First-Term Board Members. Sacramento, CA: California School Boards Association.

Callahan, Raymond E. 1975. The American Board of Education, 1789–1960. In *Understanding School Boards: Problems and Prospects*, ed. Peter J. Cistone, 19–46. Lexington, MA: Lexington Books.

Cambridge Public Schools. 2005. *Schools at a Glance, 2005–2006*. Cambridge, MA: Cambridge Public Schools.

————. 2006. Cambridge Public Schools Web site. http://www.cpsd.us/.

Cannell, John Jacob. 2006. "Lake Woebegone," Twenty Years Later. *Third Education Group Review* 2:1–17.

Carter, Samuel Casey. 2000. *No Excuses: Lessons from 21 High-Performing, High Poverty Schools*. Washington, DC: Heritage Foundation.

Chall, Jeanne S., and Helen M. Popp. 1996. *Teaching and Assessing Phonics: Why, What, When, How—A Guide for Teachers*. Cambridge, MA: Educators Publishing Service.

————. 2000. *The Academic Achievement Challenge: What Really Works in the Classroom*. New York: Guildford Press.

Chubb, John E., and Terry M. Moe. 1990. *Politics, Markets, and America's Schools*. Washington, DC: Brookings Institution.

Ciotti, Paul. 2001. Money and School Performance: Lessons from the Kansas City Desegregation Experiment. In *School Reform: The Critical Issues*, ed. Williamson M. Evers, Lance T. Izumi, and Pamela A. Riley, 308–338. Stanford, CA: Hoover Institution Press.

Clinchy, Evans. 1992. *Planning for Schools of Choice: Achieving Excellence and Equity*. Vol. 4 of *Model Schools of Choice: Non-traditional Organization and Curriculum*, ed. Frances Arick Kolb. Andover, MA: Network Inc.

Coate, Douglas, and James VanderHoff. 1999. Public School Spending and Student Achievement: The Case of New Jersey. *Cato Journal* 19:85–99.

Coleman, James S., and Thomas Hoffer. 1982. *Public and Private High Schools: The Impact of Communities*. New York: Basic Books.

Committee on Governmental Affairs. 1997. *Progress Report on the Reforms in D.C. Public S*chools. Hearing before the Subcommittee on Oversight of Government Management, Restructuring, and the District of Columbia of the Committee on Governmental Affairs. U. S. Senate, 105th Congress, 1st Session, September 8. S. Hrg. 105-364. Washington, DC: U.S. Government Printing Office.

———. 1998. *Lessons Learned in the D.C. Public Schools*. Hearing before the Subcommittee on Oversight of Government Management, Restructuring, and the District of Columbia of the Committee on Governmental Affairs. U. S. Senate, 105th Congress, 2nd Session, March 9. S. Hrg. 105-537. Washington, DC: U.S. Government Printing Office.

Committee on Government Reform and Oversight. 1998. *Oversight on the Academic Plan for the District of Columbia Public Schools*. Hearing before the Subcommittee on the District of Columbia of the Committee on Government Reform and Oversight. U. S. House of Representatives, 105th Congress, 2nd Session, April 3. Serial No. 105-147. Washington, DC: U.S. Government Printing Office.

Council of the Great City Schools. 2004. *Restoring Excellence to the District of Columbia Public Schools: Report of the Strategic Support Team of the Council of the Great City Schools*. Washington, DC: Council of the Great City Schools.

Cunningham, George K. 2004. Learning from Kentucky's Failed Accountability System. In *Testing Student Learning, Evaluating Teaching Effectiveness*, ed. Williamson M. Evers and Herbert J. Walberg, 245–301. Stanford, CA: Hoover Institution Press.

Damon, William. 1995. *Greater Expectations: Overcoming the Culture of Indulgence in America's Homes and Schools*. New York: Free Press.

Denton, Peter. 2002. Abbott Reform: Is It about Civil Rights, or Funding? http://www.nje3.org/articles/battlefield.html.

Division of Educational Accountability. 2002. *A Five Year Statistical Glance at DC Public Schools: School Years 1996–97 Through 2000–01*. Washington, DC: Division of Educational Accountability, Student Accounting Branch.

Downs, Anthony. 1967. *Inside Bureaucracy*. Boston: Little, Brown.

Eberstadt, Mary. 2001. The Schools They Deserve: Howard Gardner and the Remaking of Elite Education. In *School Reform: The Critical Issues*, ed. Williamson M. Evers, Lance T. Izumi, and Pamela A. Riley, 17–33. Stanford, CA: Hoover Institution Press.

Education Data Partnership. Education Data Partnership Web site. http://www.ed-data.k12.ca.us/.

Education Management Accountability Board. 2000. *Cambridge Public Schools Review*. Report of the Education Management Accountability Board. Boston: Massachusetts Department of Revenue, Division of Local Services.

Education Trust. 1999. *Dispelling the Myth: High Poverty Schools Exceeding Expectations*. Washington, DC: Education Trust.

Education Week. 1998. Sausalito Recall Certified. *Education Week*, January 21.

Eliot, Thomas H. 1959. Toward an Understanding of Public School Politics. *American Political Science Review* 53:1032–1051.

Evers, Williamson M. 1998. From Progressive Education to Discovery Learning. In *What's Gone Wrong in America's Classrooms?*, ed. Evers, 1–21. Stanford, CA: Hoover Institution Press.

———. 2001. Standards and Accountability. In *A Primer on America's Schools*, ed. Terry M. Moe, 205–247. Stanford, CA: Hoover Institution Press.

———. and Paul Clopton. 2003. The Curricular Smorgasbord. In *Our Schools and Our Future: Are We Still At Risk?*, ed. Paul E. Peterson, 239–279. Stanford, CA: Hoover Institution Press.

Fimrite, Peter. 1997. Sausalito Schools Get Low Grades. *San Francisco Chronicle*. August 22.

———. 1998. Marin DA's Office in an Uproar Over Election. *San Francisco Chronicle*. May 24.

Finn, Chester E., Jr. 1997. The Politics of Change. In *New Schools for a New Century: The Redesign of Urban Education,* ed. Diane Ravitch and Joseph P. Viteritti, 226–250. New Haven, CT: Yale University Press.

Fiscal Crisis and Management Assistance Team. 1997. *Management Assistance Audit for the Sausalito Elementary School District.* Bakersfield, CA: Financial Crisis and Management Assistance Team, State of California.

Freebairn-Smith, Martha, ed. 1968. *Something That's Happening: A Portrait of Sausalito School District.* Sausalito, CA: Sausalito School District.

Gardner, Howard. 1983. *Frames of Mind: The Theory of Multiple Intelligences.* New York: Basic Books.

Geary, David C. 1994. *Children's Mathematical Development.* Washington, DC: American Psychological Association.

Gehring, John. 2000. Students Boycott Tests in Mass. To Protest Emphasis on Exams. *Education Week.* April 19.

———.2002. Vote to Award Diplomas Defies State Testing Policy. *Education Week.* May 8.

Gewertz, Catherine. 2000. A Hard Lesson for Kansas City's Troubled Schools. *Education Week.* April 26.

Grady, Elizabeth. 1994. New Frontiers: Moving the Humanities Model of Curricular Development. *Teaching the Humanities* 1 (Summer): 13–21.

Graham, Steve, and Karen R. Harris. 2000. The Role of Self-Regulation and Transcription Skills in Writing and Writing Development. *Educational Psychologist* 35:3–12.

———. 2006. Strategy Instruction and the Teaching of Writing. In *Handbook of Writing Research*, ed. Charles A. MacArthur, Graham, and Jill Fitzgerald, 187–207 New York: Guilford Press.

Hanushek, Eric A. 1986. The Economics of Schooling: Production and Efficiency in Public Schools. *Journal of Economic Literature* 24(3): 1141–1177.

———. 1989. The Impact of Differential Expenditures on School Performance. *Education Researcher* 18(4): 45–51.

———. 1996. School Resources and Student Performance. In *Does*

Money Matter? The Effect of School Resources on Student Achievement and Adult Success, ed. Gary Burtless, 43–73. Washington, DC: Brookings Institution.

———. 1997. Assessing the Effects of School Resources on Student Performance: An Update. *Educational Evaluation and Policy Analysis* 19(2): 141–64.

———. 2002. Teacher Quality. In *Teacher Quality*, ed. Lance T. Izumi and Williamson M. Evers, 1–12. Stanford, CA: Hoover Institution Press.

Hays, Samuel P. 1964. The Politics of Reform in Municipal Government in the Progressive Era. *Pacific Northwest Quarterly*, 55: 157–169.

Hirsch, E. D., Jr. 1985. Literacy and Formalism. In *Challenges to the Humanities*, ed. Chester E. Finn, Jr., Diane Ravitch, and P. Holley Roberts, 47–65. New York: Holmes and Meier.

———. 1996. *The Schools We Need and Why We Don't Have Them*. New York: Doubleday.

———. 2004. Comment on The Ed School's Romance with Progressivism by David F. Larabee. In *Brookings Papers on Education Policy, 2004*, ed. Diane Ravitch, 112–117. Washington, DC: Brookings Institution.

Hofstader, Richard. 1963. *Anti-Intellectualism in American Life*. New York: Alfred A. Knopf.

Homfeld, Melville J. 1959. Schools for Everything. *Atlantic Monthly* 203 (March): 62–64.

Iannaccone, Lawrence, and Frank W. Lutz. 1967. The Changing Politics of Education. *AAUW Journal* (American Association of University Women) 60:160–162, 191.

———. 1977. Three Views of Change in Education Politics. In *The Politics of Education: The Seventy-Sixth Yearbook of the National Society for the Study of Education*, pt. 2, ed. Jay D. Scriber, 255–286. Chicago: National Society for the Study of Education.

———. 1982. Changing Political Patterns and Governmental Regulations. In *The Public School Monopoly: A Critical Analysis of*

Education and the State in American Society, ed. Robert B. Everhart, 295–324. Cambridge, MA: Ballinger.

Innes, Richard G. 2006. *Bang for the Buck: How Cost Effective Are Kentucky's Public Schools?* Bowling Green, KY: Bluegrass Institute.

Izumi, Lance T., and K. Gwynne Coburn. 2000. *California Index of Leading Education Indicators 2000*. San Francisco: Pacific Research Institute.

———. K. Gwynne Coburn, and Matt Cox. 2002. *They Have Overcome: High-Poverty, High-Performing Schools in California*. San Francisco: Pacific Research Institute.

Johnston, Robert C. 1997. Dollars Don't Mean Success in CA District. *Education Week*. December 3.

Kirp, David L., and Donna R. Leff. 1979. Sense and Sentimentality: Race and Schooling in Sausalito. Pts. 1, 2. *Urban Education* 14: 131–160, 321–332.

Kirst, Michael W. 1984. *Who Controls Our Schools? American Values in Conflict*. Stanford, CA: Stanford Alumni Association.

———. 2004. Turning Points: A History of American School Governance. In *Who's in Charge Here? The Tangled Web of School Governance and Policy*, 14–41. Denver: Education Commission of the States and Washington, DC: Brookings Institution.

Klahr, David, and Milena Nigam. 2004. The Equivalence of Learning Paths in Early Science Instruction: Effects of Direct Instruction and Discovery Learning. *Psychology Science* 15:661–667.

Kvasager, Whitney. 2005. State Rethinking School Takeovers. *North Jersey Herald and News* (Passaic). March 6.

Ladd, Helen F., Rosemary Chalk, and Janet S. Hansen, eds. 1999. *Equity and Adequacy in Education Finance: Issues and Perspectives*. Washington, DC: National Academy Press.

LaGanga, Maria L. 1997a. Sausalito Schools: Money Isn't Enough. *Los Angeles Times*. May 16.

———. 1997b. Audit Sees "Chaos" in Sausalito Schools. *Los Angeles Times*. September 26.

Lartigue, Casey J., Jr. 2004. Educational Freedom for D.C. Schools. In *Educational Freedom in Urban America: Brown v. Board After*

Half a Century, ed. David Salisbury and Lartigue, 69–108. Washington, DC: Cato Institute.

Lee, Valerie E. 1997. Catholic Lessons for Public Schools. In *New Schools for a New Century: The Redesign of Urban Education*, ed. Diane Ravitch and Joseph P. Viteritti, 145–163. New Haven, CT: Yale University Press.

Lerner, Barbara. 1985. Self-Esteem and Excellence: The Choice and the Paradox. *American Educator* (American Federation of Teachers) 9 (Winter): 10–16.

Loveless, Tom. 2001. A Tale of Two Math Reforms: The Politics of the New Math and the NCTM Standards. In *The Great Curriculum Debate: How Should We Teach Reading and Math?*, ed. Loveless, 184–209. Washington, DC: Brookings Institution.

Lutz, Frank W. 1975. Local School Boards as Sociocultural Systems. In *Understanding School Boards: Problems and Prospects*, ed. Peter J. Cistone, 63–76. Lexington, MA: Lexington Books.

Malanga, Steven. 2005. Jersey's Urban Meltdown: The Problem Isn't Sprawl; It's Collapsing Cities. *City Journal*, Eye on the News Web log, January 19. http://www.city-journal.org/html/eon_01_19_05sm.html.

Martin, Roscoe C. 1962. *Government and the Suburban School*. The Economics and Politics of Public Education, ser., no. 2. Syracuse, NY: Syracuse University Press.

Massachusetts Department of Education. School and District Profiles. http://profiles.doe.mass.edu/.

Mayer, Richard E. 2004. Should There Be a Three-Strikes Rule Against Pure Discovery Learning: The Case for Guided Methods of Instruction. *American Psychologist* 59:14–19.

Mayer, Susan E. 1997. *What Money Can't Buy: Family Income and Children's Life Chances*. Cambridge, MA: Harvard University Press.

Minorini, Paul A., and Stephen D. Sugarman. 1999. Educational Adequacy and the Courts: The Promise and Problems of Moving to a New Paradigm. In *Equity and Adequacy in Education Finance: Issues and Perspectives*, ed. Helen F. Ladd, Rosemary

Chalk, and Janet S. Hansen, 175–208. Washington, DC: National Academy Press.

Mises, Ludwig von. 1944. *Bureaucracy*. New Haven, CT: Yale University Press.

Mitchell, Nancy, and Berny Morson. 2006. No Winning Number: Survey Shows That Funding Alone Can't Boost School Scores. *Rocky Mountain News*. January 3.

Moe, Terry M. 1997. The Positive Theory of Public Bureaucracy. In *Perspectives on Public Choice: A Handbook*, ed. Dennis C. Mueller, 455–480. Cambridge, England: Cambridge University Press.

———. 2006. Union Power and the Education of Children. In *Collective Bargaining in Education: Negotiating Change in Today's Schools,* ed. Jane Hannaway and Andrew J. Rotherham. Cambridge, MA: Harvard Education Press.

Morantz, Alison. 1996. Money and Choice in Kansas City: Major Investments with Modest Returns. In *Dismantling Desegregation: The Quiet Reversal of* Brown v. Board of Education, ed. Gary Orfield, Susan E. Eaton, and the Harvard Project on School Desegregation, 241–263, 391–396. New York: The New Press.

Moynihan, Daniel Patrick. 1972. Equalizing Education: In Whose Benefit? *The Public Interest* 29:69–89.

Murnane, Richard J., and Frank Levy. 1996. Evidence from Fifteen Schools in Austin, Texas. In *Does Money Matter? The Effect of School Resources on Student Achievement and Adult Success*, ed. Gary Burtless, 93–96. Washington, DC: Brookings Institution.

Murphy, Jerome T., and David K. Cohen. 1974. Accountability in Education—The Michigan Experience. *The Public Interest* 36:53–81.

Nappi, Chaira R. 1999. Local Illusions. *Wilson Quarterly* 23:44–51.

National Center for Education and the Economy. 2002. *America's Choice School Design: A Research-Based Model*. Washington, DC: The Consortium for Policy Research in Education, National Center for Education and the Economy. http://www.ncee.org/acsd/research/index.jsp.

National Reading Panel. 2000. *Teaching Children to Read: An Ev-*

idence-Based Assessment of the Scientific Literature on Reading and Its Implication for Reading Instruction. NIH Pub. No. 00-4754. Washington, DC: National Institute of Child Health and Human Development, National Institutes of Health.

Neuman, Susan B., and David K. Dickinson, eds. 2001. *Handbook of Early Literacy Research.* New York: Guilford Press.

Newark (NJ) Public Schools. 2005. Budget Statement for 2005–2006.

———. 2006. Comprehensive Annual Financial Report for the Fiscal Year Ended June 30, 2005.

New Jersey Department of Education. 2005. New Jersey Department of Education Web site. http://www.nj.gov/cgi-bin/education/csg/05/csg.pl?string=dist_code3570&maxhits=1.

Niskanen, William A., Jr.. 1994. *Bureaucracy and Public Economics.* Brookfield, VT: Edward Elgar.

Office of Accountability. 2006. *A Five-Year Statistical Glance at D.C. Public Schools, School Years 2000—2001 through 2004–2005.* Washington, DC: District of Columbia Public Schools Office of Accountability.

Ohanian, Susan. 1999. *One Size Fits Few: The Folly of Educational Standards.* Portsmouth, NH: Heinemann.

Osborne, Evan. 2005. Education Reform as Economic Reform. *Cato Journal* 25:297–316.

Ostrom, Vincent. 1961. Education and Politics. In *Social Forces Influencing American Education: The Sixtieth Yearbook of the National Society for the Study of Education,* pt. 2, ed. Nelson B. Henry, 8–45. Chicago: National Society for the Study of Education.

Peladeau, Mormand, Jacques Forget, and Francois Gagne. 2003. Effect of Paced and Unpaced Practice on Skill Application and Retention: How Much Is Enough? *American Educational Research Journal* 40:769–801.

Peltzman, Sam. 1993. The Political Economy of the Decline of American Public Education. *Journal of Law and Economics* 36:331–370.

Perry, Mary. 2006. Shedding Light, Reducing the Heat. *Leadership* (Association of California School Administrators) 35 (3): 16–19.

Peterson, Paul E., and Thomas L. Williams. 1972. Models of Decision Making. In *State, School, and Politics: Research Directions*, ed. Michael W. Kirst, 149–168. Lexington, MA: Lexington Books.

———. 1976. *School Politics, Chicago Style*. Chicago: University of Chicago Press.

Picus, Lawrence O. 1997. Does Money Matter in Education? A Policymaker's Guide. In *Selected Papers in School Finance 1995*, NCES 97-536. Washington, DC: National Center for Education Statistics. http://nces.ed.gov/pubs97/97536-2.html.

———. Scott F. Marion, Naomi Calvo, and William J. Glenn. 2005. Understanding the Relationship Between Student Achievement and the Quality of Educational Facilities: Evidence from Wyoming. *Peabody Journal of Education* 80:71–95.

Pogrow, Stanley. 2003. Rescuing Abbott. Trenton (NJ) *Times*. June 8.

Postrel, Virginia. 2006. The Poverty Puzzle. Review of *The White Man's Burden* by William Easterly. *New York Times Book Review*, March 19.

Ravitch, Diane. 2000. *Left Back: A Century of Failed School Reform*. New York: Simon & Schuster.

Renaissance Newark Foundation. 2006. Newark, NJ. http://www.GoNewark.com.

Rich, Wilbur C. 1996. *Black Mayors and School Politics: The Failure of Reform in Detroit, Gary, and Newark*. New York: Garland Publishing.

Richard, Alan. 2000. Mass. Audit Cites Accountability Problems in Cambridge Schools. *Education Week*. February 23.

Roberson, Rose Marie. 2005. Interview with Williamson M. Evers. Marin County, CA, September 1.

Rone, Dana. 2004. Testimony before the New Jersey State Assembly Budget Committee, March 24. http://www.nje3.org/articles/ronetestimony.pdf.

———. 2005. The Issue Is Education. Newark (NJ) *Star Ledger*. July 25.

Rutter, Michael L., Barbara Maughan, Peter Mortimore, Janet Ouston, and Alan Smith. 1979. *Fifteen Thousand Hours: Secondary Schools and Their Effects on Children*. Cambridge, MA: Harvard University Press.

San Francisco Examiner. 1998. Kamena Tops Colleague to Claim Marin DA Post. *San Francisco Examiner*, June 3.

Schlichtman, Paul. 2003. School Committee Member Supports Upcoming Override. Arlington (MA) *Advocate*. May 22.

SchoolMatters. SchoolMatters, a service of Standard and Poor's. Web site, http://www.schoolmatters.com.

Schrag, Peter. 2005. *Final Test: The Battle for Adequacy in America's Schools*. New York: New Press.

Segal, Lydia G. 2004. *Battling Corruption in America's Public Schools*. Cambridge, MA: Harvard University Press.

Shanker, Albert. 1994. Where We Stand: Noah Webster Academy. *New York Times*. July 3.

Shokraii, Nina H., Christine L. Olson, and Sarah Youssef. 1997. *A Comparison of Public and Private Education in the District of Columbia*. F.Y.I. ser., no. 148.Washington, DC: Heritage Foundation.

Siegler, Robert S. 1998. *Children's Thinking*, 3rd ed. Upper Saddle River, NJ: Prentice Hall.

Solo, Len. 1992. Getting Support from the Community. *Principal* (National Association of Elementary School Principals) 71 (3): 26–27.

Sowell, Thomas. 2005. *Black Rednecks and White Liberals*. San Francisco: Encounter Books.

Spear-Swerling, Louise, and Robert J. Sternberg. 1996. *Off Track: When Poor Readers Become "Learning Disabled."* Boulder, CO: Westview Press.

State Education Office. 2004. *Establishing a Baseline: A Report on the State of Education in the District of Columbia*. Washington, DC: District of Columbia State Education Office.

Stone, J.E. 1996. Developmentalism: An Obscure but Pervasive Restriction on Educational Improvement. *Education Policy Analysis Archives* 4 (8), http://olam.ed.asu.edu/epaa/v4n8.html.

Stotsky, Sandra. 1995. The Uses and Limitations of Personal or Personalized Writing in Writing Theory, Research, and Instruction. *Reading Research Quarterly* 30:758–776.

Thornton, Shirley A. 2005. Interview with Williamson M. Evers. Sausalito, CA, September 1.

Timar, Thomas B. 2004. *Categorical School Finance: Who Gains, Who Loses?* Working Paper Series 04-2. Berkeley, CA: Policy Analysis for California Education (PACE).

Toma, Eugenia Froedge. 1979. Review of *Scholars, Dollars, and Bureaucrats* by Chester E. Finn Jr. *Southern Economic Journal* 46:675–676.

———. 1980. Education. In *Agenda for Progress: Examining Federal Spending*, ed. Eugene J. McAllister 197–215. Washington, DC: Heritage Foundation.

———. 1981. Bureaucratic Structures and Educational Spending. *Southern Economic Journal* 47:640–654.

———. 1983. Institutional Structures, Regulation, and Producer Gains in the Education Industry. *Journal of Law and Economics* 26:103–116.

———. 1986. Rent Seeking, Federal Mandates, and the Quality of Public Education. *Atlantic Economic Journal* 14:37–45.

Torgesen, Joseph K. 1998. Catch Them Before They Fall: Identification and Assessment to Prevent Reading Failure in Young Children. *American Educator* (American Federation of Teachers) 22 (Spring-Summer): 32–39.

Traub, James. 1998. Multiple Intelligence Disorder. *The New Republic.* October 26.

Trotter, Mark. 2006. Interview with Williamson M. Evers. Marin County, CA, March 6.

Tucker, Marc S., and Judy B. Codding. 1998. *Standards for Our Schools.* San Francisco: Jossey-Bass.

Tullock, Gordon. 1965. *The Politics of Bureaucracy.* Washington, DC: Public Affairs Press.

Tyack, David B. 1969. Needed: The Reform of a Reform. In *New Dimensions in School Board Leadership: A Seminar Report and*

Workbook, ed. William E. Dickinson, 29–51. Evanston, IL: National School Boards Association.

———. 1974. *The One Best System: A History of American Urban Education*. Cambridge, MA: Harvard University Press.

———. and Elisabeth Hansot. 1982. *Managers of Virtue: Public School Leadership in America, 1820–1980*. New York: Basic Books.

———. 1993. School Governance in the United States: Historical Puzzles and Anomalies. In *Decentralization and School Improvement: Can We Fulfill the Promise?*, ed. Jane Hannaway and Martin Carnoy, 1–32. San Francisco: Jossey-Bass.

U.S. Department of Education, 2004. *Digest of Education Statistics 2003*, NCES 2005–025, Washington, DC: National Center for Education Statistics.

Viadero, Debra. 1994. A World of Difference, *Education Week*. February 2.

Walberg, Herbert J., and Rebecca C. Greenberg. 1998. The Diogenes Factor. *Education Week*. April 8.

———. 2002.Teaching Methods. In *Teacher Quality*, ed. Lance T. Izumi and Williamson M. Evers, 55–72. Stanford, CA: Hoover Institution Press.

Ward, James Gordon. 1990. Implementation and Monitoring of Judicial Mandates: An Interpretive Analysis. In *The Impacts of Litigation and Legislation on Public School Finance: Adequacy, Equity, and Excellence*, ed. Julie K. Underwood and Deborah A. Verstegen, 225–248. Tenth Annual Yearbook of the American Educational Finance Association. New York: Ballinger.

Ward, Nelly. 2005. *Hancock v. Driscoll* Case Concludes in Massachusetts. ACCESS (a Project of the Campaign for Educational Equity, Teachers College, Columbia University). http://www.schoolfunding.info/news/litigation/2-27-05hancockdecision.php3.

Washington Post. 2006. A Shrinking School System. Editorial. *Washington Post*, February 21.

Wenders, John T. 2005a. The Extent and Nature of Waste and Rent Dissipation in U.S. Public Education. *Cato Journal* 25:217–244.

————. 2005b. Idaho Public School Spending and Student Performance. http://www.edexidaho.org/news_views/TaxConference.htm.

West, E. G. 1968. *Economics, Education, and the Politician*. Hobart Paper no. 42. London: Institute of Economic Affairs.

White, Kerry A. 1999. Student Protesters in Massachusetts Sit Out State Exams. *Education Week*. June 2.

Wildavsky, Aaron. 1970. A Program of Accountability for Elementary Schools. *Phi Delta Kappan* 52:212–216.

————. 1979. Learning from Education: If We're Still Stuck on the Problems, Maybe We're Taking the Wrong Exam. In his *Speaking Truth to Power: The Art and Craft of Policy Analysis*, 309–325. Boston: Little, Brown.

Willingham, Daniel T. 2004. Ask the Cognitive Scientist: Practice Makes Perfect—But Only If You Practice Beyond the Point of Perfection. *American Educator* (American Federation of Teachers) 28 (Spring): 31–33, 38–39.

————. 2005. Ask the Cognitive Scientist: Do Visual, Auditory, and Kinesthetic Learners Need Visual, Auditory, and Kinesthetic Instruction? *American Educator* (American Federation of Teachers) 29 (Summer): 43–45, 51–53.

Wirt, Frederick M., and Michael W. Kirst. 1972. *The Political Web of American Schools*. Boston: Little, Brown.

Wu, Hung-Hsi. 1999. Basic Skills Versus Conceptual Understanding: A Bogus Dichotomy in Mathematics Education. *American Educator* (American Federation of Teachers) 23 (3): 14–20.

Yecke, Cheri Pierson. 2005. *Efficiency and Effectiveness in Minnesota School Districts: How Do Districts Compare?* Minneapolis: Center of the American Experiment.

Zeigler, L. Harmon, M. Kent Jennings, and G. Wayne Peak. 1974. *Governing American Schools: Political Interaction in Local School Districts*. North Scituate, MA: Duxbury Press.

Zoch, Paul A. 2004. *Doomed to Fail: The Built-In Defects of American Education*. Chicago: Ivan R. Dee.

5

Thorough and Efficient Private and Public Schools

Paul E. Peterson

THE CONSTITUTIONS OF many states require schools to be "thorough and efficient," or use words to similar effect.[1] The constitutional language is well chosen since it appears to ask of schools that they operate at the highest level of productivity (that is, that they provide the highest-quality schooling at the lowest price) for all students in the state. But many state courts have interpreted these clauses differently. When schools are found to be less than "thorough and efficient," they have ordered as a remedy not more efficient operations but a higher level of expenditure instead. Such a remedy assumes existing schools to be efficient already and inadequate only in that they have limited resources. Yet it remains unclear whether increases in financial support, even substantial ones, can by themselves bring school

1. Elena Llaudet provided extensive research assistance for this paper.

performance up to the desired standard (Burtless 1996; Berry 2006).

In considering the connection between expenditure and school performance, much can be learned by examining the quality of schooling in the private sector. Private schools currently educate over 11 percent of students in the United States. They spend considerably less per pupil than public schools do. Yet the average performance of their students is as high or higher than that of students attending public schools. In this paper I identify various factors that could account for greater private school productivity, placing emphasis on the educational role played by "co-producers," that is, family, peers, and students themselves. In conclusion, I suggest that public schools, in order to become genuinely "thorough and efficient," need to attend to the lessons provided by private schools.

The Private School Market

Many well-educated opinion leaders, when thinking of private schools, speak of New England's Andover and Exeter, or Washington, D.C.'s St. Albans and Sidwell Friends, that is, exclusive, expensive, quite secular institutions that serve the nation's economic, political, and social elite. If they did not attend such schools themselves, their impressions have been formed by reading J. D. Salinger's *The Catcher in the Rye* or by viewing such films as *Dead Poets Society* or *Finding Forrester,* fictional insights into the educational world of the privileged.[2]

---

2. The examples are taken from Howell, Peterson with Wolf and Campbell (2006), the source for other details provided in this paper that are not otherwise attributed.

Mainly Religious Schools

Yet according to the U.S. Department of Education's Center for Education Statistics (2005a), most of the more than six million students, or 11.6 percent of those enrolled in school, attend a much less well-endowed private school, one that is likely to have a religious affiliation.[3] Forty-seven percent of private school students attend Catholic schools; another 15 percent are enrolled in Evangelical Protestant schools; 4 percent go to Lutheran schools; 16 percent to other religious schools (Jewish, Episcopal, Presbyterian, Islamic, Greek Orthodox, and others); and just 17 percent attend a nonsectarian private school, whether an exclusive one or simply a local Montessori or Waldorf school or one that is seeking to preserve a particular ethnic tradition. Altogether, secular private schools serve less than 2 percent of the school-age population, while schools with a religious affiliation serve about 9 percent.

Whether sectarian or not, private schools in the United States face potent competition, perhaps more so than entities, for-profit or nonprofit, in any other industry. Admittedly, small technology firms fear the market power of Microsoft, Intel, and Google. And many small-town businesses have not been able to survive the overwhelming retail power exercised by such giants as Wal-Mart or Target. But private schools face a stronger competitor, namely, the public school system, which has not only captured close to 90 percent of the schooling market but operates with massive subsidies from the government, allowing it to offer most services free of charge. Further, there is a set of in-

3. Throughout this paper, we will report data from various sources and years, making the assumption that variation from year to year is minor enough to be ignored for the purposes of this paper. Data reported in this sentence are projected enrollments for 2005. The percentage falls to a little more than 10 percent if preschool enrollment is excluded.

stitutions—teacher unions, school board associations, schools of education—that fight aggressively to preserve the public school's market position. Above all, the quasi-monopolistic position that public schools enjoy is indisputably legitimate, free of the threat of antitrust lawsuits that leaders in the technology and retailing sector must take into account (Moe 2001).

Only certain kinds of private schools have survived such exceptional competition. Some are prestigious, exclusive ones that cater to those who can afford the $15,000 to $40,000 annual tuition that must be paid out of after-tax income. But most private schools serve those who have strong religious commitments or those who feel their values and beliefs are not adequately respected by the public school system. Many of these private schools were formed in the nineteenth century by Roman Catholics, who wanted their children's education to be infused with their church's religious beliefs and traditions. Catholics took particular umbrage at the fact that students in public schools were asked to pray Protestant prayers and read from a Protestant version of the Bible. To protect their children from such influences, Catholics set up an alternative, low-cost system of education staffed mainly by members of religious orders who swore lifelong oaths of poverty (Ravitch 1974). On a smaller scale, members of conservative Lutheran synods, most especially the Wisconsin and Missouri Synods formed by immigrants from Germany, created their own schools not only for doctrinal reasons but also because they wished to provide children instruction in their treasured German language (Peterson 1985).

Throughout the twentieth century, Catholic and Lutheran schools began to lose market share. The price of tuition rose as women became less willing to take vows of poverty and labor costs began to rise. And as doctrinal and linguistic considerations declined in significance, fewer church members were willing to make the substantial financial sacrifice to pay for tuition when a free public school was readily available nearby. Yet the size of the private sector remained quite constant. As the number of Catholic and Lutheran schools waned, they were replaced by those formed by Evangelical Protestants. At first, these schools were little more than a knee-jerk response to the racial and social turmoil brought about by the desegregation of southern schools. However, they gradually acquired a broader mission, the preservation of a culture that objected to the increasing secularization of the public school system (no more daily prayers, Bible reading, or Christmas pageants) and to its more permissive approach to sexuality (explicit sex instruction, tolerance of homosexuality, and provision of contraceptives).

So the preservation of distinctive religious and cultural traditions remains the driving force in private education today. This becomes evident when school vouchers that reduce the cost of private schooling are made available to low-income families. In prior research, my colleagues and I discovered that Catholics and Evangelical Protestants, especially when actively engaged in their parish or church, were more likely to apply for a school voucher, more likely to accept a voucher when offered one, and more likely to keep their child in the private school of their choice over time. In summarizing our findings, we observed that

> while much of the public debate over school choice focuses on the possibility of social stratification, the reality of student differentiation looks quite different, at least in small targeted voucher initiatives. Far more important [than class distinctions] are a family's religious identity and level of engagement. On reflection, one should not be particularly surprised by these findings. Most private schools in the United States have always been religious. Meanwhile, public schools . . . must remain strictly secular. Families that prefer to have their child educated in a religious environment can be expected to be among the first to seek and make use of vouchers. (Howell, Peterson, with Wolf and Campbell 2006, 213–214)

Other data on private schools are consistent with these results. For example, a survey of principals conducted by the U.S.
Department of Education (2003a, 10) found that those working
in the private sector are much more likely than are public school
principals to say that "religious development or multicultural
awareness" is one of the three most important goals for their
school. Sixty-four percent of private school principals stated this
as one of their top goals, as compared with just 11 percent of
public school principals.

Cost-Sensitivity

Despite the religious commitment of many of those who send
their children to private schools, the schools themselves cannot
be indifferent to economic considerations. Their clientele is often
only of moderate income, and school tuition and fees are not tax
deductible. If schools charge too much, they risk pricing themselves out of existence, no matter how sincere the religious con-
victions of their clientele. As a result, the average amount paid
by students attending private schools in 2000 was only $4,689,
a remarkably low number when one considers that public
schools receive per-pupil funding of roughly twice that amount
(U.S. Department of Education 2005b).[4] Presumably, private
schools would charge more if they felt the market would bear it.
But since parents always have the option of sending their child
to a free public school, private schools must be realistic about
the price they can set for the services they render.

Price sensitivity is greatest among low-income families, of
course. Most simply cannot afford a private school. But when
school vouchers are made available to this population and tuition costs are paid by the government, then the demand for pri-

4. In 1999–2000 the average private school tuition was $4,689, while per-
pupil expenditures in public schools were an average of $8,149.

vate schooling expands fairly quickly. In Milwaukee it took only eight years after their constitutional status was clarified for all the vouchers available at the time—enough to serve 15 percent of the city's public school population—to find takers. Yet when a voucher covers only half the tuition, only about a third to half of those who express an interest in the option of sending their children to a private school exercise it when the opportunity arises (Campbell, West, and Peterson 2005). Clearly, the demand for private schooling fluctuates rapidly with the price of the service.

Educational Expenditures in Public and Private Schools

Because most private schools charge only a modest tuition, private schools spend considerably less per pupil than the amount spent by public schools. According to information reported by the U.S. Department of Education (2005b), average public school expenditures in 2003 were $9,929 per pupil, while private school expenditures were only $5,634 per pupil.[5] In other words, private schools spent per pupil only 57 percent of what public schools did. With their more substantial resources, public schools offer a broader range of services. They also have a more elaborate administrative structure; provide many students free transportation to school; design specialized educational services for those with mild, moderate, and severe disabilities; and arrange alternatives for those whose native tongue is other than English.

---

5. In this U.S. Department of Education report, per-pupil expenditures were calculated using enrollment figures from table 3 and total expenditures from table 30. Data on private school expenditures are estimates. Total expenditures for public schools include current expenditures, interest on school debt, and capital outlay.

Some might feel that such services are irrelevant to the quality of education a child receives and should not be included in any public-private comparisons. If that is so, then it is not clear why the public expenditure takes place. But even when such expenditures are stripped from comparisons with private schools, differences remain considerable, at least in the several big cities for which information is available. My colleagues and I (Howell, Peterson, with Wolf and Campbell 2006, 92) were able to obtain fairly comparable data from both public and Catholic schools in three New York City boroughs—the Bronx, Brooklyn, and Manhattan. We deducted from the public school ledger all costs that most private schools do not incur—among others, all monies spent on transportation, special education, school lunches, and other ancillary services. We even excluded the very substantial costs of the bureaucracy that manages the operations of the public schools at the city, borough, and district level. All these deductions constituted no less than 40 percent of total public school costs. But even after the expenditures for all of these items were subtracted, New York City's public schools still spent more than twice the amount spent by the Catholic schools. We obtained similar results in Washington, D.C., and Dayton, Ohio.

Because of their more limited resources, private schools have less elaborate facilities. In the evaluation of three school voucher programs in New York, Washington, D.C., and Dayton, Ohio, it was possible to compare parental judgments of the physical plant of public and private schools attended by comparable students. In those cities children attending public schools were more likely to attend a school that had a nurse's office, a cafeteria, a library, a gymnasium, an art program, and a computer laboratory. (I will draw on information from these evaluations throughout this paper, referring to them as the "three city study." Because the evaluations were randomized field trials, they provide comparable data about public and private schools.

For a full discussion of the methods used and the full set of findings, see Howell and Peterson, with Wolf and Campbell (2006).

Quite apart from their inferior facilities, private schools pay their teachers considerably less. Public school teachers reported their 2000 earnings to be, on average, close to $43,000 a year, while private school teachers said their earnings were, on average, less than $30,000 (U.S. Department of Education 2005b, table 76). Perhaps because of their lower salaries, the private school workforce turns over more quickly, leaving teachers less experienced than those working in the public sector. Twenty-four percent of private school teachers had fewer than three years of experience, as compared with just 13 percent in the public sector. Nearly 30 percent of public school teachers had more than twenty years of experience, as compared with just 18 percent of private school teachers. Also, private school teachers were slightly less likely to be teaching in the same school from one year to the next. While 85 percent of the public school teachers had remained in the same school in 2001 as in 2000, the last year for which this information is available, in private schools the percentage was just 79 percent (U.S. Department of Education 2005b, tables 67 and 74).

Salaries of private school principals also trail their public school counterparts. Their average salary in 2000 was little more than $43,000 yearly, while that of public school principals was over $66,500, a better than 50 percent pay differential (U.S. Department of Education 2005b, table 84). This, despite the fact that private school principals tended to be somewhat more experienced. In 2000 the average principal in the private sector had served in that position for more than ten years, as compared with fewer than nine years for principals in the public sector.

In sum, private schools would certainly be judged fiscally "inadequate" by those state courts that have reached such conclusions in suits concerning public schools. As compared with the public sector, private schools have less elaborate facilities, their teachers are less experienced, and both their teachers and principals are less well paid.

How, then, do private schools convince families that their education is worth the difference in cost between the free public school and the tuition the private school charges? In making the case to parents, the school's religious identity and contrasting set of cultural values are certainly critical. But that would hardly suffice if students in private schools were not also receiving comparable instruction in reading, writing, arithmetic and other basic subjects. As much as parents may wish to preserve certain values, they cannot be expected to ignore their child's need to acquire basic educational skills. To make sure their schools are educationally comparable to the public schools in their community, private schools have found a kitbag of productivity-enhancing tools that public schools would be well advised to emulate.

Organizational Solutions

The most easily adopted, though probably not the most important, of the productivity-enhancing tools used by the private sector are simple organizational ones. As compared with public schools, private schools tend to be smaller, are run with less administrative complexity, impose fewer transfers on the child as he or she ages, and have smaller, or at least equally small, classes.

School Size

Private schools, on average, are about a third the size of those in the public sector. According to U.S. Department of Education (2004) data, the average private school in the United States enrolls 184 students as compared with 573 students in the average public school. Among elementary schools, the average private school enrolls 160 students as compared with 436 students in the average public school. In central cities similar differences are observed. In our three-city study, private school parents estimated an average of 278 schoolmates at their child's school, as compared with an estimate of 450 fellow students at the public schools (Howell and Peterson 2006).

The smaller size of the private school is very likely to enhance productivity. Although some have argued that larger schools are more efficient and can provide a broader curriculum, most studies have found smaller ones to be more educationally effective. (For a summary of the existing research on the effects of school size, see Chubb and Peterson 2005.) Principals can maintain tighter supervision over staff and students, a sense of community is more easily created, and social control can be established through informal networks rather than by means of bureaucratic regulation.

Administrative Simplicity

It is not only because private schools are smaller that bureaucratization is reduced but also because most private schools operate with greater independence and autonomy (Chubb and Moe 1990). Many private schools are incorporated independently as nonprofit institutions, with their own board of trustees, to whom the head of the school reports. Relations between heads and employees are handled informally. Hardly any private school head must negotiate salaries with representatives of employee organizations.

The one set of schools administered within a larger-scale institutional structure is operated by Catholic archdioceses. In this system the central office, though it retains ultimate control, devolves most decisions to the school level. With few constraints, school heads determine policies governing student admission; the hiring, compensation, and retention of teachers; and the allocation of fiscal resources. Although needy Catholic schools may receive some financial assistance from the archdiocese, most schools are expected to find, on their own, the bulk of the resources necessary to maintain their operations.

The greater administrative simplicity in the private sector is evident from teacher reports about their working conditions. According to a U.S. Department of Education survey (2005b, table 73), "routine duties and paperwork interfere with my job of teaching" is said to be the situation for 71 percent of public school teachers but for only 45 percent of private school teachers. Also, private school teachers were much more likely than were their public school colleagues to feel they had "a lot of influence" on such school policies as setting standards for student performance, establishing curriculum, and setting discipline guidelines.

Two-Tier versus Multi-Tier System

Private schools prefer the traditional two-tier division between elementary and high school to the three-tier system that has become increasingly popular in the public school system. As shown in table 5.1, no less than 27 percent of public school students are enrolled in middle school, but the institution is almost nonexistent in the private sector. Even the separation between elementary and high school is not always maintained in the private sector, since 26 percent of students in private schools attend what the U.S. Department of Education labels "combined" schools, which either extend beyond eighth grade and admit students before seventh grade or have ungraded classes.

As popular as the middle school has become, the old-fash-

Table 5.1 Percentage of Schools and Enrollment in Public and Private Schools by Grade Span, 2003–2004

	Public schools		Private schools	
	Schools (%)	Enrollment (%)	Schools (%)	Enrollment (%)
Elementary	57	44	68	60
Middle	15	27	1	0[a]
Secondary	21	26	8	14
Junior high	1	1	0[a]	0[a]
Combined	7	3	23	26
Total percentage:	100	100	100	100
Total number:	94,420	54,055,110	28,783	5,303,806

Notes: Elementary schools are considered to be those with at least one grade lower than five and no grade higher than eight. Middle schools are considered to be those with no grade lower than five and no grade higher than eight. Secondary schools are considered to be those with no grade lower than seven and at least one grade higher than eight. Junior high schools are considered to be those with a seven-to-nine grade span, and they are also included as secondary schools. Combined schools are considered to be those with at least one grade lower than seven and at least one grade higher than eight and schools with only ungraded classes.
[a] Negligible amount.
Source: U.S. Department of Education 2004.

ioned two-tier system appears to be more educationally productive. Most scholarly studies find that young adolescents learn more if they attend K–8 schools rather than middle schools (e.g., Moore 1984; Becker 1987; Simmons and Blyth 1987; Wihry, Coladarci, and Meadow 1992; Franklin and Glascock 1998; Offenberg 2001; and Baltimore City Public School System 2001). For example, a recent study of Milwaukee's public schools found that students in K–8 schools outperformed those in middle school (Cook 2005). The study was undertaken when it was discovered that families were preferring private and charter schools over public middle schools, an important fact in this city, where 30 percent of the students are attending either charter schools or private schools with a government-funded voucher that covers their tuition. Faced with these findings and this heavy competition, public schools in Milwaukee are gradually reverting to the K–8 format.

Class Size

Despite their limited fiscal capacities, private schools appear unwilling to make sacrifices in classroom size. Although researchers disagree about whether students learn more in smaller classes (e.g., Hoxby 2000; Krueger 1999), private school leaders have organized their schools on the assumption that smaller classes are better. Rather than pay teachers higher salaries, they use their scarce dollars to hire more staff and thus keep classes as small as those in the public sector, perhaps even smaller. According to one government report (U.S. Department of Education 1997), the average class size of schools in 1994 was just twenty in private schools, as compared with twenty-three in public schools. According to another, the pupil-teacher ratio in 2002 was roughly the same—about sixteen students—in the two sectors (U.S. Department of Education 2005b, table 64). In a national evaluation of a voucher program that my colleagues and I conducted, parents reported an average of twenty students in the classroom of the private school, as compared with twenty-four in the public school classroom (Howell and Peterson 2006, 100).

It is not clear whether private school administrators find smaller classes more educationally effective or whether they just find them a valuable marketing tool. But in the trade-off between employee salaries and the size of the pupil-teacher ratio, they seem to prefer more staff to higher-paid staff.

In summary, private schools have several organizational characteristics—smaller school size, administrative simplicity, a broader age-structure, and smaller class sizes—that enhance their productivity. Yet no one of these policies, nor all of them together, provides the most important mechanism for achieving high levels of educational efficiency. Most important is the greater ability of the private sector to enlist the services of others in the provision of educational services, a practice we will characterize as "co-production."

Co-Production

Co-production takes place whenever a product is created or a service is performed by those who do *not* receive monetary reimbursement as well as by those who do (Ostrom et al. 1982). A pervasive fact of modern life, co-production is found in both the public and private sectors. In the public sector, examples are readily identified. Safety is preserved by paid police and fire officials but also by watchful citizens. Streets are kept clean not only by paid sanitary engineers but also by ordinary citizens who throw their trash in publicly provided barrels. In the private sector, groceries are distributed by paid clerks but also by shoppers who put groceries in their carts. Similarly, gasoline is pumped by drivers, cash is retrieved by ATM cardholders, and soft drinks, junk food, and newspapers are all retrieved by inserting coins in vending machines. Indeed, a well-known principle of efficient retailing is shifting the cost of (co-) production from paid employees to unpaid customers.

To achieve efficient co-production, firms must attend to the interests and concerns of those *not* paid for their services. If ATM cards are not easy to use, customers will wait for the teller. If trash barrels are not emptied by paid employees, unpaid pedestrians will discard their junk promiscuously. If groceries are not attractively displayed by store employees, customers will not buy them.

Education that takes place in schools is co-produced by those who do *not* receive monetary reimbursements for their services as well as by those who do. Paid for their services are teachers, principals, maintenance personnel, bus drivers, and the myriad other specialized personnel needed to maintain complex, modern school systems. They are motivated to provide educationally relevant services in part by the wages and salaries they receive. If shirking is excessive, an employee can be asked to leave.

No less important are educational co-producers who cannot be asked to leave, even if they are low performing. (To simplify the presentation, I will, from this point on, refer to paid personnel as producers and to unpaid personnel as co-producers.) The most important co-producer is the student himself or herself. Peers, parents, relatives, neighbors, and friends, too, are co-producers. Altogether, the actions of the co-producers are almost certainly more important for educational production than are the actions of paid producers.

To enlist cooperative behavior from co-producers, private schools must consider their incentives and concerns. To engage students in their own education, these incentives may be both intrinsic and extrinsic and both long-range and immediate. Extrinsic incentives are generally regarded as the most effective for most producers, but it is often assumed that when it comes to educating themselves, students respond (or at least should respond) mainly to intrinsic ones, such as the love of learning, or if extrinsic, to long-term ones, such as the opportunity to go to college or to enter the workforce as a highly skilled, well-paid worker. Thus, much attention is given to the ways of encouraging students' love of learning, by enhancing their self-esteem, or by providing entertaining, enjoyable educational experiences in an attractive setting. To encourage attention to the long-term consequences of education, teachers emphasize the importance of finishing high school and pursuing a college degree.

Such intrinsic or long-term extrinsic incentives may work for some students, especially those who find it easy to learn and who are surrounded by co-producers (parents, peers, and others) ready and willing to reinforce the messages teachers convey. But for those students not so privileged, intrinsic incentives may need to be supplemented by short-term, extrinsic incentives, such as requiring a minimum level of performance (both in deportment and accomplishment) for a student to remain at the school, or to be promoted to the next grade at the end of the year, or eventually, to graduate. Other co-producers are also responsive to these extrinsic incentives.

Co-Production in Public and Private Schools

Generally speaking, private schools are better designed than public schools to motivate co-producers, whether parents, peers, or students themselves. For one thing, parents must pay money to send their children to private schools. Once a financial sacrifice has been made, the family has a strong incentive to make sure its resources are well spent, and parents can be expected to be more engaged with their child's education. Even a young child may appreciate whether or not the family is making a financial sacrifice on his or her behalf. As one public school parent (herself a public school teacher but one who had attended private school) reported in a focus group conversation:

> Last year one of the little boys in my daughter's class was a trouble-maker, was serving after-school detention. And he was just being a little pill. And I looked at him, and I said, "Joshua, you're lucky, when I was in second grade, if I would have had detention, I would have had to have written one thousand times. "I will behave." He looked at me and said, "Well, I wouldn't do it." I said, "Well, my parents were paying $300 a month to send me to school. . . . " And he looked at me and

said, "Yeah, if my Mom was paying $300 a month, I would
have to do what I was told." (Howell, Peterson, with Wolf and
Campbell 2006, 111–112)

Apart from family expectations, a student at a private school
must meet the school's own expectations in order to remain
there. First, the student must meet the disciplinary standards of
the school. Tardiness, excessive absenteeism, fighting, cheating,
disruption of the classroom's educational climate, and destruction of school property can all be grounds for suspension and
eventual expulsion. Young children, as long as they are well behaved, may not need to meet any particular academic standards,
but in most private schools older students will also be expected
to exhibit good study habits, do their homework, complete term
papers, and perform satisfactorily on tests. Otherwise, they may
not be invited to return the following academic year. In all these
respects, standards at public schools, though not entirely absent,
are generally much lower.

Peer Culture

Just as the school's expectations will create incentives for each
student, so will school expectations shape the peer culture
within a school. In private schools the fact that students are expected to adhere to the school's disciplinary code and to perform
at least at a satisfactory level affects not just each student individually but the general culture in the school. But when peer
culture is shaped by policies that rely on intrinsic incentives
(such as making learning fun and enjoyable), as is often the case
in public settings, then peer groups, as co-producers, can become highly variable, sometimes as much of a negative as a positive influence on learning, especially in urban settings where
schools serve a low-income, minority population.

In our three-city study of public and private schools, my col-

Table 5.2   Social Problems at Public and Private Schools Serving Participants in School Voucher Experiments in Three Cities[a]

	The percentage of parents who say a problem at their child's school is "very serious"	
Social problem	Private school (%)	Public school (%)
Fighting	32	63[b]
Truancy	26	48[b]
Tardiness	33	54[b]
Destruction of property	22	42[b]
Cheating	26	39[b]

[a] New York City, Dayton, and Washington, D.C.
[b] $p < .01$
Source: Howell and Peterson (2006, 111).

leagues and I asked parents questions about the educational climate at their schools. Parents were asked if fighting, truancy, tardiness, destruction of property, and cheating were a "very serious problem" at their child's school. As shown in table 5.2, low-income, inner-city parents were much more likely to report that these were serious problems if their child attended a public school rather than a private school. For example, 63 percent of parents in public schools reported fighting as a "very serious problem" if their child attended a public school, but only 32 percent of private school parents gave a similar report. The difference cannot be attributed to the parents answering the question because in our study both public school and private school parents had applied for school vouchers, though only the latter won the lottery.

A national survey conducted by the U.S. Department of Education shows findings consistent with these. Forty-one percent of public school teachers report that the "level of student misbehavior in this school interferes with my teaching," but only 25 percent of those in private schools report this as a problem. Student tardiness and class cutting is said to interfere with teaching by 32 percent of public school teachers but only by 15 percent of those in private schools. Seventeen percent of teachers in public schools, but only 4 percent in the private sector, report "student disrespect for teachers" as a "serious problem" at their schools (U.S. Department of Education 1997).

Importantly, private schools achieve a more productive educational climate without dismissing large numbers of children. In our three-city study, parents reported very few instances of expulsion from school, less than 1 percent of all children, the same percentage in the private as in the public sector. Nor did we see higher rates of student mobility from one school to another in the private than in the public sector (except for the higher percentage of public school students moving from elementary to middle school). We also did not find, in most cases, systematic differences in student suspension rates. Generally, the likelihood that a child would be suspended varied between 5 and 10 percent in both sectors. (However, among older students in Washington, D.C., we discerned higher suspension rates in the private sector.)

Apparently, students, at least if they enter private schools as young elementary students, adapt to the expectations of a school, especially when it is clear that they will otherwise be suspended or expelled. The dismissal of even one child sends a strong signal to everyone else in the school. Just as it takes but one rotten apple to spoil a barrel, so the barrel can be preserved simply by tossing out the one bad apple. And private schools have strong monetary incentives to try to keep as many of their students as possible. For that reason alone, actual exercise of the big stick is rare.

Social Capital

When a school has a healthy educational climate, that fact provides the preconditions for building a strong, educationally supportive community among the parents and friends of the school. Such communities generate what has become known as "social capital," the networks of relationships that yield positive benefits for the community over and above the contributions of any particular individual (Putnam 2001). Those who have studied Catholic schools closely have attributed their academic strength in good part to their supportive social context (Coleman and Hoffer 1987). In the view of Bryk and his co-authors (Bryk, Lee, and Holland 1993, 314):

> Catholic schools work better not because they attract better students (which is somewhat true) or because they have more qualified faculty (which does not appear to be the case). In general, these "inputs," or what economists call "human capital," are quite ordinary. Rather, Catholic schools benefit from a network of social relations, characterized by trust, that constitute a form of "social capital." . . . Trust accrues because school participants, both students and faculty, choose to be there.

Parental Communication and Involvement

Perhaps it is the social capital that comes from private school networks that accounts—at least in part—for the greater engagement of families in their children's education. According to a U.S. Department of Education survey of teachers (2005b, table 73), private school teachers are much more likely to have strong parental support for what they do. No less than 84 percent of private school parents report they receive "a great deal of support from parents for the work I do." Only 58 percent of public school teachers say they receive the same level of support.

Admittedly, parents who pay for their child's education can be expected to be more motivated to assist in the child's instruction. But even if a parent is not inclined to participate, private schools have incentives to do everything they can to make sure parents become as engaged as possible. They need to establish records of accomplishment, if they are to remain viable institutions. To do that, they need to engage parental co-producers as much as possible. Not surprisingly, nationwide surveys provide ample evidence that private schools, as compared with public schools, communicate more extensively with parents, contacting and involving them in a wide variety of ways (Vaden-Kiernan 2005). In another U.S. Department of Education survey of parents (2005b, table 25), those with children in private school were much more likely to report that they volunteered in school, attended a class event, attended a general school meeting, and attended a parent-teacher conference. For example, 69 percent of the private school parents said they volunteered at school, as compared with just 38 percent of the public school parents. Attending a class event was reported by 86 percent of the private school parents, as compared with 68 percent of the public school parents.

The high involvement and communication between private schools and families could be in part a function of the greater resourcefulness of such families. However, in our three-city study of similar groups of families, my colleagues and I found that those with children in private schools, as compared with those with children in public schools, were more likely to receive a newsletter from the school, participate in instruction, speak to classes about their jobs, receive notes from teachers, be informed about their child's progress halfway through the grading period, participate in parent-teacher conferences, attend open houses, and be notified about their child if there was a behavioral problem. (See table 5.3.) That sharp differences could be observed, although the two groups of families were otherwise much the same, only underlines how much greater emphasis the

Table 5.3   Parental Outreach at Schools Serving Participants in School Voucher Experiments in Three Cities[a]

	Percentage of parents who answer "yes"	
Outreach	Private school (%)	Public school (%)
Parents receive newsletters about school.	88	68[b]
Parents participate in instruction.	68	50[b]
Parents receive notes from teachers.	93	78[b]
Parents are notified when child sent to office for first time because of disruptive behavior.	91	77[b]
Parents speak to classes about their jobs.	44	33[b]
Parents are informed about student progress halfway through the grading period.	93	84[b]
Regular parent-teacher conferences are held.	95	90[c]
Parent open houses are held at school.	95	90[c]

[a] New York City, Dayton, and Washington, D.C.
[b] $p < .01$
[c] $p < .05$
Source: Howell and Peterson (2006,106).

private school places on the involvement of parents in the educational process.

Homework

Perhaps the most direct way of involving co-producers in the educational process is to ask students to do a substantial amount of homework. From the point of view of the school, this form of education is low cost (though it does require that teachers check and grade the homework). Perhaps it is for this reason that teachers in private schools are much more likely to assign homework. When similar groups of families were compared in our three-city study, 72 percent of private school parents said their child did at least an hour of homework every night, as compared with only 56 percent of public school parents. Also, 90 percent of private school parents said the homework was "appropriate" for their child, as compared with 72 percent of public school parents. Anecdotal information from the evaluation was consistent with these quantitative data. For example, one focus group conversation yielded this exchange:

> MOTHER: My kids never even had homework in the public schools.
> MODERATOR: You're saying no homework. . . .
> MOTHER: No, he didn't even have a concept of how to come home every day and do homework.
> MODERATOR: But now. . . .?
> MOTHER: He has homework every day. I look in his bag. His teacher writes notes. They have a homework book where they have to write their homework in a book. I have to sign the book every day.

Clearly, this school, by asking parents to sign off and therefore take responsibility for the child's homework, is making every effort to enlist co-producers into the educational production process.

Significance

The debate over public school adequacy, with its heavy emphasis on financial considerations, assumes that the critical factors affecting educational adequacy can be altered by fiscal policy. With more money, schools can pay their teachers and principals more; they can build new, more sophisticated buildings; they can feed children breakfast, lunch, and an after-school snack; they can transport children near and far to settings considered most educationally appropriate; and they can supply nursing and other medical services, as well as a plethora of focused services for those eligible for bilingual or special education.

Most of these strategies for achieving educational adequacy

are unavailable to all but the most exclusive private schools. The rest, operating on budgets little more than half the size of those in the public sector, must find low-cost or costless ways to enhance learning, if they are to achieve some degree of adequacy. Some of these tools are simple organizational devices. Keep the school small, reduce bureaucracy, and until they reach high school, do not ask students to change schools as they grow older. But more important than any of those organizational strategies, it is the private school's ability to enlist the help of co-producers—students themselves, their peers, their parents, and others in their lives—that is the secret to its success.

In private schools students are given strong, immediate incentives to adopt educationally appropriate behavior and to focus on their studies. If they are to stay in the school, they must avoid becoming a discipline problem, and, as they grow older, they often must reach at least a minimal standard of achievement. By giving the same incentives to all its students, the school creates a peer group that learns self-discipline and appropriate learning habits. For most students, then, the peer group in a private school is an educational asset, not a liability. Parents are given a strong incentive to participate in their child's education by asking them to pay for it. When one pays for something, one acquires ownership in the activity. And by asking parents to pay, the school forces itself both to listen to and communicate its expectations to its clients, if only to maintain enrollment. Homework assignments, compulsory teacher-parent conferences, extensive communications between home and school: all reinforce and sustain the family as educational co-producers.

With students, peers, and families all contributing to the education process, it matters less that teachers are less well paid, less experienced, less credentialed, perhaps even less able, than their public school peers. However important the teacher is to a child's educational success—and there is plenty of evidence that teachers are the most important educational element that can be *purchased*—enlisting the active, positive engagement of co-producers is even more crucial. At least that is what one concludes when one looks at the evidence on student achievement in public and private schools.

Student Achievement

Despite levels of financial inadequacy that would provoke severe sanctions from many state judges who have ruled on adequacy lawsuits, private school performance, as shown by students who attend their schools, is not obviously deficient. Instead, students who attend private schools perform at a higher level than do students attending public schools. Whether or not their higher performance can be attributed to the private school—or to the students themselves—has been a matter of considerable disputation. Still, when all is said and done, few doubt that private schools do at least as well as the public schools at educating the children entrusted to their care.

Recent NAEP Findings

The most recent evidence on private school performance comes from a report issued by the U.S. Department of Education (2005a). Based on standardized tests administered to a national sample of both public and private schools, the National Assessment of Educational Progress (NAEP), also known as the nation's report card, provides information, by combining data for the years 2000 and 2003, on the educational achievement of students in fourth and eighth grades.[6] As shown in table 5.4, in

6. The National Assessment of Educational Progress (NAEP) achievement data for private schools are spotty; if information on private school performance is not reported in this paper, it is because NAEP did not have an adequate sample and chose not to report the information.

Table 5.4   Private School Performance Advantage: Difference in Performance of Students in Private and Public Schools on National Assessment of Educational Progress, Combined Results for 2000 and 2003.

The private school performance advantage was . . .

	Fourth grade		Eighth grade	
	In test-score points	*In s.d.*	*In test-score points*	*In s.d.*
Math	10	0.36	16	0.44
Reading	19	0.51	21	0.60
Science	15	0.44	17	0.47
Writing	13	0.36	18	0.47

By race/ethnicity, fourth grade, math, 2003

	In test-score points	*In s.d.*
White	5	0.18
Black	5	0.18
Hispanic	10	0.36
Asian	4	0.14

By parent's highest level of education, eighth grade, reading, 2003

	In test-score points	*In s.d.*
Less than high school	18	0.51
Graduated from high school	15	0.43
Some education after high school	11	0.31
Graduated from college	16	0.46

Notes: s.d. = standard deviation, N/A = not available.
Sources: U.S. Department of Education (2005a, 2003b).

all comparisons, whether in math, reading, writing, or science, students in private schools were performing at a higher level. In fourth grade, private school students performed 10 test-score points higher in math and 19 points higher in reading, differences that are about 36 percent and 51 percent of a standard deviation, respectively. Since one standard deviation is about the difference between a fourth grader and an eighth grader, private school students in fourth grade were about one to two years ahead of their public school peers.[7] This difference was also observed for students in other grades and subject levels.

For the most part, these differences were fairly constant among types of private schools. In nearly all comparisons Catholic and Lutheran schools performed at or above the private school average. In some instances Evangelical Protestant schools performed below the private school average, though still above the public school average. In fourth grade math, for example, Evangelical Protestant schools scored ten points above the public school average but four points below the private school one. Similar results were obtained in fourth grade writing achievement.[8]

But according to the NCES study (Braum and others 2006), the private school advantage disappears once statistical adjustments are made for student characteristics. Among 4th graders, a 4.5-point public school advantage was detected in math, while in reading parity between the sectors was observed. After the same adjustments were made for 8th graders, private schools

7. The standard deviation for the 2003 NAEP for fourth graders was 0.28 in mathematics and 0.37 in reading (U.S. Department of Education 2003b).

8. The NAEP report refers to Evangelical Protestant schools as "Conservative Christian" schools. In our view this is a misnomer, since Catholic and Lutheran schools classified separately in the NAEP report are also Christian. "Evangelical Protestant" better captures the distinctive religious heritage of the many schools often characterized as "Christian."

retained a 7-point advantage in reading but achieved only parity in math.

Although this seems to indicate that private schools are no more effective than public ones, the analysis from which these results are derived depends on measures of student characteristics that inconsistently estimate student background in the public and private sectors. Using the same data but substituting better measures of student characteristics, Elena Llaudet and I (2006) identified a consistent private school advantage.

The most serious flaw in the NCES study is its reliance on student participation in four federal programs—Title I, free lunch, programs for those with Limited English Proficiency, and special education for the disabled—as information about the students' background characteristics. Reliance on that participation information inconsistently classifies public and private school students as disadvantaged, because public and private schools have quite different obligations and incentives to classify students as participants. As a result, NCES undercounted the incidence of disadvantage in the private sector and overcounted its incidence in the public sector.

For example, if a public school has a schoolwide Title I program, which is permitted if 40 percent of its students are eligible for free or reduced-price lunch, then every student at the school—regardless of poverty level—is said to be a recipient of Title I services. By contrast, private schools cannot directly receive Title I funds nor can they operate Title I programs. Instead, private schools must negotiate arrangements with local public school districts, which then provide Title I services to eligible students. Many private schools lack the administrative capacity to handle these complex negotiations or do not wish to make available services that they will not administer, making private school participation haphazard. In the 2003–04 school year, only 19 percent of private schools were reported by the U.S.

Department of Education (DOE) to participate in Title I, compared to 54 percent of public schools. Similar problems bedevil the use of participation in the other three federal programs as well.

To check the sensitivity of NCES results to the use of this inconsistent classification scheme, Llaudet and I estimated program effects with a model that excluded the variables that measured participation in federal programs but included measures of the following background characteristics: race, ethnicity, gender, parents' education, location of the school (regionally and by urban, suburban, or rural area), absenteeism at school, availability of a computer in the home, the number of books in the home, frequency with which a language other than English is spoken at home, and teacher reports of whether the child suffers from a profound or moderate disability.

Results from this model reveal a consistent private school advantage. In 8th grade math, that advantage was 5 test points, in reading it was 11 points. Among 4th grades in math, the private schools outperformed the public schools by 2 points, while in reading the private sector had an 8-point advantage.

The results for Catholic schools using the alternative models are very similar to those of the private sector as a whole. Lutheran schools are estimated to have a larger advantage in math and a similar one in reading when compared to the results of the private sector taken together. And Evangelical Protestant schools are found to perform at a similar level to public schools in math but at a higher level in reading.

Systematic Comparisons

Although based on an improved model, these results cannot be taken as definitive because the data on which they were based were collected at a single point in time, making it extremely difficult to estimate how much a student was learning. For better estimates one needs to turn to other research that dates back to the seminal work of James S. Coleman and his colleagues.

Under the auspices of the Department of Education, the Coleman team, in 1980 and 1982, directed the "High School and Beyond" survey collected from a cross-section of United States high school students. By testing a national sample of students in public and private schools in two waves, the Department of Education generated data on the determinants of academic gains in high school from a student's sophomore to senior years. The Coleman research team (Coleman, Hoffer, and Kilgore 1982; Coleman and Hoffer 1987) found that students in private schools performed at a higher level than did students in public schools, even after observable family background characteristics were taken into account.[9]

Critics, however, pointed out flaws in the data collected and the procedures used to evaluate them. In a 1985 issue of *Sociology of Education,* three particularly well-crafted essays reported, analyzed, and interpreted the data. The authors of these essays disagreed about whether the data showed that private schools had significant effects on student achievement. Thomas Hoffer, Andrew Greeley, and James Coleman (1985) found that private schools had substantial, positive effects on student test performance, while Douglas Wilms (1985) found trivial effects, if any. Christopher Jencks (1985) mediated the conflict, reaching Solomonic conclusions somewhere in the middle. Debate on the issue has continued along much the same lines since the Coleman research. Later studies have come to rival conclusions, some showing positive private school effects on students, others showing no such effects.

9. The following discussion follows closely that presented in Howell and Peterson, with Wolf and Campbell (2006).

There is one point, however, on which most researchers agree: private schools help close the education gap between ethnic groups. Surveying the literature on school sector effects and private school vouchers, Princeton University Economist Cecilia Rouse (2000, 19) says that "the overall impact of private schools is mixed, [but] it does appear that Catholic schools generate higher test scores for African-Americans." Similarly, University of Wisconsin economists Jeffrey Grogger and Derek Neal (2000, 153) conclude that "urban minorities in Catholic schools fare much better than similar students in public schools" while the effects for urban whites and suburban students generally are "at best mixed."[10]

The first scholarly recognition of the private school contribution toward the closing of the test-score gap was contained in the *Sociology of Education* disputation. The Coleman research team found strong positive effects on low-income, minority students. Catholic schooling increased minority test scores by an estimated 0.15 standard deviation yearly, nearly three times as much as the estimated effect on white students (Hoffer et al. 1985, tables 1.7 and 1.8, 80–81).[11] Jencks showed that Wilms's data, despite its exclusion of dropouts, also contained positive (though not statistically significant) effects of attending a Catholic school on African Americans' reading scores. Taking all the evidence from both studies into account, Jencks (1985, 134) concluded, "the evidence that Catholic schools are especially helpful

10. The findings presented in this paper come from analyses conducted on the National Educational Longitudinal Study.

11. These are the estimates of effects when controlling for background characteristics and years in Catholic school. Effect size is estimated from information provided in Jencks, who estimates an annual effect size of Catholic schools for all students of around 0.05 in math and reading but does not estimate an effect size for black or minority students, separately. Hoffer et al., however, estimate effects on minorities that are about three times those for whites.

for initially disadvantaged students is quite suggestive, though not conclusive."

Later studies have generally affirmed the Coleman team's findings. In an analysis of the National Longitudinal Survey of Youth, Derek Neal (1997) found that students who attend Catholic schools are more likely to graduate from high school and college and score higher on standardized tests. The effects, Neal notes, are the greatest among urban minorities. Catholic schools also have a significant, positive effect on black earning potential, but not on that of whites. In separate studies David Figlio and Joseph Stone (1999, 133) as well as William Evans and Robert Schwab (1993) reached similar findings for African Americans. They also found that the effect of Catholic schools was particularly large in central cities. In Figlio and Stone's words: "The estimated treatment effect is more than twice as large for African Americans in big cities than for African-Americans in general." (Other studies finding positive educational benefits from attending private schools include Coleman et al. [1982], and Chubb and Moe [1990]. Critiques of these studies can be found in Goldberger and Cain [1982].)

These findings from national surveys indicate that private schools can help close the education gap. They are supported by results from a randomized experiment, the three-city study that my colleagues and I conducted. We found positive private school effects on the educational performance of African Americans but found little effect, one way or another, on the performance of other groups. African American students, after attending private schools for three years, reached, on average, a performance level somewhere from one to two years higher than a comparable group of African American students who remained in public schools.

That similar differences were not always observed for groups from other ethnic backgrounds is to be expected. Private schools, to survive, do not need to realize higher levels of achievement as long as they are offering something else that parents desire. In a market environment where the competitor is able to offer similar services free of charge, private schools, to attract a clientele, must keep costs low but still match public schools on achievement, and offer something else besides, usually an education that comports more closely with the family's values. To make sure students learn, private schools place high expectations on students and their families. Interestingly enough, such policies have the biggest positive benefit on the educational experience of African American students. In a school that insists on student self-discipline, family engagement, and appropriate behavior by peers, African American students are the ones who benefit the most, simply because in a public setting those elements of co-production are especially hard to realize.

Conclusions: The Road to Adequacy in Public Education

For those concerned about adequacy in public education, there is much to be learned from the private sector. Even if we assume that, for the white majority, the rate of learning in the private sector is only just as good, and not greater, than the rate of learning in the public sector, productivity is higher in the private sector because private schools are doing equally well at little more than half the cost. Any automobile maker who could do the same would drive the competition into oblivion. Only the public schools' access to government subsidies prevents the same from happening to them. When the public and private schools are put on a more similar financial footing, as in Milwaukee, Wisconsin, a steady flight to the private sector takes place. That public schools fiercely fight all voucher initiatives only reveals that they are aware of this.

But can any of the productivity-enhancing elements in the private sector be exported to the public one? Is there a way of achieving more adequate public education other than pursuing a financial strategy that has so far proven illusory? Certain organizational steps can easily be taken—indeed, they are already being undertaken in places where public schools are facing strong competition. In Milwaukee, the most competitive environment in the United States, middle schools are being phased out, elementary schools are expanding up through eighth grade, high schools are being divided into smaller units, and authority is being decentralized to the building level.

All these are important first steps, but can public schools do a better job of enlisting the help of educational co-producers? Here, the place to begin is with the students, who need to be given strong incentives to learn. Ideally, attendance at desired public schools should depend on self-discipline and, as a child grows older, on educational achievement. Short of that, students should not be promoted from one grade to the next unless they reach a stated level of proficiency. Students should reach a certain level of achievement in a range of subjects before they are given their high school diploma. And high school examinations should be subject-based, comprehensive, and allow for a range of achievement beyond the bare minimum. Results should be incorporated into high school diplomas and, if the student so authorizes, scores should be made available to employers and institutions of higher learning. Then, the higher-performing students will be given incentives to reach still higher levels of accomplishment.

All these steps will affect students, peers, and families alike. With goals well specified, achievement rewarded, failure penalized, and peers who interfere with the learning process removed from the educational setting that most students enjoy, the conditions for learning in public schools will be greatly enhanced.

All this can be done at a minimum cost, well within the budgets of almost all school systems.

Courts cannot mandate these reforms, of course. The search for adequate education cannot be legalized. But once courts understand that co-producers play a key, if not the primary, role in the educational process, then financial issues that are currently given preeminence will be placed in appropriate perspective.

References

Baltimore City Public School System. 2001. *An Examination of K–5, 6–8 versus K–8 Grade Configurations.* A research study conducted for the new Board of School Commissioners by the Division of Research, Evaluation, and Accountability. Baltimore, MD: Baltimore City Public School System.

Becker, H. J. 1987. *Addressing the Needs of Different Groups of Early Adolescents: Effects of Varying School and Classroom Organizational Practices on Students from Different Social Backgrounds and Abilities.* Report No. 16. Baltimore, MD: Center for Research on Elementary and Middle Schools, Johns Hopkins University.

Berry, Christopher. 2006. The Impact of School Lawsuits on Expenditure. In *School Money Trials*, ed. Martin R. West and Paul E. Peterson. Washington, D.C.: Brookings Institution Press.

Braun, Henry, Frank Jenkins, and Wendy Grigg. 2006. Comparing Private Schools and Public Schools Using Hierarchical Linear Modeling. U.S. Department of Education, Institute of Education Sciences, National Center for Education Statistics, NCES 2006-461.

Bryk, Anthony S., Valerie E. Lee, and Peter B. Holland. 1993. *Catholic Schools and the Common Good.* Cambridge, MA: Harvard University.

Burtless, Gary, ed. 1996. *Does Money Matter? The Effect of School Resources on Student Achievement and Adult Success.* Washington, D.C.: Brookings Institution Press.

Campbell, David E., Martin R. West, and Paul E. Peterson. 2005. Participation in a National, Means-Tested School Voucher Program. *Journal of Policy Analysis and Management* 24, no. 3 (Summer): 523–541.

Chubb, John E., and Terry M. Moe. 1990. *Politics, Markets, and America's Schools.* Washington, D.C.: Brookings Institution Press.

Chubb, John E., and Paul E. Peterson. 2005. Consolidate Districts, Not Schools. In *Reforming Education in Arkansas.* Stanford, CA: Hoover Institution Press.

Coleman, James S., Thomas Hoffer, and Sally Kilgore. 1982. *High School Achievement.* New York: Basic Books.

Coleman, James S., and Thomas Hoffer. 1987. *Public and Private High Schools: The Impact of Communities.* New York: Basic Books.

Cook, H. Gary. 2005. *What's Best in the Middle? Student Engagement, Achievement, Attainment, and Growth Differences between K–8 and Middle School Grade Configurations at Milwaukee Public Schools.* Research Report #0501. Milwaukee Public Schools. Division of Assessment & Accountability.

Evans, William N., and Robert M. Schwab. 1993. *Who Benefits from Private Education? Evidence from Quantile Regressions.* Department of Economics, University of Maryland.

Figlio, David N., and Joe A. Stone. 1999. Are Private Schools Really Better? *Research in Labor Economics* 18:115–140.

Franklin, B.J., and C.H. Glascock. 1998. The Relationship between Grade Configuration and Student Performance in Rural Schools. *Journal of Research in Rural Education* 14, no. 3:149–153.

Goldberger, Arthur S., and Glen G. Cain. 1982. The Causal Analysis of Cognitive Outcomes in the Coleman, Hoffer, and Kilgore Report. *Sociology of Education* 55 (April–July): 103–122.

Grogger, Jeffrey, and Derek Neal. 2000. Further Evidence on the Effects of Catholic Secondary Schooling. In *Brookings-Wharton Papers on Urban Affairs*: 2000. Washington, D.C.: Brookings Institution Press.

Hoffer, Thomas, Andrew Greeley, and James Coleman. 1985.

Achievement Growth in Public and Catholic Schools. *Sociology of Education* 58 (April):74–97.

Howell, William G., Paul E. Peterson, with Patrick J. Wolf and David Campbell. 2006 [2002]. *The Education Gap*. Revised ed. Washington, D.C.: Brookings Institution Press.

Hoxby, Caroline M. 2000. The Effects of Class Size on Student Achievement: New Evidence from Population Variation. *Quarterly Journal of Economics* 115, no.4:1239–1285.

Jencks, Christopher. 1985. How Much Do High School Students Learn? *Sociology of Education* 8 (April): 128–135.

Krueger, Alan B. 1999. Experimental Estimates of Education Production Functions. *Quarterly Journal of Economics* 114 (1999): 497–532.

Moe, Terry M. 2001. *Schools, Vouchers, and the American Public*. Washington, D.C.: Brookings Institution Press.

Moore, D. W. 1984. *Impact of School Grade-Organization Patterns on Seventh and Eighth Grade Students in K–8 and Junior High Schools*. Paper presented at the annual meeting of the New England Educational Research Organization. Rockport, ME.

Neal, Derek. 1997. The Effects of Catholic Secondary Schooling on Educational Achievement. *Journal of Labor Economics* 15, no. 1, pt. 1:98–123.

Offenberg, R. M. 2001. The Efficacy of Philadelphia's K-to-8 Schools Compared to Middle Grades Schools. *Middle School Journal* 32, no. 4 (March): 23–29.

Ostrom, Elinor, Roger B. Parks, Paula C. Baker, Larry L. Kiser, Ron Oakerson, Vincent Ostrom, Stephen Percy, Martha Vandivort, Gordon P. Whitaker, and Rick Wilson. 1982. Coproduction of Public Services. In *Analyzing Urban-Service Distributions*, ed. Richard C. Rich, 185–199. Lexington, MA: Lexington Books.

Peterson, Paul E. 1985. *The Politics of School Reform, 1870–1940*. Chicago University.

Peterson, Paul E., and Elena Llaudet. 2006. On the Public-Private School Achievement Debate. Paper presented before the annual meetings of the American Political Science Association.

Putnam, Robert D. 2001. Community-Based Social Capital and Educational Performance. In *Making Good Citizens: Education and Civil Society,* eds. Diane Ravitch and Joseph Viteritti. New Haven, CT: Yale University.

Ravitch, Diane. 1974. *The Great School Wars: New York City, 1805–1974*. New York: Basic Books.

Rouse, Cecilia Elena. 2000. *School Reform in the 21st Century: A Look at the Effect of Class Size and School Vouchers on the Academic Achievement of Minority Students.* Working Paper no. 440. New Jersey: Princeton University.

Simmons, R., and D. Blyth. 1987. *Moving into Adolescence: The Impact of Pubertal Change and School Context.* Hawthorne, NJ: Aldine.

U.S. Department of Education, Institute of Education Sciences, National Center for Education Statistics (NCES). 1997. *Findings from the Condition of Education 1996: Teachers' Working Conditions.* Washington, DC: U.S. Government Printing Office.

———. 2003a. *A Brief Profile of America's Private Schools, 1999–2000.* Washington, DC: U.S. Government Printing Office.

———. 2003b. *National Assessment of Educational Progress. Reading and Mathematics Assessments.* http://nces.ed.gov/nationsreportcard/nde/.

———. 2004. *Common Core Data: Public Elementary/Secondary School Universe Survey, 2003–04 (Preliminary) and Private School Universe Survey Data, 2003–2004.* www.nces.ed.gov.

———. 2005a. *Student Achievement in Private Schools: Results from 2000–2005.* Washington, DC: U.S. Government Printing Office.

———. 2005b. *Digest of Education Statistics 2004.* Washington, DC: U.S. Government Printing Office.

Vaden-Kiernan, Nancy. 2005. *Parents' Reports of School Practices to Provide Information to Families: 1996 and 2003.* U.S. Department of Education, Institute of Education Sciences, NCES. Washington, DC: U.S. Government Printing Office.

Wihry, D.F., T. Coladarci, and C. Meadow. 1992. Grade Span and Eighth-Grade Academic Achievement: Evidence from a Predominantly Rural State. *Journal of Research in Rural Education* 8, no. 2:58–70.

Wilms, Douglas J. 1985. Catholic School Effects on Academic Achievement: New Evidence from the High School and Beyond Follow-up Study. *Sociology of Education* 58 (April): 98–114.

6

How Can Anyone Say What's Adequate If Nobody Knows How Money Is Spent Now?

Marguerite Roza and Paul T. Hill

THE PLAINTIFFS IN adequacy lawsuits presume that school districts know how to use additional funds effectively. This chapter examines that presumption. We show that urban school districts do not know how they spend their existing funds, and often fail to direct extra funds to the students and programs to which they claim to attach high priority. In fact, the way urban districts currently convert dollars to resources undermines existing attempts to determine what's adequate. We therefore question whether new funds gained through adequacy lawsuits will be spent more purposively or to greater effect.

Adequacy lawsuits are generally brought on behalf of the poor and disadvantaged students served by urban public school systems. Plaintiffs argue that disadvantaged students cost more to educate, and unless the districts that serve them get extra money, the education of the disadvantaged will be underfunded. Though a lot of money is at stake in school finance disputes, the claimants usually ignore the biggest pot of money available to support schools: current school funding. As has become evident in recent years, there is very little clarity on exactly how this money is spent, who receives what, or how effective alternative uses of funds are.

Much activity surrounding the adequacy movement is centered on determining the right amount of funds to support desired student outcomes. What this view misses, however, is the importance of the choices districts make about how they spend their money. The big hole in the adequacy logic is the assumption that districts now use their resources strategically to benefit children and will use new resources to do so in the future. In truth, many schools in urban school districts already receive much more money than the minimum "adequate" amounts the plaintiffs seek, while others funded by the same pot of revenue get much less. Moreover, as we shall show, districts often spend less of their money for the education of disadvantaged students than for others, and even when they try to favor the neediest students, districts often inadvertently spend disproportionate amounts of their money on others.

Data Show Pervasive Patterns of
Uneven Spending among Schools

There is growing evidence of a dark secret about big city school spending: a great deal is spent on some schools while other schools in the same district get shortchanged. In an analysis of spending patterns in Denver, we found the district spent over fourteen thousand dollars more per pupil in one school than in another. There is a high school in Chicago in which the district spends more than five times as much per pupil as it does in another. While these examples are particularly extreme, our research has uncovered spending disparities of more than five thousand dollars per pupil among selected schools in Austin, Seattle, Baltimore, Fort Worth, and other urban districts, generating more than hundreds of thousands (and at times, millions) of dollar differences in total spending at the school level.

One might speculate that the higher spending at some schools is driven by student needs, but the examples used here focus only on the expenditure of general purpose funds, not the special category program funds that are supposed to go for some children and not for others. In other words, these spending differences have nothing at all to do with the presence of children with special needs. The reality is that spending varies significantly from school to school in a district, driven not by policy or by strategy but by budgeting practices that accommodate teacher preferences, political forces, and the haphazard distribution of many uncoordinated programs and services.

How can district policymakers and parents support this state of affairs? The bottom line is that they probably don't know how money is actually spent and how large the discrepancies among schools are. School district budgeting and accounting practices make it difficult to determine exactly how much a district spends on any one school. Reams of district budget and accounting data detail districtwide spending on particular items (e.g., teacher salaries, supplies, and administration) and by departments (e.g., elementary education, professional development, student services, and bilingual education), but typically tell us nothing about how much is spent on any one school as opposed to another.

For the last five years, researchers at the Center on Reinventing Public Education have been digging deep into district spending, uncovering spending patterns in more than thirty different districts. We began in the first district by asking what we thought was a simple question: how much does the district spend on each school it operates? After studying many districts, we are no longer surprised that this question is not easily answered. We are now accustomed to getting the answer to this question only by starting at the school level and tracing where every dollar comes from and how it is used.

The results of our work in several major urban districts are startling. They suggest that spending among schools varies substantially and often indiscriminately within districts, and that district leaders are largely unaware of where their dollars are going. And while this state of affairs has lain hidden for years, now in the midst of debates about how much *should* be spent on public education, there is good reason to take stock of where the dollars are going. Our research highlights three ways in which district budgeting practices shape spending on individual schools—often to the disadvantage of the groups of students whom the district claims to be trying hardest to serve.

Staff Allocation Practices Invite Disparities

In most districts a staff-based formula is used to allocate full-time staff to schools based on increments of student enrollment (e.g., a teacher for every twenty-five students and a vice principal when enrollment exceeds four hundred). While these base-formula-driven allocations seem innocuous enough, problems arise when districts allocate additional staff on a case-by-case basis, such as a music teacher for a specific magnet school or a technology specialist in an innovative high school. The district then totals up the number of full-time-equivalent (FTE) staff positions and converts them into dollars, using districtwide average salaries for each type of staff.

In many districts real spending disparities are created because of the case-by-case (or line-item) staff additions. Sometimes the staff allocations make sense because they address the particular needs of a school's student population (such as a bilingual education teacher for higher concentrations of non-English-speaking students). Other times, staff additions are best explained by history, parents' political influence, or special relationships between people in a particular school and members of the school board or central office staff. When tracing the source of various staff allocations, we often heard explanations such as "that school has always had an extra counselor" or "that additional vice principal was placed as part of a deal with a board member years ago" or "we put the extra art teachers in schools where art was really valued." Additional staff allocations for a Montessori program in one school amounted to a 74 percent increase in spending over the district average.

With staff-based allocations, year-to-year adjustments are made by cutting people (not dollars), which is particularly difficult in the context of local politics. In one district, when the budget cuts threatened to eliminate a music teacher specially placed in one school, students playing instruments turned out en masse at school board meetings until the idea was abandoned. Staff positions, whether justified or not, become sacred and untouchable. School principals who know how to work the system can often rake in the lion's share of these special allocations. In Denver, without exception, the newest schools, with no history of working the system, receive fewer staff per pupil than the rest of the district's schools. In Chicago the more elite lakefront schools have captured 17 percent more staff resources per pupil than what is spent districtwide (Myers 2005).

Uneven allocations of staff positions alone were responsible for spending differences of more than five thousand dollars per pupil between schools in both Cincinnati and Houston before these districts converted to a student-based allocation system in 1999–2000. With this new system, instead of allocating staff positions, districts allocate *dollars* formulaically based on student needs. While research has demonstrated the extent to which student-based allocation can reduce this source of inequity, to date only a handful of districts have been willing to abandon their staff-based allocation practices.

The Distribution of Experienced Teachers
Hurts the Poorest and Lowest-Performing Schools

Further spending differences surfaced when we converted staff FTEs into the dollar costs associated with real salaries of the teachers assigned to each school. For schools with more junior teachers, real salaries are lower, and thus real spending is lower than in schools with more senior teachers. For schools with more experienced teachers, the opposite is true. As a 2002 analysis of Baltimore City Schools showed, teachers at one high-poverty school were paid an average of $37,618 as compared with more than $57,000 at another school in the same district.

These salary differences add up to real-dollar spending differences among schools. In the same year in Cincinnati, the average salary at Rockdale was $42,431 and $59,334 at North Avondale. This gap in salaries meant that the district spent 35 percent more on North Avondale than on Rockdale.

Spending patterns that result from salary differences are not random. As has been widely documented, teacher preferences dictate assignment in such ways that the greenest teachers generally serve in the most struggling schools. In most districts, the real spending on teachers in high-poverty, low-performing schools is less than on teachers in more affluent, higher-performing schools. In Baltimore, despite nominal incentives from the state to keep more qualified teachers in low-performing schools, the average teacher in a low-performing school is paid four thousand dollars less than in the average higher-performing school. These spending differences amount to systemic "gaps" between what districts spend on teachers in different kinds of schools. Table 6.1 shows some of those gaps between the high-

Table 6.1   Teacher Salary Gap between Highest- and Lowest-Poverty
Quartiles, Selected Urban Districts

	Salary Gap
Austin	$3,837
Baltimore	$4,000
Cincinnati	$4,357
Dallas	$2,494
Denver	$3,633
Ft. Worth	$2,222
Houston	$1,880
Sacramento[a]	$4,846
San Francisco[a]	$2,247
Seattle	$2,094

[a] *Source:* Education Trust West (2005). All other data are from the Center on Reinventing Public Education (CRPE) analysis. Data in all cases are from 2003–2004,
except Baltimore (2001–2002) and Cincinnati (2000–2001).

est-poverty and lowest-poverty quartiles of schools in urban districts around the country.

These are persistent patterns. An Education Trust West report shows that for 80 percent of the fifty largest districts in
California, teachers in the highest-poverty quartile of schools are
paid less than those in the wealthiest quartile. Los Angeles Unified is a notable exception where the district has aggressively
placed more experienced teachers in the highest-poverty
schools. Without such deliberate intervention, it is unlikely that
most districts will reverse this state of affairs.

Further confounding reform in this area is that most districts
bury these patterns by accounting for labor costs using the average district salary for each school staff position, rather than
the real salary earned by individual employees. As a result, two
schools may appear to have the same per-pupil budgets while,
in reality, the district spends significantly more at the school
with more experienced teachers. As long as districts report only

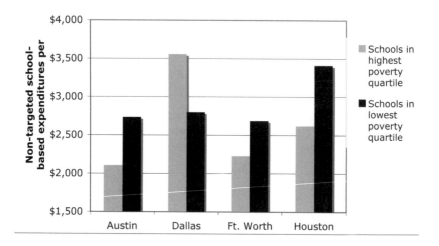

Figure 6.1   School Expenditures among High- and Low-Poverty Schools
in the Four Largest Texas School Districts (2002–2003)
Source: Data developed in original studies by CRPE.

average salaries, they will hide spending practices that shortchange high-poverty schools.

Targeting Special Program Funds to Needy
Populations Doesn't Force Spending Parity

Various federal and state funding streams attempt to aim additional funds at the neediest students, including high-poverty and
non-English-speaking children. The intent of these programs is
that the funds be used to layer on top of an even distribution of
state and local monies, so that these students get something extra.

A comparison of expenditures among schools in the four
largest districts in Texas (figure 6.1) shows the extent to which
state and local monies are *not* evenly distributed, so that in three
of the districts, the highest-poverty schools are not getting an
even share of these dollars.

In Austin, Ft. Worth, and Houston, the districts spend $629, $456, and $792, respectively, more nontargeted dollars per pupil in more affluent schools than in the highest-poverty schools. In Dallas, where the trend is the opposite and the district spends $763 more per pupil in the highest-poverty schools, state officials attribute the pattern to various court orders dictating increased spending on selected high-poverty and high-minority schools.

While the intent of federal (and some state) law is clear that targeted dollars should be providing something extra to disadvantaged populations that would not be provided otherwise (Jennings 2000), many district officials do not follow this logic. In one interview, the superintendent eagerly pointed out that he had recently placed a reading specialist in every school; he then went on to say that he funded those in the high-poverty schools with federal Title I funds, and the rest with local dollars. Contrary to the intent of the federal program, the Title I funds brought nothing extra to the neediest schools that other schools didn't also receive. Others have acknowledged that once one school in the district gets something new (like full-day kindergarten, a teacher mentor, etc.) then all the schools want it. The challenge, as some district leaders see it, is to move funds around to keep everyone happy. The effect is that not all schools have equal access to the nontargeted funds, and the targeted (or categorical) funds don't have their intended effect of boosting spending for schools that need it the most.

Funds supposedly targeted to needy students are also distributed haphazardly. In one district the incremental spending on a non-English-speaking student ranged from zero to almost four thousand dollars, depending on which school the child attended. Similarly, depending on the school, an identified gifted child could receive no extra services, or services costing more than twenty thousand dollars per gifted student. One thing is clear: the amount spent on any one kind of student—say a non-English-speaking student—varies tremendously within a district depending on what *school* the student attends.

Central Office Spending Benefits
Some Schools Much More than Others

Central budgets reflect spending not represented in school budgets, amounting to 40 to 60 percent of a district's total operating expenditures. While some of this spending pays for intrinsically central functions (e.g., the superintendent's salary, debt financing, Office of the General Counsel, and personnel), other spending is allocated to individual schools in the form of services, and the expenditures reflected in school budgets. Often, central spending benefits some schools far more than others, since some schools get special program staff, focused professional development, roaming specialists, truancy programs, and so on.

In our research, the allocation of centrally controlled resources drove more inequality in school spending than school budget staffing formulas or real salary differences. Yet districts have little means for assessing (or even coordinating) the distribution of these resources. Much of central spending is carved up and overseen by heads of central office units who create their own unique rules for distribution of their resources. For example, central budgets might fund a special art appreciation program in three schools, planetarium field trips for two schools, specialists instructed to respond to school requests, roaming therapists that can choose where to spend their day, matching funds for elective teacher education costs, and so on.

The allocation of central budgets is anything but strategic. In our tracking of every dollar expended centrally in one urban district, we found cases where the distribution of staff time was completely dependent on the individual preferences of central office staff members. One psychologist noted that she spent most of her time in the school closest to her home, even though she was supposed to serve three different elementary schools. Another gifted specialist spent the most time in a school where "the principal really valued her work." When we added it all up, some schools benefited by more than $3,000 per pupil, while others received less than $400 in centrally managed services. The findings suggest that the differences aren't just at the extremes, with schools at the twenty-fifth percentile receiving $717 per pupil and schools at the seventy-fifth percentile receiving more than double that at $1,525.

When we layered resources from centrally managed budgets over the uneven distributions created by the other patterns described earlier, we found that funds did not reverse the inequities apparent in direct school allocations but added a new layer of complexity to them. In Denver the difference between the extremes on either end of the scale showed that some schools received over $18,000 more per pupil than others, even after taking into account funds targeted for student needs. Unlike the variations in spending across districts, these variations within districts have nothing at all to do with access to resources.

How is it possible that local leaders and constituents accept such erratic spending patterns? While these patterns probably exist in nearly all urban districts, our experience suggests that district leaders simply aren't aware of the real spending patterns, and often their assumptions are wrong about what kinds of schools are getting the most money. In one district we studied, a school board was determined to increase funding for middle schools, which it thought received less money than other schools received. Our detailed analysis of that district's spending showed that middle schools were already receiving more money per pupil than elementary and high schools but the district didn't know it. Another district proposed closing two of its small schools, thinking they were more expensive on a per-pupil basis, but in fact these two small schools were operating at a lower than average cost per pupil. As the next sections will demonstrate, this state of affairs has important implications for the adequacy movement.

Current Spending Patterns Make for a
Misguided Focus on District Level Resources

Legal analysts have argued that low performance in New York City can be blamed, at least in part, on the fact that New York City spends an average of some four thousand dollars less per pupil than Westchester County. What they fail to acknowledge, though, is that individual schools in New York spend more than six thousand dollars more per pupil than other schools do in the same city. In fact, despite litigation arguing for fiscal equity across districts, recent data suggest that the real problem is spending differences across schools *within* districts, not differences across districts.

Even in Texas, where the state has worked aggressively to equalize resources across districts with the state's now-famous Robin Hood law, evidence suggests that these efforts have had no real effect on the continuing spending differences across schools within districts. As reported in Roza and Guin (2006), figure 6.2 shows that there is greater spending variation *within* Texas' four largest school districts than *among* districts statewide. In each of the four independent school districts (ISD) shown, school-based expenditures were weighted by student need—related attributes and compared across schools. A higher coefficient of variation (cv) suggests more dispersion. The cv's are consistently higher for spending across schools within districts than across districts (with enrollments greater than ten thousand). These data bluntly demonstrate that efforts to equal-

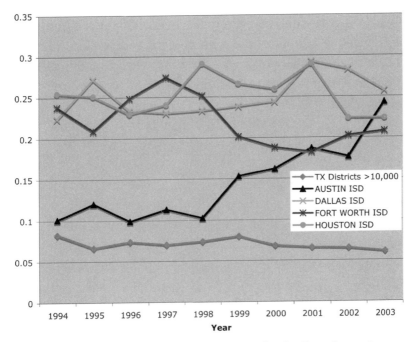

Figure 6.2   Weighted Per-Pupil Expenditures for the Four Largest Districts in Texas

ize gross district spending do little to raise the level of spending on the most disadvantaged students.

District Resources Are Not Closely Linked to Spending at any One School

These kinds of data point to one of the flaws in the adequacy logic that argues that if only districts had access to identified "adequate funds," schools would have enough resources to provide an "adequate education." The flaw is in assuming that spending at any given school is closely related to average spending as computed at the district level.

In Denver, for example, 24 percent of the schools receive more than 110 percent of the district-weighted average expenditure (a figure that takes into account the differing student needs at each school). Some 30 percent receive less than 90 percent of the district average. Deciding where spending is adequate and where it isn't in Colorado certainly requires more than an examination of this district's average expenditure.

In 2004 a Texas A&M study indicated that something near $6,200 per pupil is needed to provide an adequate education for districts in Texas. In Ft. Worth, where the average nontargeted expenditure is $5,850 in 2003–2004, the district was already spending at least this much on 17 of the district's 111 schools. In Houston, expenditures exceeded $6,200 in 121 of the district's 260 schools. At one school, the district actually spends as much as $9,400, while at another, the district spends only $3,750.

These findings suggest that the question is not what the average expenditure is at the district level, but how evenly the funds are spread among schools. Whether or not a school receives adequate funding ultimately has a lot to do with the district's allocation practices.

Determining What's Adequate at the District Level
Depends on How Resources Are Allocated

While adequacy calculations differ in their approach, data, and finally their determinations, it goes without saying that adequacy calculations based on existing district spending averages are inherently flawed, since these averages aggregate across substantial variation in spending from one school to another. Moreover, deciding what amount of resources is adequate is highly dependent on how the resources will be used. In other words, the amount of resources needed to provide a particularly defined quality of education if resources are used efficiently is very different from the amount needed if resources are used inefficiently. With higher-paid teachers teaching higher-performing students, one can hardly argue that the current allocation systems are efficient in relation to the district-proclaimed goals of closing achievement gaps.

Fiscal Practices Will Undermine the Strategic Use of New Funds

Current district fiscal practices do more than just hinder our understanding of how districts spend money. Clear spending information is critical for both financial stability and for efforts to spend money strategically. With many districts managing some two hundred thousand line items, and with averages used in place of real costs, it is no surprise that district leaders struggle to keep track of spending.

And without good spending data, most district leaders must make difficult decisions about where to place, or whether to cut out, programs without any insight into how these decisions affect the relative spending at any one school as compared with another. In one district a recent decision to cut out a three-hundred-thousand-dollar program benefiting Latino students was made without recognition that the schools benefiting from the program were already shortchanged by more than four hundred thousand dollars each year because of salary averaging. In another case, a superintendent commended his staff for diverting a greater share of the district's centrally managed resources to low-performing schools without knowing that centrally controlled programs were disproportionately benefiting the highest-performing schools.

The existing fiscal practices are not only difficult to manage, they reward political influence and fuel distrust of district leaders. In a system that lacks transparency, school leaders assume that the squeaky wheel gets the grease, and as a result, the savvy ones squeak a lot. Teacher unions assume district leaders are hiding pots of cash, so contract negotiations start out in an atmosphere of distrust. Since constituents distrust district spending decisions, voter-approved levies come with increasingly prescriptive instructions for how levy money can be used; and reporters on the education beat stay on the lookout for spending scandals. The distrust creates an adversarial environment for district leadership, further complicating an already nearly impossible job.

District Spending Practices Thwart
Policy Efforts to Improve Education

For years state and federal policymakers have attempted to do their part in addressing achievement with designated funding for high-needs students, accountability requirements, and incentives for new school models. Yet these policy efforts have undoubtedly been hindered by school districts' fiscal practices.

Billions of dollars in categorical aid are spent by states and the federal government to help districts educate high-needs students. But because of district budgeting practices, the potential effect of programs like that established by federal Title I legislation is not fully realized. As described earlier, the targeted funds layer over fragmented and incoherent spending patterns. Most notably, attempts to boost resources for high-needs populations run counter to central office staff preferences and to policies dictating the allocation of the most experienced teachers.

In the case of accountability legislation that holds schools accountable for student performance, without a doubt, success hinges on the equitable allocation of resources. Yet as we have seen, district budgeting practices do little to ensure that schools have access to similar resource levels and mask the resources that they actually receive. Current budgeting practices that yield erratic spending differences among schools undermine efforts to hold all schools to the same standards.

In recent years we have also seen efforts to encourage new options for schooling—another effort that requires spending data at the level of the school. For new schooling options to be workable, policymakers must have confidence that they receive the same funds as are spent on existing public schools. Similarly, there is no way for policymakers to assess the cost-effectiveness of new schooling models without accurate cost estimates. And on a practical level, districts with school choice will need some mechanism by which public funds can be transferred as students transfer from one school to the next in a district.

Simply layering on new funds will most likely reinforce the existing spending patterns among schools. A recent adequacy calculation from Illinois suggests that the state should be spending $2.2 billion more, amounting to just over a thousand dollar increase in spending per pupil. Despite its funding challenges, the Chicago Public Schools already spends more than that on sixty-seven of its schools. New funds brought into the existing resource allocation system will undoubtedly result in even more dollars for these sixty-seven schools. What we can't assume is that new funds will lead to comparable boosts in spending at all schools.

The Implications for the Adequacy Agenda

Nothing in the pleadings of pro-adequacy lawyers weakens the forces that lavish some schools with resources and starve others. Teachers will still prefer working in wealthier schools. The newest and least-qualified teachers will still be left in the toughest schools, just as the students in those schools will be left with them.

The real drivers of spending inequity are hidden, and the

people who most benefit from them—middle-class parents in nicer neighborhoods, as well as senior teachers and the union that works in their interest—benefit from keeping them off the table.

We know that more is already being spent on some schools than the adequacy lawsuits claim is appropriate. As we have shown, district decision making favors such schools because of their stability, the quality of leadership and teaching staff they can attract, and the activism of influential parents. What's to prevent such schools getting the lion's share of additional funds obtained through adequacy lawsuits? Nothing whatever. The lawsuits leave the districts' decision-making processes intact, making it likely that new funds will follow the same patterns as current funds do.

Districts and their lawyers who demand more money in the name of disadvantaged students must show how they will change their funds allocation methods so that money—what they now get and what they hope to get in the future—will benefit the disadvantaged children on whose behalf the lawsuits are brought. The leaders of city school systems and their lawyers must first acknowledge that practices that shortchange the poorest schools are wired into the system. And they need to make sure the wiring is pulled out.

This requires real accounting for central office costs and the transparent spending that is at least as high in poor neighborhood schools as in wealthier ones. Plaintiffs and judges also need to open their eyes to the realities that drive the distribution of teachers, teacher quality, and salaries.

Teachers should get cash incentives to teach in challenging schools, a no-no under most collective bargaining agreements. Eliminating salary averaging—and instead giving schools real-dollar budgets based on enrollment—would put a lot more money in schools in impoverished neighborhoods, which they could use to offer higher salaries, reduce class size, or buy new technology.

Especially in today's policy environment, a clear case can be made for gaining transparency in district spending. The good news is that change is taking place in a few districts, so new models do exist. New formulas and online tools are being developed to help districts take stock of their spending, which a few districts are electing to do.[1] New accounting methods help districts adapt their old systems with minimal changes to yield accurate spending data by school (Miller, Roza, and Schwartz 2005). And some districts, as mentioned earlier, are even adopting new methods for allocating resources to schools. By opting to fund students rather than school staff positions, and by identifying different spending increments for a regular student as opposed to a bilingual student, a gifted student, and so on, districts are trying to use student needs as the primary driver in allocations. Oakland, California, has gone a step further and is now experimenting with using real salaries in its school allocations. In Chicago a switch to a student-based allocation system with real-dollar accounting would relocate some $96 million (6 percent of the district's direct allocation to schools) to schools currently shortchanged by the existing system.

What is the right way to spend district money, whether existing or additional? Our data do not answer that question, and indeed no one answer is likely to be right. Some general principles are obvious—money should be spent on things that matter for student learning, in the amounts intended and for defined activities, and in ways that can be traced and evaluated. But

1. School Communities That Work, an initiative of the Annenberg Institute for School Reform, has an online tool, entitled Assessing Patterns of Resource Distribution, that allows school-spending variations, taking into account the differing needs of students, at http://www.schoolcommunities.org/resources/APRD/welcome.php.

those principles do not resolve questions about whether money should be spent according to a central district plan or allocated on a per-pupil basis to schools and then spent according to each school's own needs and strategies. We have proposed elsewhere that devolution to schools is the approach most compatible with the transparent use of funds, but that might not always be the most educationally productive course.

As state and district leaders wrestle over formulas for disseminating funds, they miss the one variable that matters most in the current system. Every state has formulas for disseminating funds to districts, and districts usually use staffing formulas to allocate teacher resources to schools. Yet we have found that the most consistent driver of unintended variations in spending has nothing to do with the complicated mix of data feeding the formulas. Schools that receive more than their share of the funds are simply better at working the system. There are principals who know how to get the best teachers, and those who skate through budget cuts. And there are vice principals who know how to get the most from the three psychologists working in the central office. There are parent-teacher clubs that make sure that when a grant ends, the grant-funded specialist stays on the district budget. And there are even school board members who manipulate formulas so as to tip the balance to their schools.

It is not news that school districts are weak stewards of money. In the past five years, nearly half of all big city superintendent firings have been directly or indirectly due to financial mismanagement. Baltimore, Seattle, and Oakland are all recent examples: superintendents persuaded their school boards to invest in big school-improvement plans just weeks before it became evident that the district was broke and could not even keep its existing commitments.

Adequacy lawsuits claiming that the addition of specific amounts to district budgets will lead to effective schooling for all children look implausible in this context. If districts don't know where their money is going now, how can they know how to use new money? Because of the way budgetary control is fragmented and driven by political bargains, is there any reason to think districts will drastically alter their practices to use new money strategically or efficiently? The data presented here suggest the answers to these questions is no.

References

Jennings, John F. 2000. Title I: Its Legislative History and Its Promise. *Phi Delta Kappan* 81, no. 7 (March): 516–522.

Miller, L. J., M. Roza, and C. Swartz. 2005. A Cost Allocation Model for Shared District Resources: A Means for Comparing Spending Across Schools. *Developments in School Finance.* U.S. Department of Education. Washington, DC: National Center for Education Statistics.

Myers, J. 2005. Some More Equal than Others. *Catalyst Chicago* (February): 2.

Roza, M., and K. Guin. 2006. *Does the School or the District Matter More in Terms of Access to Resources? A Longitudinal Study of Inter- and Intra-District Spending in Texas.* Seattle: Center on Reinventing Public Education.

7

Science Violated: Spending Projections and the "Costing Out" of an Adequate Education

Eric A. Hanushek

THE RECENT MOVEMENT to hold schools accountable for student performance has highlighted a simple fact: Many students are not achieving at desired levels.[1] Moreover, it takes little additional evidence to realize that many schools are not on an obvious path toward eliminating the gaps. These simple facts have led people with widely varying reform perspectives to enter into the fray with plans and solutions. And a natural follow-on question is invariably "what will it cost?" To answer this important question, a series of very misleading methods for estimating the costs of an improved education have evolved, but the problems

1. This analysis benefited from helpful comments by Alfred Lindseth, Paul Peterson, Martin West, and Michael Wolkoff and from the research assistance of Brent Faville. An earlier version of this paper was presented at the conference on *Adequacy Lawsuits: Their Growing Impact on American Education,* Kennedy School of Government, Harvard University, October 13–14, 2005, and a companion analysis of costing out studies is found in Hanushek (forthcoming).

with these methods are generally unrecognized (or ignored) in the public and judicial debate.

"Costing out studies" should be interpreted as political documents, not as scientific studies. They are most frequently contracted for by parties interested in increasing spending for education (including teachers unions, state departments of education, and litigants), although they sometimes involve defensive reactions of parties trying to neutralize a rival costing out study that calls for large increases in spending. They are seldom used as analytical tools to aid in policy deliberations.

The greatest premium is placed on finding "a number," because—regardless of its validity—a number for total "required" state spending can be used easily in a public relations campaign.[2] Discussion of the underlying basis for the number is usually relegated to the status of arcane academic debate, while the number itself frames the discussion. The debate about the basis for the number is not news, but the number is.

These studies *inherently* fail to provide usable information about the resources that would be required to meet a given student achievement level, at least when the resources are used efficiently and effectively. Instead, as described below, the studies merely provide spending projections that incorporate, and in general lock in, current inefficient uses of school funds.

But the other side is equally as important. Even if the specific method used in the spending projections is based on programs that have a proven track record of effectiveness—an infrequent occurrence in itself—there is no mechanism that will ensure the funds provided will be used in a way that is consistent with the effective programs. In fact, the final reports on spending projections invariably include a disclaimer that indicates one should

---

2. This explains why the Web sites for advocacy organizations give top billing to costing out studies. For example, see the ACCESS Project at http://www.schoolfunding.info.

not really expect the outcomes they consider because a variety of other forces are likely to dissipate any results. In other words, none of these studies suggests that the projected spending would actually have an effect on student achievement. To deflect criticism these studies frequently couch the analysis in terms of "opportunity" instead of outcome, but there is no scientific or objective way to define such an approach.

The warning of lack of results is perhaps the most accurate statement in a number of these studies. Little evidence supports the case that improvements have followed past court infusions of funds. This chapter concludes with additional data on such ineffectiveness, and Evers and Clopton (chapter 4) provide detailed case studies of the failure of large increases in funds to lead to noticeable improvements in student outcomes.

The fundamental issues surrounding the design and execution of these studies, described in this chapter, make these studies an inappropriate basis for judicial or legislative deliberations on school finance.

Approaches to Costing Out Adequacy

The pressures to solve the widely perceived problems with public schools have led courts and legislatures to look for a scientific determination of the amount of spending by schools that would be adequate to achieve the state standards. Indeed there has been no shortage of consultants who are prepared to provide an analytical answer to what level of spending is needed. This activity, dubbed "costing out studies," has been conducted in more than thirty-three states, and the demand for such analyses has only increased.[3] Courts are willing to write the specific numbers

3. A review of past costing out studies can be found in *Education Week* (2005). See also the ACCESS Project Web site, a project of the Campaign for Fiscal Equity (CFE), the plaintiffs in the New York City adequacy case, *Campaign*

from costing out studies into judgments,[4] and legislatures come back repeatedly to these studies to guide their appropriations. Plaintiffs entering into lawsuits about school funding, recognizing the political power that can be generated by them, now tend to make a requirement for an official costing out study as the first remedy they seek.

Much of the allure of the existing study approaches derives from their commonsensical and logical approaches to analysis, all wrapped in a patina of science. These perceived traits benefit, however, from misconceptions about the underlying analyses. They do not meet the most basic standards of scientific inquiry.

A set of now-standard approaches has been developed to answer the question "how much would it cost to make all students achieve proficiency?" These approaches differ in important ways, but they share one common feature—none can provide a valid and reliable answer to this question. As a leading proponent of the use of these costing out studies concedes, "the aura of 'scientific' decision-making that is associated with these studies can be misleading. It is not, in fact, possible to definitively identify the precise amount of money that is needed for an adequate education. Although these studies use a variety of complex statistical and analytic techniques, all of them are premised on a number of critical judgments which strongly influence their ultimate outcomes" (Rebell 2006, 5).

There is little scholarly research on these analyses. A small number of firms have conducted contract work with organiza-

---

for Fiscal Equity v. State of New York, 100 N.Y.2d 893 (N.Y. 2003). CFE states that its primary mission is to "promote better education by conducting research, developing effective strategies for litigation and remedies (including cost studies), and providing tools for public engagement." The count of earlier costing out studies comes from http://www.schoolfunding.info/index.php3, accessed on October 7, 2005.

4. See, for example, *Campaign for Fiscal Equity v. State of New York* and *Montoy v. State of Kansas,* No. 92032 (Kan. S.Ct. June 3, 2005).

tions in specific states. These analyses are, however, similar across states and across firms applying a common approach. It is also true that the common nomenclature for each type of study is itself misleading and does not accurately reflect the underlying approach to obtaining a cost estimate.

Perhaps the most commonly applied approach is the "professional judgment" method.[5] With a few nuances, the underlying method involves convening a panel of educators—teachers, principals, superintendents, and other education personnel such as business officers—and asking them to develop an educational program that would meet certain specified outcome standards. Their efforts typically produce "model schools" defined through class size, guidance and support personnel, and other programs that might be necessary. The analysts running the process then provide elements missing from the model schools (e.g., central administration costs or computers and materials) and use externally derived cost factors (e.g., average teacher or principal salaries) to the model schools. Depending on the details of the panel activities, the panels may provide guidance on the extra resources for disadvantaged children, special education, and English language learners, or these extra resources may come from cost factors assumed by the consultants.

An alternative but similar approach directly substitutes the judgment of the analysts themselves for the judgment of the professional panels. This approach has been immodestly called the "state of the art" approach by the primary firm associated with it.[6] At other times, building on the current mantra of educational

5. Examples of this (coupled with the leading groups applying the methodology) include Augenblick & Myers (2002), Augenblick, Myers, Silverstein, and Barkis (2002), Augenblick, Palaich, and Associates (2003), AIR/MAP (2004a), Picus, Odden, and Fermanich (2003), and Verstegen and Associates (2003).

6. See Odden, Fermanich, and Picus (2003).

policy, the consultants refer to it as the "evidence-based" method. The consultants sort through available research, select specific studies that relate to elements of a model school, and translate these studies into precise implications for resources in schools. It is advertised as applying research evidence to develop a set of model schools that are subsequently costed out in the same manner as the professional judgment model schools.

Neither of the previous methods makes any use of the actual spending and achievement experiences of districts in the specific state. The remaining two approaches rely on data from the schools and districts in a state.

The "successful schools" model begins by identifying a subset of the schools in a state that are effective at meeting educational goals. (Note that this is also conducted at the district rather than the school level.) The identification of successful schools may use differing methods but usually concentrates on the level of student achievement, possibly including identified input levels that relate to state policies and regulations and, infrequently, making adjustments to allow for the background of students.[7] Spending on special programs—say, remedial education or special education—is stripped out of budgets in the successful schools to obtain a "base cost" figure for each district. Typically, then, the base costs for a portion of these schools— derived from excluding some number of schools in the tails of the distribution that are presumed to be outliers—are averaged to develop a level of spending that can feasibly yield effective performance. To get the full costs of the school, expenditures on special programs are then added back, based on the distribution of students with such special needs for each school.

The "cost function" approach, sometimes referred to as the

7. See, for example, Augenblick and Myers (1997), Myers and Silverstein (2005), and Standard & Poor's School Evaluation Service (2004).

"econometric" approach, also uses the experiences of the state's schools in spending and achievement to derive what different levels of achievement would cost according to the available observations on the current practices of schools.[8] The exact methodology, while invariably involving a series of complicated statistical steps, differs in its application across states but has similarities to the successful schools analysis in attempting to characterize districts that are meeting desired achievement standards. Through statistical methods, the approach estimates how spending is affected by different student outcome levels and different student characteristics—which in turn can be used to derive the spending for different districts attempting to meet different performance levels. This approach may or may not attempt to distinguish between efficient and inefficient producers of outcomes, that is, between districts that spend more for some given level of achievement than others do.[9]

As explained below, each name is but a nom de guerre, used to market methods as serious scientific approaches to costing out adequacy. In reality, each method suffers from serious shortcomings, and each fails to provide a reliable or scientific way to estimate the needed expenditures for achieving prescribed levels of outcomes.

Why the Methods Don't (Can't) Work

Each of the approaches to determining the costs of an adequate education has some surface appeal, but their validity and reli-

8. Examples of this analysis include Duncombe, Lukemeyer, and Yinger (2003), Reschovsky and Imazeki (2003), and Gronberg, Jansen, Taylor, and Booker (2004).

9. Gronberg, Jansen, Taylor, and Booker (2004) explicitly analyzed the efficiency of districts, but this analysis was not well received in the courtroom; see the decision of Judge John Dietz in *West Orange-Cove Consolidated Independent School District et al. v. Neeley et al.,* No. GV100528 (Dist. Ct. Travis County, Texas, Nov. 30, 2004).

ability depend on their treatment of several important steps. The evidence about costing out studies is drawn from a selection of existing analyses. This selection was not drawn because the examples were particularly better or worse in application than others. Instead, they are used as convenient illustrations of the larger problems.

The theme of the discussion is that the identified problems with each approach are not ones of application that can be fixed by doing better. The problems are fundamental flaws that are not readily dealt with through fine-tuning one or the other of the approaches.

The Co-existence of Alternative Outcome Standards

The outcome standards that are considered should have a significant effect on the analysis of costs. For example, bringing all New York State students up to the level of having an elite diploma (a New York State Regents Diploma) is one of the loftiest goals of any state in the nation.[10] This standard is clearly different from the constitutional requirement which, by the interpretation of the court of appeals, was a sound basic education—a standard explicitly below the Regents Diploma. Different outcome standards frequently coexist. In fact the existence of multiple standards has proliferated, since the states moved to more comprehensive accountability systems, and the federal government intervened in linking accountability to student performance under the No Child Left Behind Act of 2001 (NCLB). All estimation of performance and costs depends directly on the outcome standard that is applied.

10. New York State traditionally had two different diplomas with varying requirements. In 1996 the New York Regents decided that all students would have to qualify for a Regents Diploma (the previously optional high standard undertaken by roughly half of the students in New York State). This requirement has had a long phase-in period with altered testing requirements.

The choice of standards is a political decision, reflecting a variety of factors. Often the state department of education or the state board of education promulgates its standards, but they are not necessarily the views of the elected officials in the executive or legislative branches of the state. More important, these standards rarely bear any relation to constitutional standards, which are often phrased in broad generalities. Nor are they the same as the mandatory standards that might exist under state or federal accountability standards.

Clearly, decisions about the standards that should be applied are not within the purview of the hired researchers doing the costing out studies. But since many costing out studies are commissioned and paid for by parties with a position on what they would like the answer to be and with an understanding of the political import of the results, neither should the definition of outcome be left to the organization that contracts for the study to be done.

None of the extant methods for costing out adequacy avoids this issue. Each must explicitly or implicitly base estimation on a definition of outcomes, but this definition requires political judgments that are seldom introduced.

Take some examples. The New York City adequacy suit, after a full round of legal decisions, was remanded to the lower court to determine a final judgment on actions to deal with the constitutional failure of the extant system. The plaintiff in the case, the Campaign for Fiscal Equity, hired two consulting firms—the American Institutes for Research (AIR) and Management Analysis and Planning (MAP)—to cost out an adequate education in New York City under the New York State constitutional requirement for providing a "sound basic education."[11] This group of

11. Details of the costing out exercises in the *CFE* case can be found in Hanushek (2005).

consultants chose, in consultation with their clients, to evaluate the costs of meeting the Regents Learning Standards that all children in New York should get a Regents Diploma. The Governor's commission, appointed to assess the appropriate State response to the court's decision, adopted a lower standard in its estimation of costs, conducted with Standard & Poor's School Evaluation Service (2004). The judicial referees, who were appointed by the court to advise it on the decision, simply ignored differences in the standards for cost estimation and were pleased by the consistency of the estimates—even though they were based on different outcome standards and should not have been the same by the logic of costing out (Hanushek 2005). The referees then went on in their report to recognize that the highest court had already said that the Regents Learning Standards were inappropriate, apparently oblivious of the fact that standards should affect any cost estimates.[12]

Take the studies commissioned in Kentucky. Three separate studies were conducted by two firms: Verstagen and Associates and Picus and Associates (who conducted parallel studies using a professional judgment and a "state of the art" approach). Picus and Associates (Odden, Fermanich, and Picus 2003) are generally willing to let their professional judgment panels define what the vague seven constitutional requirements of education laid down by the Kentucky Supreme Court mean as long as the requirements are fully met by 2014.[13] Verstegen and Associates

---

12. John D. Feerick, E. Leo Milonas, and William C. Thompson, *Report and Recommendations of the Judicial Referees* (*CFE*, Nov. 30, 2004).

13. The instructions given to the panelists about student outcomes to be achieved were: sufficient oral and written communication skills to enable students to function in a complex and rapidly changing civilization; sufficient knowledge of economic, social, and political systems to enable the student to make informed choices; sufficient understanding of governmental processes to enable the student to understand the issues that affect his or her community, state, and nation; sufficient self-knowledge and knowledge of his or her mental

(2003), on the other hand, call for these requirements along with an extensive set of input and process requirements included in the current Kentucky school regulations.

Or take Augenblick, Myers, Silverstein, and Barkis (2002) in Kansas. This analysis, which was later written into the judgment of the Kansas State Supreme Court, provides the following insight into the consultant's role in setting student outcome standards:

> A&M worked with the LEPC [Legislative Education Planning Committee] to develop a more specific definition of a suitable education. We suggested using a combination of both input and output measures. For the input measures, it was decided that the current QPA [Quality Performance Accreditation] requirements would be used, along with some added language provided by the LEPC. This additional language included vocational education as a required course offering, and identified other programs and services that might be provided as part of a suitable education. Next we set the performance measures that would be used. Again, A&M worked with the LEPC. Together we determined which content areas and grade levels would be used. The math and reading tests are given in the same grade levels every year, the writing, science and social studies tests are given in alternating years. A&M felt that the reading and math tests, which are given every year, gave us the most flexibility in setting the output measures.

Perhaps more interestingly, the definition of adequacy is not always related to outcomes. In North Dakota, Augenblick, Palaich, and Associates (2003), the successor firm to Augenblick &

---

and physical wellness; sufficient grounding in the arts to enable each student to appreciate his or her cultural and historical heritage; sufficient training or preparation for advanced training in either academic or vocational fields so as to enable each child to choose and pursue life work intelligently; and sufficient levels of academic or vocational skills to enable public school students to compete favorably with their counterparts in surrounding states, in academics or in the job market.

Myers, noted that the state did not have explicit outcome standards but instead had input requirements. For their analysis, however, they layered on a set of outcomes that were related to state goals under No Child Left Behind. (Of course, if one were just interested in providing a well-defined set of inputs and did not have to worry about the relationship with student outcomes, it would be relatively easy to calculate the level of "adequate" funding using existing spending on the inputs.)

Duncombe, Lukemeyer, and Yinger (2004) analyze the effects of different goals on the estimated costs under alternative estimation approaches. They demonstrate that reasonable differences in the loftiness of the educational goal can lead to 25 percent differences in estimated costs in their own estimation approach and 50 percent differences across alternative estimation approaches, including the professional judgment approach.

The organizations commissioning different costing out studies appear to recognize the importance of the standard chosen, often arguing for the highest standard on record (e.g., the Regents Learning Standards in CFE's instructions) or at least a full NCLB standard of 100 percent proficient. The exception is the successful schools approach, where the method *requires* that some schools meet the standard, that is, are successful. This requirement implies that the outcome standard chosen cannot be too far from current operations, and probably also explains why relatively few studies commissioned by special interest groups use the successful schools method (Baker, Taylor, and Vedlitz 2005).

The application of any standard, particularly in the professional judgment or the state-of-the-art approach, is usually left vague and up to the interpretation of the individual panel members or the consultants. This vagueness is entirely understandable, because it is far from obvious how the precise standard (or variations on it) could enter into the costing out approach. The two approaches that build on observed outcomes in a state (the successful schools and cost function methods) have a different problem. They must have actual data on how close any school is coming to meeting the standard, and more important, the methods cannot feasibly consider more than one or two explicitly measured outcomes. These constraints often call for the consultants basing studies entirely on data availability and their own outcome choices.

But arbitrary choices of objectives yield arbitrary estimates of costs. The courts on the other hand seldom focus on the standard used by the consultant and instead tend to grasp the cost identified without apparent regard for the importance of the chosen objectives.

The appropriate outcome standard clearly differs by purpose, and a variety of people enter into setting the definition in varying circumstances. But in the judicial adequacy deliberations, it is simply inappropriate to divorce these definitions from the democratic policy process and to deed it over to consultants and interested parties.[14]

The Empirical Basis of the Cost-Performance Relationship

Costing out studies address questions of the relation between a desired outcome ("adequate education") and the set of resources needed to reach that outcome. Put differently, the key to any such study is whether it accurately identifies how much achieve-

---

14. Surprisingly, not everybody would agree that outcome standards should be politically interpreted. Michael Rebell, a central figure in the New York City adequacy case and others, holds that the consultants *should* be the ones to determine the appropriate standards. In his words, "Education finance analysts should be held responsible for articulating and justifying the output measures used in their studies, and they should not be allowed to 'pass the buck' by stating that they are accepting vague or illogical output measures simply because they have emerged from the political process" (Rebell 2006, 53).

ment will change with added resources. Providing a reliable answer to this question has defied all past research, and none of the approaches to costing out an adequate education solve it.

The school systems in each state generate information about the relation between current spending and achievement, but this is seldom easy to interpret. Different school districts have different advantages in terms of the clientele they serve, and different districts make different choices about curriculum, programs, and personnel. These interact with spending decisions, often leading to little obvious relation between resources and achievement.

Decades of scientific research across a wide range of school experiences has focused on uncovering the contribution of schools to student outcomes. This substantial body of work shows, contrary to widely held popular beliefs, that there is not a consistent relation between school resources and student achievement (see Hanushek 2003). Such a finding of course presents a challenge to the consultants who attempt to describe the expanded resources needed to push student performance to the desired levels.

In the courtroom the plaintiffs seeking more resources have developed a variety of approaches to deal with this fundamental problem for their cases. One is simply to ignore the accumulated evidence, relying instead on common beliefs. Another is to set up a straw man by translating the research findings into the trivial question, "does money matter?" Some minimal level of resources is obviously necessary. Moreover, the research neither says that resources *never* matter nor that resources *could not matter*. It does, however, show that providing resources without changing other aspects of schools, such as the incentives for performance by teachers and administrators, is unlikely to boost student performance. The research evidence also fails to identify conditions or uses of money that translate resources into student performance, making it impossible to specify a combination of resources and programs that will reliably boost achievement.

The challenge of squaring actual observations with costing out studies is best seen in a candid statement in Augenblick & Myers (2002), which is also repeated in most of their other studies:

> The effort to develop these approaches stems from the fact that no existing research demonstrates a straightforward relationship between how much is spent to provide education services and performance, whether of student, school, or school district.
>
> In the absence of such a simple relationship, and in light of the fact that some people believe that there is no clear association between spending and performance, four rational approaches have emerged as ways to determine a base cost level: (1) the professional judgment approach; (2) the successful school (district) approach; (3) the comprehensive school reform approach; and (4) the statistical approach.

In other words, the *advantage (!)* of the various methods is that they do not require any basis in the empirical reality of the specific state or, more generally, any state. The professional judgment panels or the state-of-the-art researchers in particular are completely free to declare anything without worry about being contradicted by the data.

The professional judgment panels employ professional educators to develop programs and model schools, but there is never any indication that the members of these panels have any particular relevant expertise in terms of a knowledge of the extant research base, of an understanding of outcomes either inside or outside of their own locality, or of the effects of varying amounts of resources, especially when outside of their own experience. Indeed, no indication is generally given of the selection criteria for panelists. Were they chosen because they came from particularly innovative or high-quality districts? Were they chosen because of previously expressed views on programs or resources? Or were they just the subset of a larger invited group representing those willing to attend a weekend session in exchange for added pay?

The consultants performing the study seldom know any of the education personnel in the state, so they obviously need to solicit nominations—frequently from the organization commissioning the study. But since these organizations generally have a direct interest in the outcomes of the study, it seems unlikely that they will produce a random selection of educators to serve on the professional judgment panels. The nature of the selection process ensures that the judgments of any panel cannot be replicated (a fundamental concern of any truly scientific inquiry).

But reality is worse than that. The educators recognize by the nature of the exercise that their input to the process may have an effect on their future well-being. This bias and conflict of interest is most apparent in the highly publicized court cases, such as that in New York City where the professional judgment panels were employed to suggest a remedy to an already decided liability (Hanushek 2005). Such a conflict is nonetheless also generally present in less publicized circumstances when educators are asked to develop a wish list of what they might like in their schools and districts. As noted in Massachusetts, "A review of the study (ex. 35, the professional judgment study by Dr. Verstegen) suggests that the resource needs identified represent to some extent a wish list of resources that teachers and administrators would like to have if they were creating an ideal school with no need to think about cost at all."[15]

---

15. Exhibit 35 is the professional judgment study of Dr. Verstegen. The judgment goes on to note: "In this regard, as the defendants' witness Dr. Robert Costrell pointed out, if Dr. Verstegen's professional judgment model is applied to the comparison districts of Brookline, Concord/ Concord-Carlisle, and Wellesley, it appears that none of the three is spending enough to provide an adequate

The lack of any empirical linkage described in Augenblick & Myers (2002) is precisely true for the professional judgment work and close to true for the state-of-the-art work. The empirical basis of the state-of-the-art analyses is a small number of selected research studies that relate to some schooling experiences, although not the experiences in the individual state. And most important, because these are highly selective studies from the research base, there is no reason to believe that they can be generalized or that they reflect the empirical reality *anywhere*.

The successful schools analysis uses information on a selected subset of the schools, based on the performance of their students. The identification and selection of the successful schools is obviously an important step. From a scientific perspective, simply taking high performing schools defined by the level of student test scores and other outcomes is inappropriate, because performance is affected by a host of nonschool factors including family background, peers, and prior schooling experiences. If these other factors are ignored, the interpretation of the observed spending-achievement relationships in the successful schools or successful districts is unclear, because there is no sense that the relation is causal or could be reproduced by simply altering the spending of a district. Nonetheless, virtually all existing successful schools studies rely on success defined just by the level of student achievement, not by the value added of schools.

The various cost function estimation approaches explicitly rely on the spending and achievement of the schools in a state,

---

education. Dr. Costrell could identify only five school districts in the Commonwealth that are spending at a level that would be considered appropriate according to the Verstegen model (see ex. 5449), and none of the five is included in Myers' seventy-five 'successful school' districts." This latter point reappears elsewhere, as noted in the analysis below. See trial record in *Hancock , et al v. Commissioner of Education, et al,* 882 N.E.2d 1134 (2005).

thus appearing to be closer to actual schooling experiences. But, the key to interpreting these remains whether or not they have adequately identified the *causal* relationship between student performance and spending.

A simple way to understand these cost function estimates is to begin with the closely related estimation contained in the extensive literature on educational production function. A wide range of past studies—as underscored by the quotation from Augenblick & and Myers (2002) above—have looked for a relation between resources and achievement. This work involves estimating the statistical relation between achievement and a series of individual characteristics along with various measures of the resources available. This research has generally found little in the way of a consistent relationship between spending and student outcomes, and moreover almost all estimates that suggest such a resource-achievement relation often show a very small effect of resources on student outcomes (Hanushek 2003). If one were to take the estimates of the effect of resources from these, there would be the immediate implication that large amounts of resources were needed to obtain a noticeable achievement gain (again, because resources have little effect on achievement).

But now consider cost function estimates, which generally involve a statistical relation between spending as the dependent variable and achievement and characteristics of the student population as the explanatory variables.[16] This analysis essentially moves spending from the right-hand side of the equation to the

---

16. Note that these estimates bear little relationship to classic cost functions in microeconomic theory that would use an underlying assumption of optimal firm behavior to translate the production function (achievement as related to various inputs) into a cost function that describes how cost relates to the prices of inputs. None of the work in education observes any variations in input prices (e.g., teacher wages, textbook costs, and the like). The empirical work in education described here relates spending to outputs and inputs such as the number or kind of teachers, the poverty rate, and so forth.

left, and achievement to the right.[17] If the estimated effect of spending on achievement is small, this approach reverses it to indicate that it takes a lot of spending to obtain a little more achievement. But they have not necessarily identified the cost, or the expenditure needed, to obtain any outcome. They have only shown that the current pattern of spending is not very productive, exactly like the more extensive production function estimation.

This estimation is directly related to the production function estimation. It is given the new clothing of being a "cost function," but it simply describes the existing spending patterns across districts with different achievement levels.[18] The expenditure function does not indicate the minimum expenditure (or cost) of reaching any achievement level but instead identifies average spending behavior seen in districts.

No scientifically valid method is used to answer the question "how will achievement change for a given change in resources or spending?" even though the question is central to all the costing out approaches. This issue proves to be beyond the current

17. Some approaches to cost estimation are not done in this way but instead use various optimization methods to obtain the minimum cost of achieving some outcomes. They are nonetheless subject to the same interpretative issues about causation.

18. There are some serious statistical complications in this work. The econometric methodology places requirements on the modeling that are almost certainly violated in this estimation. The cost function estimation essentially assumes that districts first specify the outputs they will obtain and that this chosen achievement level and the characteristics of the student body determine the spending that would be required (i.e., achievement is exogenous in statistical parlance). This approach, while summarizing the average spending patterns of different districts, is inconsistent with the interpretation that the level of resources available to a district determines student outcomes.

The specific data and modeling are also very important. As Gronberg, Jansen, Taylor, and Booker (2004) state, "The measurement of efficiency in producing a set of outcomes is directly linked to the particular set of performance measures that are included in the cost model and the particular set of input measures."

capacity of extant scientific investigations and is not overcome by the limited investigations of the costing out consultants.

The Treatment of Inefficiency

It seems clear, and the evidence supports the case, that not all school systems use their funds as effectively as others. This fact raises a serious problem if one studies spending to understand the cost of an adequate education. Should the starting point be the current spending, accepting whatever is being done, or should there be some attempt to deal with the inefficiency issue? And should there be allowance for the fact that some districts, when given extra funds, will not use them productively to increase student performance? Without accurately identifying current inefficiencies by schools and without specifying how added resources for a district will be used, the costing out methods lack any predictive value.

In fact, the natural definition of "cost" is the *minimum* spending needed for a given outcome. It is likely in the case of schools that some districts spend more to achieve a given outcome than others do. Inefficiency is simply spending more than the least that is required. It is apparent why cost must refer to just the minimum spending to obtain a level of achievement, because otherwise the value of cost would be completely arbitrary, depending on the whim of what a district wanted to spend.[19]

The problem is that it has proven difficult, if not impossible,

19. In education discussions, efficiency often has a bad name, in part because it is taken to mean least cost without regard to the outcome. The classic misstatement of efficiency in education is found in Callahan (1962), which like many subsequent considerations failed to hold outcomes constant but instead looked at pure minimization of spending. The spending of two schools that are producing very different amounts of learning does not, by itself, say anything about the efficiency of the two schools unless, of course, the high producer is also the low spender.

for researchers to identify the true costs of meeting any goal. In fact, only rarely do studies mention possible inefficiency in spending, let alone attempt to deal with it.[20]

The divergence between observed spending and true costs has been almost entirely ignored or dismissed in past judicial proceedings. One line of judicial rulings (e.g., Wyoming and Montana) even elevates the distinction to dizzying heights by declaring that any differences in the financing of districts must be "cost based," while meaning for practical purposes "spending based." When the court retains jurisdiction and financing decisions are regularly revisited to verify the "cost basis," districts are given a clear incentive to increase their spending, regardless of the efficacy or efficiency of the spending.

An example of the idea of how inefficiency is bizarrely dealt with can be readily found from the referees in the New York City case. The plaintiffs offered the estimates of AIR/MAP (2004a), while the State, using the much lower estimates of Standard & Poor's School Evaluation Service (2004), had suggested that it was reasonable to concentrate on the spending patterns of the most efficient of the successful schools—those that did well in student performance with lower expenditure. They thus excluded the top half of the spending distribution by successful districts in their calculations. But when the referees attempted to reconcile the state's recommendation of $1.9 billion with the AIR/MAP estimates of more than $5 billion, they insisted on adding in all the high-spending districts, even when such districts did not produce better academic outcomes. After all, the referees reasoned, "there was no evidence whatsoever indicating that the

20. An exception is Gronberg, Jansen, Taylor, and Booker (2004). The academic studies of cost functions have concentrated more on efficiency issues but have been subject to potentially severe specification issues that bias the results.

higher spending districts . . . were in fact inefficient."[21] In other words, spending more to achieve the same outcomes should not be construed as being inefficient. One might then ask "what would indicate inefficiency?"

The importance of this is immediately obvious. If spending must be enough to raise achievement regardless of how efficiently resources are used, the answer is likely to be a very large number.

The existing studies are clearly best described as spending studies and spending projections, and not as cost studies. Accurate language is not, of course, used because even sympathetic readers and judges would question simple reliance on spending without a demonstration that the spending was effective. And indeed plaintiffs have been very effective in avoiding the discussion of this issue.

The deeper conundrum is that the courts cannot simply rule that districts should spend money well, particularly when the districts have no past experience with using resources well. Thus, if courts are restricted just to dictating spending levels, they are confronted with having to decide how to treat the inefficiency that is built into the conclusions derived from empirical evidence for a state. Dealing with such issues is generally far beyond the expertise of the courts.

---

21. John D. Feerick, E. Leo Milonas, and William C. Thompson, *Report and Recommendations of the Judicial Referees*" (*CFE*, Nov. 30, 2004). Much of the testimony and discussion with the referees revolved around what proportion of the high spending (or high and low spending districts) was appropriately left out of the calculations. The S&P calculations omitted the top 50 percent of the spending distribution for schools that had sufficiently high achievement to be successful, while the plaintiffs argued that this was not the general norm of those who did this type of work. Again, because it is not a scientific procedure, there is no objective way to decide among alternative cutoffs for inefficient schools. In contrast, the "efficient schools" according to the econometric approach will be many fewer—generally less than a dozen, depending on the specific analytical model.

Minimum Costs and Costing Out Approaches

Analyzing the minimum cost needed to achieve any given outcome—the putative job of the costing out consultants—requires
that cost estimation be built on the joint consideration both of
program effectiveness and of costs. Obtaining an estimate of the
minimum costs to reach the achievement goal is seldom even a
consideration in the costing out studies. Ignoring this ensures
that the results are biased above the true costs of adequacy.
Indeed such a bias is a design feature of most of the work.[22]

The professional judgment panels are generally instructed at
the beginning of the process not to consider where the revenues
would come from or any restrictions on spending. In other
words, dream big—unfettered by any sense of realism or trade-
offs. (Indeed, one reason for taking adequacy cases to the courts
is that the democratic appropriations process necessarily takes
these matters into account—and the courts might be induced to
avoid them). But those instructions to the panels apparently do
not always work to the satisfaction of consultants and clients. As
Augenblick, Palaich, and Associates (2003) state about the operation of the professional judgment panels in North Dakota,
"Finally, we should say that the members of all of the panels
behaved in a way that can best be described as parsimonious.

---

22. Rebell (2006, 59) wants to define ignoring efficient spending as a purposeful virtue of costing out studies, perhaps because he realizes that they miss
the mark in this area: "Although efficiency and accountability are obviously
major public policy concerns which should be vigorously pursued, it is ques-
tionable whether cost analysis *per se* is an appropriate venue for pursuing these
concerns. After all, the basic purpose of costing-out analysis is to determine
what level of resources, *using the best mix of current practices* [his emphasis],
will meet stated achievement goals. The extent to which major changes in current practices might produce acceptable results for lower costs is not part of
the stated mission of these studies, nor could it be without postulating a set of
hypothetical variables that would be inconsistent with the methodological prem-
ises of professional judgment panels and successful school district studies."

. . . We worked hard to push people to identify resources they thought were needed to help students meet state and federal standards in spite of their natural tendency to exclude items because local voters might not approve of them or schools could 'get by' without them." This process, more openly acknowledged in this case than in others, hardly suggests a quest for the minimum expenditure needed to achieve an outcome.

Similarly, AIR/MAP (2004a) used a two-stage panel process in analyzing the New York adequacy case where a superpanel was given the various inputs of the separate panels and could, input by input, aggregate across the panels. This process ensures that any trade-offs between programs and resources of the individual panels are lost, and the process essentially arrives at the maximum resource use sketched by the panels and not at the minimum resource use.

But the apparent irrelevance of focusing on minimum cost is nowhere as clear as in an oft-repeated discussion in the state-of-the-art analyses. Allan Odden, before he began consulting on costing out studies, wrote that educational policy should recognize that improved performance could be obtained by redirecting existing expenditures and did not have to rely on added expenditure. Such an answer does not square with the orientation of many organizations purchasing costing out studies, which are uninterested in an answer that current resources are sufficient. (If so, they would be unlikely to incur the expense of a costing out study). This incongruence of past perspectives and funders' objectives apparently leads to their standard disclaimer (Odden, Fermanich, and Picus 2003):

> Odden (1997) identified the costs of seven school wide designs that were created by the New American Schools. In subsequent analyses he showed how via resource reallocation, they were affordable at schools spending at the average or median level of expenditure per pupil in the United States (Odden & Busch,

1998; Odden & Picus, 2000). His analysis, however, did not include adequate planning and preparation time for teachers and did not standardize costs across various designs, so his 1997 cost figures are underestimated.

The standardization across designs refers specifically to the fact that some whole school models require less expenditure than others. The state-of-the-art costing out studies proclaim that in such a case one should use the *maximum* expenditure level for any of the models.

This spirit of maximizing expenditure also comes through in their programmatic recommendations. The specific programs (repeatedly recommended across states) include ones that, according to their evidence, have widely varying effectiveness and costs. Yet, instead of recommending programs that yield high achievement per dollar invested, the consultants recommend doing everything. Some parts of their program, however, would purportedly produce ten times the achievement of others for each dollar spent.

The expenditure function approach with few exceptions simply traces out the past spending of districts. Thus, unless one can assume that all districts are spending money wisely—an assumption broadly contradicted by existing research—these estimates cannot be interpreted as tracing out the minimum costs.[23]

Only the successful schools approach potentially considers such issues if high-spending districts are trimmed from the sample of successful districts that are used to calculate the cost estimate. But even here there is no uniformity, and the study might trim not only high-spending but also low-spending districts.

23. Other techniques found in the scholarly literature have been developed to consider cost minimization (see Hanushek [2002]). Even when considered, the problem is that it is generally impossible to describe how efficiency is achieved (see Gronberg, Jansen, Taylor, and Booker [2004]).

In any event, there is no way for a court or the legislature to determine how it could require other districts to behave like the successful low-cost districts. One cannot realistically specify that spending must be effective—because the existing research and knowledge base in districts is insufficient to support that. Moreover, the expenditure function analyses that consider efficiency and the successful schools analyses may be able to point to districts that are doing relatively well, but they cannot describe why they are doing well or how some other district might be able to replicate their performance.

Projecting Outcomes to an Adequate Level

All costing out studies are motivated by an argument that achievement falls short of desired levels and thus it is necessary to provide the resources needed to reach the state goals. The important question for assessing costing out studies is whether they can describe policies and resources that will reliably lead to the new, higher achievement levels. None can.

States have developed varying goals, but many of the goals have not been thoroughly tested in the sense that it is known how to reach them. Indeed, as mentioned previously, it is popular to link costing out studies to achieving the goals of No Child Left Behind, even if NCLB is generally not an obvious constitutional requirement. And no state has yet shown how it will reach the goal of having all students "proficient" in core subjects by 2014.

The professional judgment approaches assume that because the goal was given in general terms to the panel at its inception, the panelists have come up with a model school that will produce the desired results. None of the reports ever discusses this or evaluates that possibility. In fact, just the opposite. When the reports are produced, there is generally a disclaimer that indicates there is little reason to expect that students will actually achieve at these levels. Take, for example, the statement in the New York City study (AIR/MAP 2004a):

> It must be recognized that the success of schools also depends on other individuals and institutions to provide the health, intellectual stimulus, and family support upon which public school systems can build. Schools cannot and do not perform their role in a vacuum, and this is an important qualification of conclusions reached in any study of adequacy in education. Also, success of schools depends on effective allocation of resources and implementation of programs in school districts.

This "warning label" contrasts sharply with the extraordinary claim in the November 2002 AIR/MAP proposal that their study would answer the question, "What does it actually cost to provide the resources that each school needs to allow its students to meet the achievement levels specified in the Regents Learning Standards?"

Indeed, the programs and resources incorporated in the professional judgment model and its subsequent costing are predicated on just what is needed to overcome the problems in the warning label. Yet when the time comes to describe how to interpret the finished product, the consultants do not want to be judged on whether the resources actually affect outcomes.

The state-of-the-art approach relies on the consultants' conclusions about the best evidence on the effectiveness of different policies. The more recent versions of the evidence-based model (e.g., Odden, Picus, and Goetz [2006]) quantify their assessments of effectiveness of components that they include in their model school. This new information thoroughly impeaches the evidence and vividly shows its selective and biased nature. It also shows why the consultants do not use their own evidence to make any projections of achievement.

A way of seeing the problems with their work is simply to

take their analysis at face value. They design a school around a series of programs that have surface plausibility: lowered class size, full day kindergarten, expanded summer school, more professional development for teachers, and the like. For each component, they report what they believe to be the best evidence about how much achievement would be improved with each. They then advocate doing all of the components.

Looking at their evidence, however, it is easy to see why these consultants never provide an explicit projection of how achievement would improve with their model schools. The programs they advocate would, by their own reporting of the evidence, lift the achievement of the average student to beyond that of today's best performing student.[24] With the history of program outcomes in the past, it is obvious that the consultants' programs—which are simply repackaging of existing programs—will not have any such results. The easiest interpretation of this summary of their work is that the evidence is not reliable. But it also shows that the research evidence cannot provide predictions of how these overall "evidence-based" models will alter achievement.

Again, however, the authors design an "ideal" school that relies on their notions of research findings. These schools are not necessarily found anyplace in the state (where the actual schools could choose to follow such a model if they wanted to do so). The provision of resources is never accompanied by a court or legislative directive that requires the resources be used

24. The technical basis for this conclusion comes from their assessment of the "effect sizes" or the standard deviations of improvement in achievement that are predicted. (An effect size of 1.0 means that achievement would improve by one standard deviation; an improvement of one standard deviation would move the average student to the 84th percentile.) Their model school is reported to have a total effect size of 3–6 standard deviations, a completely implausible outcome that would place the average beyond the 99.9 percentile of the prior distribution.

in the way identified by the consultants. (That would probably be an even greater disaster.) Thus, providing the resources is unlikely to lead to any of the changes the consultants like, giving no reason to believe that student outcomes would increase at all.

The successful schools approach is fully rooted in the current operations of a state's schools and considers only average expenditure for the relevant group of successful schools. Therefore, it gives no information about how changing the level of spending might affect achievement. It can at best say something about meeting the generally high goals of NCLB that tend to drive court arguments *only if* some subset of schools is achieving the full standards at the time. But that appears to be unlikely.

There is no way to extrapolate the successful schools results from the currently observed outcomes of schools to a new level that is outside the range of observations on outcomes. Specifically, assume for illustration that the set of schools identified as successful has 70 to 80 percent of students reaching proficiency (which is perhaps well within current standards); there is no way to extrapolate these results to a 95 percent proficient standard.

A second extrapolation problem also occurs. When successful schools are identified just by proficiency levels on state tests, the schools identified as successful tend to have students from more advantaged families where the parents have provided considerable education to the students. The method concentrates on base spending for a typical successful school but then must indicate how much remedial spending would be needed to bring schools with students from more disadvantaged backgrounds up to the proficiency of the schools with better-prepared students. The appropriate way to do this is unclear, because again the situation is largely outside of the observations going into the successful schools analysis. The successful schools approach cannot provide any guidance to "unsuccessful" schools other than to spend the same amount of money (which many already do with poor results).

The cost, or expenditure function, approach relates spending to student performance and student characteristics. Two factors are relevant. First, it interpolates the spending differences among very disparate districts. Thus, when there are large differences in the proportions of disadvantaged students as there are in New York State (the site of analyses by Duncombe, Lukemeyer, and Yinger [2004]), it relies strongly on the functional form of the underlying statistical relationship that connects the observations of districts. Second, and more important, it does not observe districts that achieve the levels of success that are considered in the evaluation of adequacy, leading to reliance on a simple linear extrapolation of the current observations of schools with no reason to believe that this will achieve the given ends. This problem is exactly analogous to the situation above with the successful schools analysis. The problems with extrapolation for success in schools with more disadvantaged students, identified for the successful schools approach, also hold in the cost function work.

The expenditure function analysis also does not identify programmatic ways of achieving outcomes. Instead, it assumes that just adding more of the resources observed (e.g., smaller classes or more experienced teachers) will lead to higher achievement. The version of expenditure functions that includes estimates of "efficient" districts is similar to the successful schools approach—districts doing relatively well are identified but poor performers are simply told that they could do better.

In summary, each approach lacks the information needed to project outcomes outside of those currently observed, but this is precisely what the costing out exercise demands. Again, however, this is not a problem with the execution of the analyses but instead is a fundamental roadblock to the analyses. There is absolutely no reason to believe that the observed school operations provide a sufficient basis for projecting to outcomes outside of the current observations.

Incorporating Appropriate Input Prices

An integral part of all the approaches in arriving at their "cost" number is deciding on what prices to use for inputs, but the consultants not only lack appropriate data but also ignore the issues. In particular, using past salaries for teachers or past spending on administration and other inputs as the basis of calculations is inappropriate in almost all the circumstances of their projections. While some of the choices—particularly for modifying these inputs—sound reasonable, they introduce an arbitrariness that has significant effects on the resulting cost estimates.

If one wished to raise teacher quality, what would it cost? Clearly, the average salary, which is determined by the distribution of teachers of different experience levels and different amounts of academic training, cannot provide an answer to that question. What it would cost to improve teacher quality also depends markedly on whether one reproduces the current single salary schedule that does not recognize differences in quality or whether one contemplates a different pay and incentive scheme. It also depends on whether currently ineffective teachers can be replaced or whether it is necessary to wait until ineffective teachers decide to leave teaching. By considering just policies that involve adding resources to the current spending, the situation could in reality get worse. If all teachers, regardless of quality, are paid more, all teachers—including low-quality teachers—will have an incentive to remain teaching, and the ability to improve quality through replacement could become more difficult.

Such delineations of policy alternatives make it clear why the current typical behavior of a school district may not accurately indicate what improvements would cost if resources were used more effectively. It also underscores the difficulties of considering what can be done by only adjusting the funding of schools, and not considering other, more structural reforms.

The calculation of salaries is then a particularly interesting point of comparison across different studies. Sometimes the consultants simply use the average salaries for existing teachers (e.g., Odden, Fermanich, and Picus [2003]); other times they arbitrarily increase them by some amount (e.g., 10 percent in North Dakota in Augenblick, Palaich, and Associates [2003] and 18 percent in Arkansas in Odden, Picus, and Fermanich [2003]), vaguely arguing in terms of what other states spend; other times the bonus gets very high, such as the 54 percent advocated for New York City by Duncombe, Lukemeyer, and Yinger (2003), based on a regression comparison for New York districts in which New York City is a clear outlier in many of the dimensions of "uncontrollable" things such as density, poverty, and juvenile crime rates.

While the wide variance in teacher salaries has obvious and powerful effects on any cost estimates, none of these studies provides any evidence about the current quality of the teachers. Nor is there *any* research that relates teacher salary to quality, both in the ability to raise student achievement, and in the long-run supply of teachers of differing quality. So this becomes a whimsical adjustment based on the consultant's vague sense of whether average salaries are high enough or not (for some unspecified quality level). And if they say they want to improve teacher quality, they simply increase the average salary by some arbitrary percentage.

Staying with existing structures and incentives—pervasive in all the methods—makes the reliance on average spending for the components not specifically identified particularly dubious. For example, it is common to take existing central office and administrative expenditure as given and necessary. But there is no evidence that this is now the best way to organize schools or that it represents the minimum cost of providing a level of achievement.

The logic of developing estimates of the minimum cost of providing an adequate education calls for making decisions with an understanding of both the cost and the effectiveness of various inputs. The protocols of the costing out studies ensure that such decisions are never considered.

The Arbitrariness and Manipulability of Spending Estimates

While courts in various states have had differing responses to specific costing out studies, the general presumption is that all are trying to estimate basically the same thing—the resources required for adequacy. The results from past studies, however, indicate a clear arbitrariness in the results, which—because it is known to the parties supporting studies—permits strategic behavior and the manipulation of the results. Such circumstances compromise any claim to scientific underpinnings for the work.

The choice of approach for costing out is generally decided by the party requesting the work to be done. It appears that it might be a purposeful strategic choice, since many costing out studies are funded by parties with an interest in the outcome of the study (e.g., see Hanushek [2005]). For example, an analysis of differences across alternative analyses within the same state by the same researchers in four other states shows that the professional judgment method yielded estimates of "adequate" expenditure that were 30 percent above the successful schools method (Baker, Taylor, and Vedlitz [2005]). This apparently has influenced the choice of method by clients.[25]

A compilation of the estimated per-pupil expenditure for an adequate education across states and studies clearly indicates the arbitrariness of the estimates (Baker, Taylor, and Vedlitz [2005]). Even after adjusting for geographic cost differences across states and putting the estimates in real terms for 2004, the estimates differ by more than a factor of three. It is difficult to imagine what true underlying differences across states could drive such differences, since schools across the states look very similar, using similar curricula, approaches, and the like. But it is consistent with providing politically palatable estimates for the different state deliberations, because, for example, the citizens in many low-spending states would have difficulty accepting the current levels of spending in New York, let alone the post-judgment levels.

If the methods systematically produce very different results when addressing the same question, they obviously cannot be taken as giving a reliable and unbiased estimate of the resource requirements. Nor can they satisfy the most rudimentary criteria of scientific validity.

More Accurately Naming the Approaches

As with many concepts and ideas in school finance deliberations, the nom de guerre for each of the methods engenders

25. For example, Thomas Decker describes the choice of the professional judgment model for the costing out study to be commissioned by the North Dakota Department of Public Instruction: "The professional judgment approach we were aware would probably produce a higher cost estimate for achieving adequacy than successful schools." *Williston Public School District No. 1, et al v. State of North Dakota, et al,* Civil No. 03-C-507 (Dist. Ct., N.W. Jud. Cir. 2003 (Transcript of Deposition of Thomas G. Decker, August 17–18, 2005, 312).

confidence in the work, but it is a misplaced confidence. None of the names is accurate.

The professional judgment model relies on professional educators, but they generally lack expertise in designing programs to meet objectives outside of their experience. While they may have experience making trade-offs in current budgets, they do not have the research knowledge or personal experience to know how resources will change if they design a program for much higher student outcomes or of student body compositions that are outside their experience. But most important, they are asked to participate in a study where the outcomes of the study might directly affect their own pay, working conditions, and school situation, thus providing an incentive for them to distort whatever answers they might have. Thus, a much more accurate name of this approach is the *educators' wish list* model.

The state-of-the-art, or evidenced-based, model makes little effort to assess the accumulated evidence on different aspects of schooling. Instead, the highly selected evidence leads not to a scientifically grounded model but instead to the *consultants' choice* model. The results would vary dramatically if a different set of consultants, perhaps with a different focus, attempted to apply their understanding of the existing research base. In the end, the research base is simply too thin to have any consensus view about what an "evidence-based" school would look like (and, if that were not the case, it would be striking to find that none of the schools in the state already use the consultants' model).

The successful schools model begins with the identification of schools that are meeting some performance standard and then calculates the costs in an efficient subset of these successful schools. However, when the basis for judging school performance is student achievement, the resulting subset of schools conflates the various reasons why achievement may be high, including family background and other peers in the schools. By relying on the observed performance for the "successful" set of schools, it has no way to project the results to a higher performance level. This approach is better labeled the *successful students* model, because it does not separate the success or failure of the school from other factors.

The cost function approach is designed to trace out the minimum costs for obtaining given outcomes. Unfortunately, this is true only if all school districts are operating efficiently—a situation that is known not to exist. The attempts of some to deal with inefficiencies have no general scientific foundation. These approaches capture the *expenditure function* for schools by identifying the average spending of districts with different achievement levels and student characteristics. They do not trace out the necessary cost of given performance levels, and thus cannot show the cost of an adequate education.

Evidence on the Results

The approaches to costing out produce an estimate of the resources needed to achieve an adequate education. For a variety of reasons, it is difficult to link these efforts to any results. First, courts and legislatures seldom faithfully enact the consultants' dreams. Second, the consultants generally counsel not to take the results too seriously (see the AIR/MAP disclaimer above).[26]

Augenblick, Palaich, and Associates (2003, II-3), go further in their analysis of North Dakota schools to discuss a lack of empirical validation of the professional judgment work. "The advantages of the approach [professional judgment] are that it reflects the views of actual service providers and its results are

26. This admonition is particularly strange in the state-of-the-art approach, however. They claim to have chosen the best methods based on research and evidence. If that is the case, shouldn't it be mandated for all districts?

easy to understand; the disadvantages are that resource allocation tends to reflect current practice and there is *only an as-*
sumption, with little evidence, that the provision of money at
the designated level will produce the anticipated outcomes"
(emphasis added).

While Augenblick, Palaich, and Associates (2003) did not
look at the evidence, it is possible to do so in this case and in
many other such costing out exercises. The authors use the professional judgment results to prescribe the spending for each of
the K–12 districts in North Dakota in 2002. Two points are important. First, there is a wide variation in the calculated needs
of districts. Second, sixteen districts were actually spending
more in 2002 than the consultants (through their professional
judgment panels) thought needed to achieve the full performance levels for 2014.

Because we have student performance information in North
Dakota for 2002, we can see how performance is related to the
fiscal deficits and surpluses that they calculate. It seems natural
to think that districts with surplus expenditures are indeed performing above their achievement goals. It is also plausible to
think that districts with smaller fiscal deficits are closer to
achievement goals than those with larger fiscal deficits. (Note
that the method and its application are designed to account for
any different resource demands arising from the concentration
of a disadvantaged population, school size, and the like—implying that the consideration of simple, bivariate relationships of
deficits and performance are appropriate.)

A regression of reading or math proficiency percentages of
North Dakota districts on the deficits indicates a statistically significant *positive* relationship. In other words, the larger the deficit, the higher is the student performance. Figures 7.1 and 7.2
plot calculated PJ (professional judgment) deficits against student achievement, immediately casting doubt on the value of the

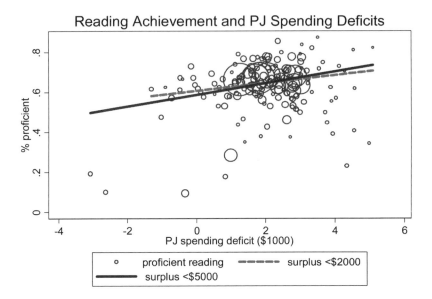

Figure 7.1   North Dakota School Districts' Professional Judgment
Results (2002 Reading)
Note: Size of circles reflects student enrollment in each district.

professional judgment approach in this case. The solid line
shows the regression of funding deficits on achievement.[27] Of
course, because there are a few very large surpluses, the regression lines in the pictures could be distorted. But, the dashed
line shows that a positive relationship between deficits and
achievement still remains when all districts with surpluses
greater than two thousand dollars are excluded from the calculations.[28]

These are hypothetical exercises, however. It would be use-

27. By their method, the estimated needs should already account for differences in student backgrounds, and therefore the simple regression corresponds
directly to their interpretation of the analysis. For this figure, the two school
districts with surpluses greater than five thousand dollars per student are excluded. Including them would make the regression line even steeper.

28. Five districts out of the sixteen with identified surpluses have surpluses
greater than two thousand dollars per student.

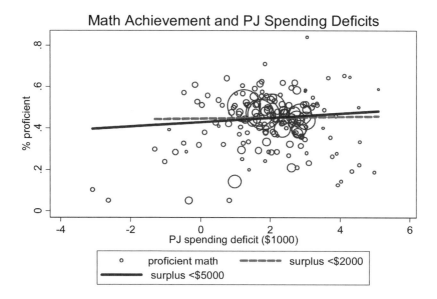

Figure 7.2   North Dakota School Districts' Professional Judgment Results (2002 Math)

Note: Size of circles reflects student enrollment in each district.

ful to see what happens when model results are introduced into actual decisions. This is difficult for a variety of reasons. First, while there is considerable current court activity, most of it has not fully worked through the courts and the legislatures and into the schools. Second, it is often difficult to obtain good comparisons to identify the effects of the court decisions.

Because Wyoming is tucked away out of sight of the East Coast media, few people outside of school finance insiders have followed the events of court decisions in Wyoming. But this example gives some insight into the effect of the adequacy decisions and court appropriations.

The Wyoming courts have considered the constitutionality of the school finance system since 1980. In *Campbell County School District v. State of Wyoming I* in 1995, the Wyoming

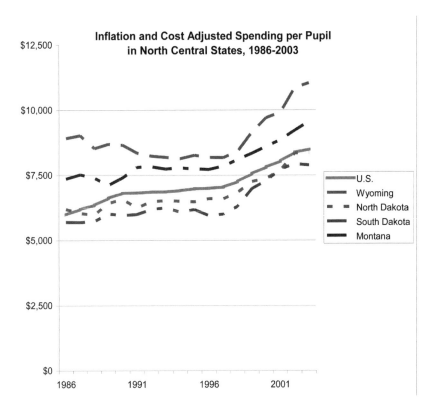

Figure 7.3   Spending History in North Central Comparison States

Supreme Court refined its schooling standard, as described in its subsequent 2001 decision:

> This court made it clear it is the job of the legislature to "design the best educational system by identifying the 'proper' educational package each Wyoming student is entitled to have." . . . Unlike the majority of states which emphasized additional funding, equalized funding, or basic education, Wyoming views its state constitution as mandating legislative action to provide a thorough and uniform education of a quality that is both visionary and unsurpassed. (*Campbell II*, 18)[29]

29. *Campbell County School District v. State*, 907 P. 2d 1238 (Wyo. 1995); *Campbell County School District v. State*, 19 P.3d 518, 538 (Wyo. 2001).

This ruling presents a license for school districts to shop for virtually any program or idea that is arguably better than what they are currently using.

An element of this history that is important, however, is that the court has ruled that the school finance system must be "cost based" (which, as noted above, really means spending based). The legislature attacked this problem by asking MAP to develop a basic funding model, which it did based on an underlying professional judgment model. The basic model has been used in developing block grants to districts in order to meet differences in circumstances (disadvantaged populations, school size, etc.).

As might be imagined, this process of developing a visionary system—based on input criteria—leads to spending increases. Figure 7.3 compares Wyoming spending with that of a set of adjoining north central states (Montana, North Dakota, and South Dakota) and with the U.S. average.[30] The courts' direct effect on spending is clear from this figure. Wyoming pulled away from the nation after the *Campbell I* decision in 1995. The

30. The other comparison states followed the normal democratic appropriations process and were not driven by court intervention in fiscal and policy decisions. Montana's future may be very different, however. In Spring 2005, the Montana Supreme Court upheld a lower court decision that the state was in constitutional violation of its requirement to "provide a basic system of free quality public elementary and secondary schools." *Columbia Falls Elem. School Dist. No. 6 et al v. the State of Montana*, No. 04-390 (Mont. S. Ct. Mar. 22, 2005). The District Court had identified the "major problems" in existing funding legislation as: "it provided no mechanism to deal with inflation; it did not base its numbers on costs such as teacher pay, meeting accreditation standards, fixed costs, or costs of special education; increases in allowable spending were not tied to costs of increased accreditation standards or content and performance standards; relevant data was already two years old when the bill was passed; and no study was undertaken to justify the disparity in ANB dollars [the 'average number belonging' entitlement] dispensed to high schools as compared to elementary schools. From these credible findings we must conclude that the Legislature did not endeavor to create a school funding system with quality in mind" (10). This reliance on input criteria could place Montana in a situation similar to Wyoming's.

Table 7.1   Rankings on 2005 NAEP Tests for North Central
Comparison States

	Math		Reading		Science[a]	
	grade 4	*grade 8*	*grade 4*	*grade 8*	*grade 4*	*grade 8*
All students						
Montana	17	6	10	6	5	1
North Dakota	8	5	8	2	4	4
South Dakota	14	4	18	8	—	—
Wyoming	7	17	14	10	7	9
Free- or reduced-lunch students						
Montana	9	5	7	5	5	1
North Dakota	3	2	3	2	2	3
South Dakota	7	1	10	3	—	—
Wyoming	1	7	1	4	4	5

[a] Science rankings for 2000 based on thirty-nine states for all students or thirty-eight states for free- or reduced-lunch students.

other states' spending patterns have not been dictated by judicial actions but instead have resulted from the democratic appropriations process. These patterns are significantly below those of Wyoming and follow roughly the national pattern.

The interesting thing is to observe the outcomes of Wyoming's court-supervised spending and how they compare with those of other states. The four north central states shown in figure 7.3 are remarkably similar in demographics, implying that simple comparisons of student achievement are appropriate.[31] Table 7.1 provides rankings on the National Assessment

31. The comparison states have similar demographics, although Wyoming has some advantages in income and education of adults. Montana and South Dakota have lower incomes and higher child poverty rates, while Wyoming has the highest income and the most high school graduates of the adult population. All states have more than 85 percent white populations with larger American Indian populations in Montana, North Dakota, and South Dakota and a larger Hispanic population in Wyoming.

of Educational Progress (NAEP) of the comparison states in 2005 for math and reading and in 2000 for science. The top panel gives comparisons for all students, while the bottom panel is restricted to students on free and reduced lunch. In fourth grade, Wyoming tends to do better than the comparison states in math and in both math and reading for low-income students. But in eighth grade, two things are important. First, Wyoming does worse across the board than the comparison states. Second, even though Wyoming consistently (and increasingly) spends more for schools, the rankings generally drop from fourth to eighth grade. In contrast, rankings in the other states generally improve from the fourth to eighth grades. Moreover, while comparisons over time are more difficult, Wyoming student performance relative to the nation declined from 1992 to 2005 in fourth grade reading and math and in eighth grade math.[32]

Table 7.2 provides comparisons on the measures of school retention and college continuation. North Dakota and South Dakota, the two lowest-spending states, consistently outperform Montana, with Wyoming performing noticeably worst on each of these outcome measures.

Although some may interpret this record as saying that it is necessary to wait longer and to mandate even more spending, the Wyoming performance information to date gives little indication that this would be a productive path.

Interestingly, under the court mandate to periodically recalibrate the spending for schools, Odden et al. (2005) investigated the funding of Wyoming schools in 2005. They concluded that the current spending—already fifth highest in the nation in 2003—was some 17 percent shy of adequate.[33] They presum-

32. While all states participated the NAEP for math and reading in 2005, only a subset voluntarily participated in the earlier grades. Eighth grade reading was not assessed until 1998 but did improve between 1998 and 2005.

33. State rankings adjust for cost of living calculated from a wage index for

Table 7.2   School Attainment for North Central Comparison States
(State Rankings in Parenthesis)

	Montana (%)	North Dakota (%)	South Dakota (%)	Wyoming (%)
Ninth graders' chance for college by age 19	42.5 (12)	61.8(1)	48.1 (6)	40.4 (20)
College continuation rate of high school graduates	54.7 (30)	73.7(1)	60.9 (13)	55.1(29)
Percent of adults aged 18–24 with high school diploma	91.1 (10)	94.4 (2)	92.0 (5)	86.5 (31)
Percent 9th–12th graders who dropped out	4.2 (22)	2.2(1)	3.9 (14)	6.4 (42)

Source: U.S. Department of Education, Digest of Education Statistics, 2003. Washington, DC: National Center for Education Statistics, 2004; NCHEMS Information Center, http://www.higheredinfo.org/dbrowser/index.php?submeasure=62&year=2002&level=nation&mode=data&state=0.

ably believe that another substantial dose of funding would produce more than the last dose of funding, but never go so far in their lengthy report as actually projecting an improvement in student achievement. And, indeed, the Wyoming legislature in 2006 voted appropriations that exceed even the Odden et al. (2005) spending plans, moving Wyoming perhaps to the highest spending state in the nation. The legislature did not, however, specify that schools must put in place the "evidence based" programs, just that they get sufficient money that they could permit it by the consultants' calculations.

The North Dakota and Wyoming data are not isolated in-

_____

nonteaching college graduates. The new estimates, according to the Access account (http://www.schoolfunding.info/news/policy/1-6-06WYcoststudy.php3 as accessed on March 10, 2006), would increase unadjusted spending from $9,965 per pupil to $11,635 per pupil. These calculations correspond to increasing total spending by $142 million to approximately $987 million, a 17 percent increase.

stances of lack of achievement gains from spending. Evers and Clopton (chapter 4) provide a series of case studies that involve significant spending increases—some from judicial actions and some from normal appropriations—that were unaccompanied by any gains in student outcomes. Their case studies cover large and very well-observed districts that nevertheless failed to use dramatically larger resources in effective ways.

Outcomes versus "Opportunity"

As previously noted, virtually none of the reports says that the calculated level of resources will yield the outcomes that the consultants are striving to obtain. When it comes time to write the reports—and to produce a document by which the consultants might be judged—the language generally changes to providing an "opportunity" to achieve the standard, not actually achieving the standard.

The motivation for the underlying costing out analyses is that children are not learning at a putative constitutional level (or an NCLB level or a state standards level), but the reports never say explicitly that the resources identified in the study are either necessary or sufficient to achieve these levels. Instead, they say that the resources will provide an opportunity to reach the standards.

This change of language means that the consultants are not predicting any level of achievement if the stated resources are provided. None of the reports states that the added resources will yield achievement that is any higher than currently observed. The reports provide no predictions about outcomes, and thus they are *completely unverifiable*. Said differently, there is no scientific basis for deciding among alternative "cost" estimates, because the data on student outcomes are not informative.

By implication of the report language, a wide range of spending could produce the same level of student outcomes. For example, why not project added spending of $10 billion a year (as opposed to $5.6 billion a year) for the New York City *CFE* case as the amount that would provide an opportunity to achieve some undisclosed higher student achievement? Why not $1 billion a year?

The obfuscation about what is being calculated is easily seen in the AIR/MAP report for the CFE litigation in New York. Remember that the report is entitled "The New York Adequacy Study: Determining the Cost of Providing All Children in New York an Adequate Education." Since an adequate education is defined in terms of student outcomes, one might think that this implies that students provided with the specified resources would achieve the adequate outcomes (in this case, achieve the Regents Learning Standards). Moreover, the report is laced with language suggesting that the AIR/MAP consortium is considering actual student achievement and not some more ethereal concept:

- In describing the purpose of the report, the AIR/MAP team states, "To remedy this injustice, Justice DeGrasse ordered a number of reforms. As a first, 'threshold task,' he charged the state with assessing 'the actual costs of providing a sound basic education in districts around the State'" (AIR/MAP 2004b, 6).

- Subsequently, when describing what was the objective, the report states, "32 organizations from throughout the state came together to initiate a one year, cutting-edge costing-out study—supported by grants from several major national foundations—that will determine the actual amount of funding needed in each school district to provide an adequate education to all students throughout the state" (AIR/MAP 2004b, 6).

- Finally, in instructing the professional judgment panels, it states, "Specifically, your task is to design adequate instructional and support programs for students in Kindergarten through twelfth grade that you are confident will meet the expectations specified in Exhibit 1 for the student populations described in the assumptions listed below" (AIR/MAP 2004b, 64). Exhibit 1 then discusses both the NCLB student outcome standards and what is necessary to reach the Regents Learning Standards.

The language is qualified, however, whenever a reader might infer that some explicit outcome is being considered in the analysis. For example, when the goals related to Regents Learning Standards are mentioned in the AIR/MAP report, they are prefaced with "an opportunity to achieve."[34] Nonetheless, there is little doubt that the reader is intended to interpret this as the actual student outcomes to be expected from providing the added resources.

This situation is not specific to the AIR/MAP report but pervades all the methods and all the available reports. The possible exception is some of the successful student or expenditure projection studies, where the authors might suggest that a given school could achieve a given level of performance *if it could figure out why some other school achieved that level and if it could reproduce it in another setting.* Yet no guidance on either the source of achievement or the way to reproduce it is ever given.

---

34. The judicial referees who declared that $5.63 billion a year was the right number consistently use the "opportunity" language. Perhaps knowing that this spending is unlikely to produce actual achievement of the kind they believe represents a sound basic education, the referees also call for regular costing out studies on a four-year cycle.

The translation of the objective into an undefined opportunity is particularly problematic when, like Wyoming, the finance system is supposed to be cost (i.e., spending) based. *Cost* necessarily refers to what is needed to purchase some good or service. But if the good or service to be purchased is undefined, and if it could mean a broad range of different things, the cost must logically also be undefined—because there is no way to link an observable outcome to an expenditure.

Instead of attempting to parse the very careful language of all the costing out studies, however, consider the opposite perspective. If the costing out studies do not provide a clear view of the outcome that would be expected, they become just the whim of the consultant—even when based on a method that has previously been applied or has a "scientific" air to it. There is no way to judge among alternative spending projections based on any evidence that will become available about outcomes, thus putting each projection in the category of personal opinion and not science. There is no obvious reason for giving deference to the personal opinion of consultants hired by interested parties in the debates.

This work also does not help the political and legislative debate on school finance. The studies are designed to give a spending number. They do not indicate how achievement is likely to be different from the current level if such an amount is spent. Neither do they suggest how achievement (or even opportunity) would differ if a state spent 25 percent more or 25 percent less than the consultants' personal opinions about what should be spent.

Conclusions

The traditional focus of courts on equity in school finance, defined simply as funding for schools, has given way to one on outcomes and adequacy. And this has moved the courts into areas in which they are completely unprepared. Specifically, if one wants to improve outcomes or change the distribution of outcomes, how can the court do it? After all, even if the courts want to do so, they cannot simply mandate a given level of student achievement. Instead they must define any judgments in terms of instruments that will lead to their desired outcomes but that can be monitored by the court. This necessity returns the decision making to a focus on money and resources.

But how much money translates into the desired schooling outcomes? For this, the courts have come to rely on outside consultants (frequently hired by interested parties) to provide the answers.

These consultants, and the people who hire them, suggest that the subsequent "costing out" exercises provide a scientific answer to the disarmingly simple question, "how much does it cost to provide an adequate education?" Nothing could be farther from the truth. The methods that have been developed are not just inaccurate. They are generally unscientific. They do not provide reliable and unbiased estimates of the necessary costs. In a variety of cases, they cannot be replicated by others. And they obfuscate the fact that they are unlikely to provide a path to the desired outcome results.

As Augenblick, Myers, Silverstein, and Barkis (2002) eloquently state in their study, which was the basis of the Kansas judgment, "None of these approaches are immune to manipulation; that is, each is subject to tinkering on the part of users that might change results. In addition, it is not known at this point whether they would produce similar results if used under the same circumstances (in the same state, at the same time, with similar data)." This possibility gives considerable latitude to the courts to pick whatever number they want. Judge Bullock in his Kansas decision speaks favorably of the Augenblick & Myers cost estimates (with the above caution included), while justifying his choice in part by noting that a parallel ruling in Montana opined:

> The testimony of Dr. Lawrence Picus of the University of Southern California (who also testified for Defendants in the instant action) was found to lack credibility in that, while testifying for the defense in Kansas and Massachusetts he had opined those systems were equitable and thus constitutional, but in Montana (while testifying for the plaintiffs) he opined Montana's funding was inadequate and violative of constitutional requirements—both opinions being based astonishingly on undisputed numbers showing Montana's system more equitable in virtually every measurement than either Kansas or Massachusetts. In other words, Dr. Picus "danced with the girls that brought him."[35]

Costing out studies are political documents, almost always purchased by clients with an agenda. When there are no accepted scientific standards for their conduct, when there are few empirical restraints, when they cannot be replicated by others, when the outcomes of any changes cannot be verified based on observed data, and when there is no requirement for consistency across applications, it should come as little surprise that the estimates please the party who has purchased them.

The history of the use of costing out studies in the New York City case highlights the political nature of such studies. During the original trial, the defense sought to introduce a professional judgment analysis of the costs of an adequate education in New York. It concluded that the school district's existing $10-billion-plus budget was sufficient to meet the constitutional requirements for a sound basic education. The plaintiffs successfully argued that the approach had not been shown to be generally

35. _Montoy v. State_, Case No. 99-C-1738 (Dist. Ct. Shawnee County, Kan., Dec. 2, 2003).

scientifically accepted and that it was inadmissible hearsay, leading to rejection of the study conducted by the MAP consulting firm. The plaintiffs then hired the same firm, MAP, along with another consulting firm to cost out an adequate New York City education, although this time based on the plaintiffs' specifications of what was adequate. The judicial referees received the plaintiffs' report and passed it back to the judge with none of the qualms that had led the judge originally to exclude such testimony or analysis.

Courts need guidance if they are to enter into the adequacy arena, because they have no relevant expertise in the funding, institutions, and incentives of schools. They are generally eager to have somebody tell them the answer, so they are willing to jump on "the number" even while recognizing that it might have problems.

The message here is that the existing costing out methods do not and cannot support such judicial decision making. There is also the distinct possibility that pursuing such a policy will actually worsen rather than help students and their achievement.

The methods provide spending projections, based crucially on existing educational approaches, existing incentive structures, and existing hiring and retention policies for teachers. Essentially, each calls for doing more of the same—reducing pupil-teacher ratios, paying existing teachers more, retaining the same administrative structure and expense. These are just the things that districts have been doing for the past three decades.

On the other side, *none* of the existing costing out studies claims that providing the resources they call for will have *any* effect on achievement. They very carefully skirt a statement that would tie them to results, couching explicit spending figures in the vague and undefined language of "opportunity." And for good reason. Past experience provides plentiful evidence of instances where funding was increased with no fundamental change and where student performance did not change. The consultants know well that even if we take a large leap of faith and believe that the programs they describe will be effective, nobody enforces the adoption of these programs when resources are added. But if the "required" spending for an adequate education is not related to an expectation about student outcome, what is the meaning of the spending that is called for? We know that it is possible to get no results while spending even more. Couldn't we also get no results by spending less?

There is a pernicious result, however. It is not just that money is wasted by investing in ways that have no payoff. Following the recommended spending projections reinforces and solidifies the existing structure of schools that has not produced, almost certainly to the detriment of students. They offer only a blind and unsupported hope of bringing about the kinds of improvements that they purport to cost out.

References

AIR/MAP. 2002. *A Proposal for Determining Adequate Resources for New York Public Schools*. American Institutes for Research and Management Analysis and Planning (November 27).

AIR/MAP. 2004a. *The New York Adequacy Study: Determining the Cost of Providing All Children in New York an Adequate Education, Volume 1—Final Report*. American Institutes for Research and Management Analysis and Planning (March).

———. 2004b. *The New York Adequacy Study: Determining the Cost of Providing All Children in New York an Adequate Education, Volume 2—Technical Appendices*. American Institutes for Research and Management Analysis and Planning (March).

Augenblick & Myers, Inc. 2002. *Calculation of the Cost of an Adequate Education in Indiana in 2001-2002 Using the Professional Judgment Approach*. Prepared for Indiana State Teachers Association. Denver, CO: Augenblick & Myers, Inc. (September).

Augenblick, John, and John Myers. 1997. *Recommendations for a Base Figure and Pupil-Weighted Adjustments to the Base Figure for Use in a New School Finance System in Ohio.* Denver, CO: Augenblick & Myers, Inc. (July).

Augenblick, John, John Myers, Justin Silverstein, and Anne Barkis. 2002. *Calculation of the Cost of a Suitable Education in Kansas in 2000-2001 Using Two Different Analytical Approaches.* Prepared for Legislative Coordinating Council. Denver, CO: Augenblick & Myers, Inc. (March).

Augenblick, Palaich, and Associates, Inc. 2003. *Calculation of the Cost of an Adequate Education in North Dakota in 2002-2003 Using the Professional Judgement Approach.* Bismarck, ND: North Dakota Department of Public Instruction (September).

Baker, Bruce D., Lori L. Taylor, and Arnold Vedlitz. 2005. "Measuring Educational Adequacy in Public Schools." Bush School Working Paper #580, Texas A&M University (September).

Callahan, Raymond E. 1962. *Education and the Cult of Efficiency.* Chicago: University of Chicago Press.

Duncombe, William, Anna Lukemeyer, and John Yinger. 2003. "Financing an Adequate Education: A Case Study of New York." In *Developments in School Finance: 2001-2002*, edited by William J. Fowler, Jr., 127–154. Washington, DC: National Center for Education Statistics.

———. 2004. "Education Finance Reform in New York: Calculating the Cost of a 'Sound Basic Education' in New York City." CPR Policy Brief No. 28/2004, Center for Policy Research of Syracuse University, New York (March).

Education Week. 2005. "Quality Counts 2005: No Small Change— Targeting Money toward Student Performance." *Education Week* (Washington, DC). January 6.

Gronberg, Timothy J., Dennis W. Jansen, Lori L. Taylor, and Kevin Booker. 2004. *School Outcomes and School Costs: The Cost Function Approach.* Texas A&M University.

Hanushek, Eric A. 1999. "The Evidence on Class Size." In *Earning and Learning: How Schools Matter*, edited by Susan E. Mayer and Paul E. Peterson, 131–168. Washington, DC: Brookings Institution.

———. 2002. "Publicly Provided Education." In *Handbook of Public Economics*, edited by Alan J. Auerbach and Martin Feldstein, 2045–2141. Amsterdam: Elsevier.

———. 2003. "The Failure of Input-Based Schooling Policies." *Economic Journal* 113, no. 485 (February): F64–F98.

———. 2005. "Pseudo-Science and a Sound Basic Education: Voodoo Statistics in New York." *Education Next* 5, no. 4 (Fall): 67–73.

———. Forthcoming. "The Alchemy of 'Costing Out' an Adequate Education." In *School Money Trials: The Legal Pursuit of Educational Adequacy*, edited by Martin R. West and Paul E. Peterson. Washington, DC: Brookings Institution.

Myers, John L., and Justin Silverstein. 2005. *Successful School Districts Study for North Dakota*. Augenblick, Palaich, and Associates, Inc. (August 15).

Odden, Allan, Mark Fermanich, and Lawrence O. Picus. 2003. *A State-of-the-Art Approach to School Finance Adequacy in Kentucky*. Lawrence O. Picus and Associates (February).

Odden, Allan, Lawrence O. Picus, and Mark Fermanich. 2003. *An Evidence-Based Approach to School Finance Adequacy in Arkansas*. Lawrence O. Picus and Associates (September).

Odden, Allan, Lawrence O. Picus, and Michael Goetz. 2006. *An Evidence-Based Approach to School Finance Adequacy in Washington*. Lawrence O. Picus and Associates (June 30).

Odden, Allan, Lawrence O. Picus, Michael Goetz, Mark Fermanich, Richard C. Seder, William Glenn, and Robert Nelli. 2005. *An Evidence-Based Approach to Recalibrating Wyoming's Block Grant School Funding Formula*. Lawrence O. Picus and Associates (November 30).

Picus, Lawrence O., Allan Odden, and Mark Fermanich. 2003. *A Professional Judgment Approach to School Finance Adequacy in Kentucky*. Lawrence O. Picus and Associates (May).

Rebell, Michael A. 2006. "Professional Rigor, Public Engagement, and Judicial Review: A Proposal for Enhancing the Validity of

Education Adequacy Studies." Paper presented at the *Annual Meeting of the American Education Finance Association*. Denver, CO.

Reschovsky, Andrew, and Jennifer Imazeki. 2003. "Let No Child Be Left Behind: Determining the Cost of Improving Student Performance." *Public Finance Review* 31 (May): 263–290.

Standard & Poor's School Evaluation Service. 2004. *Resource Adequacy Study for the New York State Commission on Education Reform* (March).

Verstegen and Associates. 2003. *Calculation of the Cost of an Adequate Education in Kentucky: Prepared for The Council for Better Education* (February).

8

Adequacy beyond Dollars: The Productive Use of School Time

E. D. Hirsch Jr.

THE INFUSION OF more dollars into poorly performing school systems often yields disappointing results, as other essays in this volume demonstrate.[1] The legal concept of adequacy needs to be broadened to ensure the adequacy not just of inputs but also of outputs. Adequate outputs are what finally count in education. In this chapter I will discuss some of the forces and practices that inhibit good educational outcomes, no matter how much increased spending is used to support schooling.

Irrespective of dollars spent, the *only* way to achieve outcomes that are excellent and equitable is through the productive use of school time. A fundamental difference between a high-performing and a low-performing school is always the degree to which school time is being used productively—through offering

1. Parts of this essay are taken from my recent book: E. D. Hirsch Jr., *The Knowledge Deficit*, Boston: Houghton Mifflin, 2006.

students cumulative, progressive, nonrepetitive learning. To illustrate this fundamental point about educational adequacy I will use the example of reading comprehension, which is known to correlate highly with academic achievement generally (McGhan 1995).

The Unproductive Use of Time in American Schools

Most instructional activities that teachers and parents engage in with young children have been shown by research to be beneficial. But research rarely asks or answers a crucial question—what is the *opportunity cost* of engaging in this activity rather than that one? Opportunity cost is an important concept from economics that reflects the fact that some benefits are forgone whenever we engage in one activity rather than another. If we teach formal reading-strategy exercises or if we read the same story three times to a child, we need to ask: how great are the benefits that will accrue to the child by doing those things as compared with the benefits that would have accrued to the child if we had used that valuable time in more productive kinds of activities such as reading further stories on the same topic?

Under the influence of the No Child Left Behind law, the principle of opportunity cost has become ever more important, since longer periods are devoted to reading in school. New York City and California have ruled that 150 minutes—two and a half hours of school time every day—must be spent on language arts in the early grades. Other states and localities require 90 minutes a day. This means that time is being allotted to language arts that formerly might have been allotted to history, science and the arts. Yet those neglected subjects are among the most essential ones for imparting reading skill.

The international comparisons of reading achievement show that our schools are among the least productive schools in the

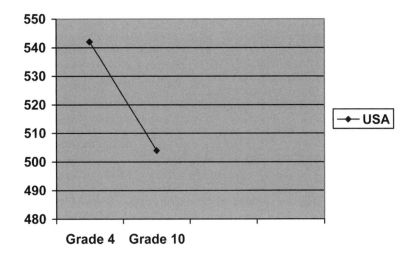

Figure 8.1   United States Reading Achievement Compared with that of
Other Nations

developed world. Our children start school knowing on average
as much as children in other developed nations, but each year
that they stay in school they fall further behind. In the third and
fourth grades, U.S. performance is on a par with that of other
developed countries. Then, in later middle-school grades, the
differences grow, and the United States gradually drifts downward. In recent studies our fourth graders scored 42 points
above the international normalized average of 500—ninth in
reading among thirty-five countries. By tenth grade they scored
just 4 points above 500—a decline of 38 normalized points between the fourth and tenth grades. They also exhibited a striking
decline in relative ranking. Figure 8.1 shows our downhill ski
slope of reading achievement from fourth grade to tenth grade,
comparing American achievement with that of the rest of the
world (NCES 2000; Lemke 2001).

A similar pattern (figure 8.2) is found in the most recent international studies of math. Our fourth graders start out knowing about as much reading and math as fourth graders do in

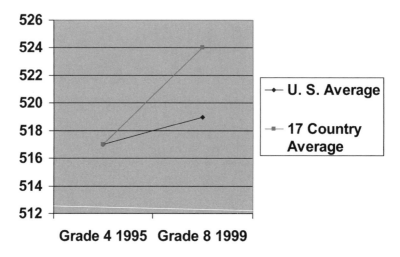

Grade 4 1995   Grade 8 1999

Figure 8.2   Math Achievement, Grade 4 to Grade 8
Note: This graph tracks the math scores for the same cohort of students from 1995 to 1999.

other countries. By eighth grade, they have fallen behind those same students (PIRLS 2001; OGLE 2003).

It's a remote logical possibility that the reason for our relative decline with each successive grade could lie in factors other than our unproductive use of school time—for instance, our distracting culture, our diversity, our racism, our unequal income distribution. But other developed nations have ethnic diversity, racism, distracting cultures, and unequal income distributions and nonetheless have higher-performing schools. Sociological explanations are not very plausible when our school curricula and teaching methods are themselves inherently unproductive. Why seek remote causes for our low educational productivity when more immediate ones are available?

Blaming Teachers

Some people blame ineffective teachers for our poor showing over time on international comparisons. But "low teacher quality" is not some innate characteristic of American teachers; it is the consequence of the training they have received and of the vague, incoherent curriculums they are given to teach, both of which result from an education school de-emphasis on specific, cumulative content. No teacher, however capable, can efficiently cope with the huge differences of academic preparation among students in a typical American classroom—differences that grow with each successive grade (Stevenson and Stigler 1992). (In other nations, the differences between groups diminish over time [Hirsch 1996].) Even the most brilliant and knowledgeable teacher, faced with such wide variations in preparation, cannot achieve as much as an ordinary teacher can in a more coherent curricular system like those found in the nations that outperform us.

The chief cause of our schools' inefficiency is this curricular incoherence (Hirsch 1996). At the beginning of the school year, a teacher cannot be sure what the entering students know about a subject because the students have experienced very different topics in earlier grades, depending on the different preferences of different teachers. Usually, the teacher must spend a great deal of time at the beginning of each year in reviewing the preparatory material that is needed for learning the next topic—time that would not have to be so extensive (and so boring to students who already have the needed knowledge) if the teacher could have been sure that the incoming students had all gained the necessary preparatory knowledge.[2]

Proposing to improve teacher quality without grasping the relation between the low effectiveness of teachers and the romantic, formalistic ideas of the education world is to mistake an effect (teachers' inadequate subject matter knowledge) for an un-

---

2. Or else the teacher, not knowing that dinosaurs and firemen were taught in the previous grade, teaches them again in the new grade—a different source of inefficiency.

derlying cause (the dominant education school ideas that cause the knowledge to be withheld from them). It is true that many American teachers are ill informed about the subjects they teach, and it is true that this reduces their productivity in the classroom. But this is not because they are inherently lazy or incompetent. It is because of the anti-fact, how-to ideas that permeate their training. American education schools consider it their job to provide teachers mainly with naturalistic and formalist ideologies. Subject matter knowledge in history, science, literature, and the arts, (to the extent that it is considered necessary at all) is an imprecisely defined area that education schools assign (without guidance) to other departments of the college or university (Clifford and Guthrie 1988; Ravitch 2000). In short, the low productivity of our schools is chiefly caused by bad theory rather than by teachers' innate incompetence. We will not improve teacher effectiveness until we change the unproductive ideas that dominate teacher preparation and guarantee poor use of school time.

The Root Causes of Unproductive Time Use

Under the schools' dominant ideas—that how-to knowledge is more important than content, and that hands-on, discovery experience is more important than mere words—our schools are bound to use time unproductively. In the teaching of reading, the formalist, how-to approach wastes time because it pursues a nonexistent will-o-the-wisp, namely, content-indifferent reading skill. This formalist approach, because of its extremely high opportunity costs, is inherently unproductive. Reading comprehension doesn't consist in *consciously* performing formal operations on a text, such as guessing what the main idea is. While it's true that we must make guesses about what an utterance means, we have all learned how to make such meaning-guesses simply by having learned to use language at all. Unproductive how-to exercises take time away from knowledge-gaining activities that really do raise reading achievement.

By the same token, a naturalistic, "hands-on," "discovery" way of teaching reading and other subjects is known to be less productive on average than a more direct approach. Many studies, summarized in the late Jeanne Chall's fine book *The Academic Achievement Challenge* have shown that the discovery approach is less time effective than the explicit, goal-directed approach to teaching (Chall 2000). While the naturalistic discovery approach certainly has a place in education, it has been shown to be wasteful of time when used as the principal method of fostering student learning. Nowhere has the inefficiency of "natural" learning been more apparent than in first-step reading—the discovery learning way of teaching young children how to translate print into sounds and words.

Many parents and teachers are familiar with the "whole language" approach to teaching phonics. In the 1920s and earlier, it was called the "whole-word" approach, so the idea is very old. Indeed, the romantic idea that decoding should be learned naturally goes back to the nineteenth century (Mann 1843). It was held then, as it is by some today, that children discover naturally how to turn printed symbols into sounds simply by being exposed to accompanying pictures and other clues about what the words are. Under this whole-word "discovery" method, therefore, children are asked to be little Sherlock Holmeses who are compelled to deduce the phonic code from indirect clues. Some children manage this feat rather well—even if slowly. But other students taught by this method do not manage it at all. Even for the more successful students, the whole-word guessing method is excessively wasteful of time, for if you want to teach a child that the letter *s* sounds like *ssss*, the fastest way to do so is to tell them that fact, help them practice their new learning, and probe to see whether they have learned it (NICH Report 2000).

Better Time Use Means Greater Fairness

An effective use of school time is especially important in all areas of learning connected with advancing language comprehension, which is inherently a slow process. For children who grow up in homes with highly articulate parents, where a toddler is hearing a wealth of language every day, the need for time effectiveness in enlarging language is less than it is for children who grow up in language-barren circumstances. Two researchers, Betty Hart and Todd Risley, have shown in detail how critical are the early pre-preschool, toddler years for enhancing later comprehension. Their path-breaking work, in which many hours of speech interactions were recorded in the homes of very young children from different social groups, showed that what toddlers heard at home in the way of speech patterns and vocabulary was hugely different, depending on social class. Not only was the sheer quantity of words heard much less in some homes than in others, but also the styles of language use were different. A child's ability to understand language turns out to be highly dependent on whether or not the parent said things like *"Do you want to play with your chalk, or do you want to get your pegs out?"* That's the kind of elaborated talk that middle-class toddlers hear. It is in contrast to the laconic utterances often used by less-well-educated parents, who say things like *"Move!"* and *"Be quiet!"* (Hart and Risley 1995, 58). Hart and Risley show that these differences in what toddlers hear currently account for most of the variation in later reading progress.

One way of changing this result would be to change the habits and speech patterns of parents. Desirable as that might be, the speech differences between low-income and middle class households are likely to persist until our educational system improves over many years and educates future parents better. From the standpoint of progress in language right now, schools themselves should try to become supereffective middle-class homes. If that is done, higher school achievement and greater equity will be the result.

When James Coleman, the great sociologist of education, analyzed the school characteristics that had the greatest effect on educational achievement and equity, he found that effective use of time was a chief factor. What was most important was "intensity," a persistent, goal-directed focus on academics that caused classroom time to be used productively (Coleman 1990). Schools with greater academic intensity produced not only greater learning but also greater equity. Such good schools not only raise achievement generally but also narrow the achievement gap between demographic groups. The first finding is obvious, since an intense focus on academics is self-evidently the most likely way to raise academic achievement. The second finding—regarding the equity effect of effective time use—is more interesting, and it has positive implications for both advantaged and disadvantaged students.

The theoretical explanation for Coleman's finding about equity is as follows: When more is learned in school during the course of a classroom period and during an entire year, disadvantaged students begin to catch up—even when their advantaged peers are also learning more or less the same things as they are. That is because disadvantaged students start out knowing less, so each added bit of learning is proportionally more enabling for them than for students who already knew more. If we are reading a story about Johnny Appleseed and some students know how plants grow while others don't, the latter group, the botanically challenged students, will be the ones who learn most from the story, although both groups will learn something new about Johnny Appleseed.

And there is a further reason for the equity effect that Coleman observed. When a lot of learning is going on in school, that fact changes the proportion between the academic knowledge gained inside school and the academic knowledge gained outside school. When many academic things are being learned *inside* school, the academic gap narrows because disadvantaged students are more dependent on schools for gaining academic information than advantaged students are. Advantaged students have a chance to learn many academically relevant things from their homes and peer groups, whereas disadvantaged students learn academically relevant things mostly from their schools. Boosting the in-school proportion thus reduces the unfair distribution of out-of-school learning opportunities.

In a productive classroom, disadvantaged students are getting proportionally more out of schooling, without holding back advantaged ones. Unfortunately, however, if the school is an unproductive one, it will have a greater *negative* effect on disadvantaged than on advantaged students (Coleman 1990). That is the reason American schools have not lived up to their democratic potential.

Examples of Effective Time Use

What students chiefly need to read well is relevant knowledge. Hence the most productive approach to imparting reading proficiency to children is to build up cumulatively the most enabling linguistic and world knowledge in the most time-effective way. When children are offered coherent, cumulative knowledge from preschool on, reading proficiency is the result. A coherent approach to content will produce this result even in the absence of a good, content-oriented language arts program, as the results in Core Knowledge schools show (Smith 2003). If besides this solid regular curriculum, students are offered a content-oriented language arts program, integrated with the curriculum as a whole, their progress in reading will be more rapid still.

The fullest evidence for the validity of this prediction comes from large-scale studies conducted by French researchers into the effects of very early school instruction on later reading achievement (French Equity 2006). The French are in a good position to perform such studies. They have been running state-sponsored preschools for more than a hundred years. By age five, almost 100 percent of French children, including the children of immigrants from Africa, Asia, and southern Europe, attend preschools. At age four, 85 percent of all children attend, and astonishingly, at age two, 30 percent of all children attend. The analyses of records from tens of thousands of students, records that include detailed information about race, ethnicity, and social class, show that the earlier the child starts, the greater will be the positive effect on reading. By the end of fifth grade in France, the relative benefit to disadvantaged pupils who start at the amazingly early age of two, rather than four, is more than one-half a standard deviation, a large effect size. Those who start at age three do better in later reading than those who start at age four, and starting school at age four is better than starting at age five. These studies show that the long-term gain in starting early is greater for disadvantaged than for advantaged students, thus confirming the theory that effective schooling is in itself compensatory.

But because progress in language is slow, the relative academic benefits revealed by these French data do not show up fully until grade five and beyond. This delayed effect is an important and understudied feature of good early schooling. A deferred effect similar to that found in the large-scale French studies was found also in an analysis by F. D. Smith of the reading

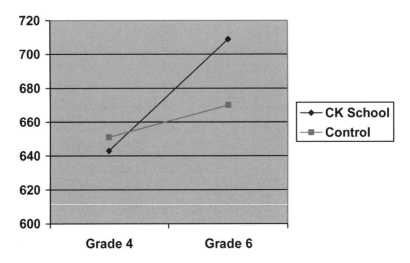

Figure 8.3   Reading Achievement Grade 4 to Grade 6 (Stanford-9 Test)—
Core Knowledge School versus Control School.

scores in a Core Knowledge school compared with those of a control school (Smith 2003). In that longitudinal study, the students in the Core Knowledge school received the Core Knowledge curriculum, a coherent, grade-by-grade curriculum designed to provide the knowledge most useful for reading comprehension. The students in the control school received the standard how-to/hands-on curriculum that prevails in most schools throughout the nation. In grades K–3, the test scores of both groups of students were on a par. In fact, Core Knowledge students were somewhat behind. But by grade six there was a large differential effect favoring the Core Knowledge students, both in equity and in reading achievement. Figure 8.3 shows the achievement effect.

Some explanation of these patterns of deferred effects may be found in the work of Joseph Torgesen and his colleagues, who show that reading tests vary in their emphases as students advance through the elementary grades (Schatschneider et al. 2004). In the earliest grades, scores on standard reading tests depend mostly on mastering the mechanics of reading—on being fluent and accurate in the decoding of words. Thus in the earliest grades, scores on standard reading tests are relatively less dependent on students' world and word knowledge. Then with each advancing grade, because of the changing nature of the tests, the factors change that are most important for test scores. In later grades, reading scores depend mostly on word and world knowledge.[3] This means that even if parents and teachers are doing everything they should to use time effectively in the early grades, they can't expect immediate, large, magic-bullet improvements in reading comprehension in the first few grades. But they are laying essential groundwork. The data show that the improvements will show up later.

Here is one practical way in which a coherent curriculum can achieve significant gains in children's reading proficiency: Everyone knows that proficient reading requires an adequate vocabulary. Everyone also knows that children's vocabularies grow when they hear or read stories. But not everyone knows how to answer the following question: What is the most effective way to build vocabulary? Is it better to read a child a short text of a different kind each day, or is it better to stay on a single topic for a period that stretches over several days or weeks? Some important research suggests that a child can learn words much faster if the teacher sticks to the same topic for several sessions. This is because word learning occurs much faster—up to *four times faster*—when the verbal context is familiar (Landuaer 1997).

---

3. If the very early tests had been designed to measure students' *oral* comprehension of utterances, it is, however, likely that the most critical factors in reading comprehension, both early and late (given adequate decoding skill), would turn out to be students' word and world knowledge. This prediction is supported by Sticht's finding that early listening skill reliably predicts later reading skill (Sticht et al. 1974).

The aim of adequacy laws in the end is to ensure both adequate educational quality and adequate fairness. Neither aim can possibly be achieved without adequate productivity in the use of school time. The *only* way to reach the long-desired educational goal of high achievement with fairness to all students is through a structure of schooling in which each grade builds knowledge cumulatively (and without boring repetitions) on the preceding grade. That structure has been lacking in the United States since the 1940s. Until it is in place, no dollar figure can produce educational adequacy.

References

Chall, Jeanne Sternlicht. 2000. *The academic achievement challenge: What really works in the classroom?* New York: Guilford Press.

Clifford, Geraldine J., and James W. Guthrie. 1988. *Ed school: A brief for professional education.* Chicago: University of Chicago Press.

Coleman, J. S. 1990. *Equality and achievement in education.* San Francisco: Westview Press.

French Equity. 2006. This research is translated and summarized on the Core Knowledge Web site,http://www.coreknowledge.org/CKproto2/Preschool/preschool_frenchequity_frames.htm.

Hart, Betty, and Todd R. Risley. 1995. *Meaningful differences in the everyday experience of young American children.* Baltimore: Peter Brookes.

Hirsch, E. D. 1996. *The Schools We Need.* New York: Doubleday.

International Association for the Evaluation of Educational Achievement. 2001. *Progress in international reading literacy study* (PIRLS). Organization for Economic Cooperation and Development, Program for International Student Assessment (PISA) 2000.

Landauer, Thomas K., and San T. Dumais. 1997. A solution to Plato's problem: The latent semantic analysis theory of acquisition, induction, and representation of knowledge. *Psychological Review* 104 (2) (April 1997): 211–240.

Lemke, Mariann, Christopher Calsyn, Laura Lippman, Leslie Jocelyn, David Kastberg, Yan Yun Liu, Stephen Roey, et al. 2001. *Outcomes of learning results from the 2000 Program for International Student Assessment of 15-year-olds in reading, mathematics, and science literacy*, Washington, DC: U.S. Dept. of Education, Office of Educational, National Center for Education Statistics Educational Resources Information.

Mann, Horace. 1843. *Seventh annual report, in report together with the report of the secretary of the board 1st-12th.* Boston: Dalton, 1838–1849.

McGhan, Barry. 1998. MEAP (Michigan Educational Assessment Program): Mathematics and the reading connection, http://comnet.org/cpsr/essays/mathread.htm.

National Institute of Child Health and Human Development (NICH). 2000. *Report of the National Reading Panel: Teaching children to read: An evidence-based assessment of the scientific research literature on reading and its implications for reading instruction.* Washington, DC: NICH, National Institutes of Health.

Ogle, Laurence T., Anindita Sen, Erin Pahlke, Leslie Jocelyn, David Kastberg, Stephen Roey, Trevor Williams, et. al. 2003. *International comparisons in fourth-grade reading literacy: Findings from the Progress in International Reading Literacy Study (PIRLS) of 2001.* Washington, DC: National Center for Education Statistics, U.S. Dept. of Education, Institute of Education Sciences.

Ravitch, Diane. 2000. *Left back: A century of failed school reforms.* New York: Simon & Schuster.

Schatschneider, Chris, Julie Buck, Joseph Torgesen, Richard Wagner, Laura Hassler, Stephen Hecht, Kelly Powell-Smith, et al. Forthcoming. A multivariate study of individual differences in performance on the reading portion of the Florida Comprehensive Assessment Test: A preliminary report.

Smith, Freddie D. 2003. The impact of the core knowledge curriculum, A comprehensive school reform model, On achievement

(Dissertation, University of Virginia) Diss. Educ. 2003.S62. Available online through Digital Dissertations, http://wwwlib.umi.com/dissertations/fullcit/3083052.

Stevenson, Harold W., and James W. Stigler. 1992. *The learning gap: Why our schools are failing and what we can learn from Japanese and Chinese education.* New York, NY: Summit Books.

Sticht, Thomas G., Lawrence J. Beck, Robert N. Hauke, Glenn M. Kleiman, James H. James, et al. 1974. *Auding and reading: A developmental model.* US AFHRL Technical Report. No. 74-36, 116. US: AL/HRPP. Jul. Alexandria, VA: Human Resources Research Organization.

U.S. Department of Education, National Center for Education Statistics (NCES). 2000. *Pursuing excellence: Comparisons of international eighth-grade mathematics and science achievement from a U.S. perspective, 1995 and 1999.* NCES 2001 (NCES 2001-028) (TIMSS and TIMSS-R), http://nces.ed.gov/programs/coe/2002/section2/tables/t13_3.asp.

9

Funding for Performance

A Policy Statement of the Koret Task Force on K–12 Education

FEW PEOPLE QUESTION the fact that American schools must improve. While the skills of American workers propelled the U.S. economy to the top of the world during the twentieth century, we enter the twenty-first century with the realization that our schools do not rank highly in comparisons with those of other developed and developing countries.

Despite substantial efforts to improve the schools, the performance of American students has remained stubbornly flat. At least portions of the problems of performance of our students and schools have been generally recognized for some time, and policymakers have responded with programs, regulations, and resources. Nonetheless, the performance situation has not materially changed.

This situation provides the backdrop for aggressive movement from one of the least likely sources: the courts. A broad coalition of groups, with diverse interests, has presented courts around the nation with an opportunity to enter into the school improvement fray. And the courts have responded.

Unfortunately, the courts' response to issues of school quality has been marked by a combination of naiveté and politics. By their nature, the courts are unprepared to devise school policy on their own, and they have consistently sided with the recommendations of largely self-interested parties. The decisions, whose full effect has yet to unfold, are unlikely to improve the schools and might well hurt them.

This assessment of court-ordered "reforms" in no way says that all is well and that our schools are firmly on the path of improvement. While there are some signs of positive change, the resource-oriented reforms of recent decades are unlikely to take us where we should be.

Having followed the fads and fantasies of the past decades, we are convinced that only more fundamental changes than those mandated by the courts or adopted by the states' legislatures will be successful. Accountability for results must be vigorously pursued. Improved incentives, including greater school choice options, are needed. And the system must be made more transparent so that those seeking more complete information about their schools can readily get it.

Improvement will not come from simply replicating, with more intensity and expense, what has not worked in the past. Instead it will come from a consistent willingness to do different things, to evaluate which of these work and which do not, and to stay with effective improvement programs. And these conditions are unlikely to come about through court intervention in the funding and operation of schools, no matter how well intentioned.

Where We Are

The U.S. economy continues to be the envy of the world. The growth rates sustained over the course of the twentieth century have moved the U.S. economy ahead of other competitors and produced the high economic well-being of Americans. As economists look at this performance, they find that a variety of factors have contributed: strong democratic institutions with a well-defined system of laws and property rights, relatively free labor and product markets, minimal governmental intrusion in the economy; and physical security. But in addition, the human capital and skills of American workers is consistently cited as one of the most important factors behind the U.S. engine of growth.

Through most of the century, the United States showed the way in skill development through an expansion of schooling for its population. The early movement to universal schooling and the progressively increasing community standards about the years of school to be completed surpassed those of nearly all other nations.

But recent decades have seen a dramatic change in this. U.S. high school completion rates have been almost constant for four decades (U.S. Department of Education 2004), while those in other developed countries have dramatically increased. At the turn of the current century, the U.S. secondary school completion rate ranked sixteenth out of twenty-one OECD countries (Organisation for Economic Co-operation and Development 2005).

As we know, however, school attainment is just one measure of student outcomes. The issue of quality, quite rightfully, has moved to the top of the policy agenda. There also the U.S. performance is a matter of concern. By our own NAEP tests, achievement of our graduates has been essentially flat since 1970 (National Center for Education Statistics 2005).[1] This sit-

1. The National Assessment of Educational Progress, or NAEP, has been

uation might not be worrisome were it not that U.S. students consistently do poorly on international tests. For example, in 2003 U.S. fifteen-year-olds ranked twenty-fourth out of twenty-nine participating OECD countries in the Programme for International Student Assessment (PISA) in mathematics (OECD 2005). The skills measured on these tests are directly related to aggregate economic growth, and the U.S. economy fails to achieve its full potential when it allows its schools to persist at current levels (Hanushek 2003b).

The other conditions favorable to economic performance and growth have in a real sense protected us from our schools. Yet even in these broader economic areas, other countries are moving to improve their economies, further threatening our international competitiveness.

These aggregate observations are also relevant for individuals. Workers with greater skills as measured by school achievement are more productive and earn more than those with less skill. Thus, the emphasis on school quality is justified also from its implications for individual earnings and economic well-being.

Finally, the patterns of educational outcomes have deep implications for our society as a whole. Racial gaps in school attainment and in achievement have stubbornly persisted. While there was convergence in both during the 1980s, the 1990s saw stagnation, leaving blacks in particular dramatically behind whites. These continuing gaps leave the distribution of incomes glaringly wide.

Even though the evidence about the economic costs of ineffective schools continues to mount, much if not all of it has been suspected for a long time. The famous government report of 1983, *A Nation at Risk* (National Commission on Excellence in

---

given to representative samples of 8-, 13-, and 17-year-olds in math, reading, and science for over three decades. Theses tests are designed to provide comparisons of students across time.

Education 1983), sounded an early alarm. While the response was largely ineffectual, it moved the issue of school quality onto the agenda with such force that it has stuck for two decades (Peterson 2003).

Concern about school quality also introduces the subject of this book—the entry of the courts as active and aggressive players in the effort to improve U.S. schools.

The Courts in School Policymaking

Although the courts have dealt with schools over a long period of time, a convenient starting point is the historic *Brown v. Board of Education* decision of 1954. The U.S. Supreme Court held that the racial segregation of schools violated the equal protection clause of the U.S. Constitution, introducing continuing oversight of schools in both the north and the south by the federal courts. Nonetheless, the Supreme Court refused to broaden *Brown* to prohibit disparities in district funding, instead ruling that the basic finance situation described in the equity cases did not rise to the level of a violation of the Fourteenth Amendment (*Rodriguez v. San Antonio*).

State constitutional claims are, however, different, because most states have both equal protection clauses and education clauses that set requirements for schooling. Beginning with the *Serrano v. Priest* case in California, most states have now faced challenges to their school financing schemes—all brought under the provisions of their separate state constitutions. The general thrust of the cases has been that unequal spending across districts is inequitable, because some students had better schools available to them than others.

Not surprisingly, the long series of such funding equity cases has produced mixed opinions, with some courts ruling their funding systems unconstitutional and others upholding their basic constitutionality. After all, both the funding schemes and the state constitutions differ substantially across states. These cases, along with related legislative actions, have tended nonetheless to yield several broad changes: spending has increased, the state share of funding has increased, and the amount of state control and regulation of local schools has increased.

The nature of school funding court cases changed during the 1990s when the arguments focused on the basic dissatisfaction with the performance of schools, as opposed to the unequal allocation of funding. The simplest version of these cases stated that even if the funding distribution were equitable, the financing program was not adequate to ensure the outcomes demanded of children once they entered the labor market.

These cases, labeled "adequacy" cases, have a very simple structure. While the testimony and cases may drag out for amazingly long periods (see chapter 1), the heart of these cases is a presentation that at least some students do not meet current state learning goals and that this must be the result of insufficient resources. Given enough resources, the argument goes, schools would be able to meet their educational goals.

The development of these court cases has been aided by the movement toward accountability in the schools, a movement that culminated in federal law under the No Child Left Behind Act (NCLB) of 2001. NCLB requires all states to introduce testing and accountability programs in their schools and sets 2014 as the year when all children will be proficient by each state's standards for learning outcomes.

The introduction of NCLB emphasized the goals for each state, but subsequent data show that not all students now meet those goals (Chubb 2005). This fact fits nicely into the stories that the advocates of adequacy lawsuits develop—achievement is unacceptable; the obvious problem is insufficient resources, and the state has a constitutional requirement to provide the added funds.

As described, however, the aspirational standards of most states, developed generally without the vote or approval of the state's legislature, seldom bear any resemblance to the language or intent of the state constitution (chapter 2). With few exceptions, state constitutions describe a floor on what is acceptable.

In looking at the history of cases, the now-well-known New York experience may appear outlandish (chapter 1), but assessing other cases suggests that it is not all that different from others. Judges recognize that schools need to be helped and want to do something to improve the situation. The stories of Kansas City, New Jersey, Cambridge, and Sausalito (chapter 4) indicate clear historical precedence for the New York case (and give a chilling foreshadowing of what may come to pass).

Indeed, the courts have been willing to be very prescriptive. In New York City the trial judge declared that the current funding for operations and maintenance should be increased by $5.63 billion a year, an amount that would push spending to double the national average. In Wyoming the legislature, under pressure from the courts, pushed spending to fifth in the nation in 2003, but consultants hired by the legislature counseled that this spending was still substantially insufficient, leading to further massive increases in funding in 2006. In Kansas the court has directed the legislature to appropriate the amount that consultants have said would be required for adequacy—a more than 20 percent increase in spending.

By the winter of 2005, almost half the states had active cases in the courts at some stage of the judicial process. Only five states had never had a school finance court case in the past three decades.

But What Is the Problem?

One simple view is just "what's the problem?" If the legislature and executive branches do not effectively deal with the obvious problems in our schools, can it hurt to have the courts weigh in to fix things?

The answer is that this decision-making process is fraught with problems—problems ranging from constitutional to educational. Indeed there is every reason to believe that aggressive judicial decision making will indeed hurt our schools, at least when measured in student outcomes.

Constitutional Structure and Judicial Incapacity

The constitutional division of powers found across the states and in the federal government is such that the appropriations process is the province of the political branches—the legislative and the executive—while the judicial branch interprets the laws in the framework offered by the constitution. In the normal course of events, the governor will submit a budget with recommendations for school funding, along with funding for other services, and with the taxes needed to support the spending. The legislature will consider this proposal and modify it during the process of arriving at an appropriation for schools and for other areas. The governor then has an opportunity to object through the veto power typically granted the executive. And if the legislature feels strongly about the appropriations amount, it can override the governor's veto.

Throughout the process, the governor and the legislature gather information, analyze the specifics of programs and policies, interact with the citizens they represent, hear from the advocates for school districts, and the like. Over time, the political branches also build up expertise through hiring specialists in the executive offices and in the legislative committees, and these specialists can provide more detailed information to the decision makers.

If these processes produce generally bad outcomes from the viewpoint of citizens, the governor and the legislators can be voted out of office. Of course, because elections are multidimensional, votes are not specific to education (or prisons or roads or . . .). Thus, the legislator seeking reelection still has considerable latitude in policy decisions without much risk of being voted out. Nonetheless, if education (or any other issue) gets too far out of line, these people can be voted out of office.

In contrast, consider the judicial appropriations process as seen, for example, in New York City. A Manhattan judge, a generalist by definition, develops expertise about schools from the material presented in the judicial proceedings, combined with whatever information or opinions he has as an individual citizen. While his opinion will be reviewed by the higher courts of the state, there is generally not a strong check or balance from the other branches. (In some states, judges are elected so that the same check from the people as found in the legislature may apply, but long term lengths, nonpartisan elections, and general lack of public scrutiny make this a weak instrument). In the New York City case, the judge hired a panel of retired judges to advise him on the correct amount to appropriate for schools. This panel took its own testimony and then ratified an analysis by consultants hired by the plaintiffs, even though similar proposed testimony by one of the consultants had been ruled inadmissible by the judge during the trial.

In other places such as Kansas, the courts skip the intervening process of a panel of judges and simply use the spending suggested by the consultants. But in each case, there is no formal review by people in the other branches—except, of course, where the judicial appropriations trigger a constitutional crisis.

(The outcome is, however, somewhat ambiguous, because the legislature can fail to assent to the judicial appropriations.)

There are many problems with this approach. The most basic is the one identified: the judicial appropriations process inverts the role of the courts and puts them in a position never envisioned by the framers of the state and federal constitutions.

Of course, the courts (and the interest groups who are plaintiffs in the cases) would argue that they have the primary role of interpreting the constitution and of ensuring compliance with it. If failures by the governor and the legislators lead to violations of the state constitution, then the courts are obligated to act. Yet on this score, it is difficult to see that the vague language of the New York Constitution requiring "free common schools," interpreted by the highest court as a requirement for a "sound basic education," implies that all students should meet the stringent requirements for a Regents diploma. Or that the Wyoming constitution, which variously calls for a "complete and uniform" or a "thorough and efficient" system of schools, means according to the courts that "Wyoming views its state constitution as mandating legislative action to provide a thorough and uniform education of a quality that is both *visionary and unsurpassed*" (*Campbell II*, 18; emphasis added).[2]

In Texas the supreme court was less expansive when it stated the general principle:

> "[W]e must decide only whether public education is achieving the general diffusion of knowledge the Constitution requires. Whether public education is achieving all it should—that is, whether public education is a sufficient and fitting preparation of Texas children for the future—involves political and policy considerations properly directed to the Legislature." (*Neeley v. West Orange-Cove*)

2. *Campbell County School District v. State*, 907 P. 2d 1238 (Wyo. 1995); *Campbell County School District v. State*, 19 P.3d 518, 538 (Wyo. 2001).

The history of judgments in different states shows clearly that the line between the proper and improper use of judicial authority has been drawn in quite different places.[3] But even if these questions are viewed as matters of interpretation where people can legitimately disagree, the judicial appropriations process fails on pragmatic grounds.

Ignoring Historical Evidence

The lack of court expertise in matters of schools is important, because it allows judgments to be made on superficial—although perhaps commonsensical—grounds that may have *little empirical basis*. The adversarial system of the courts is seldom the place to get a nuanced view of the evidence on any set of policies or school programs. Indeed the judicial system tends to rulings that fall sharply on one side of the case or the other, and the two sides are not commonly going to provide balance in their presentations.

Perhaps the most crucial element of evidence that enters into the school finance discussions of the courts is the role of funding. The constitutional violation alleged in adequacy cases is built on the basis of student performance. The fundamental issue is the lack of achievement by some students. But of course courts can-

3. In fact, some argue that the judiciary should be supreme in this area. Michael Rebell, the lead attorney in the New York City *Campaign for Fiscal Equity* case, states: "Although conventional wisdom often bemoans active judicial involvement in social policy issues, in regard to the oversight of cost studies, a continued pro-active judicial stance is vitally needed. The opportunity for an adequate education is a fundamental constitutional right which past experience has indicated will not be fully and fairly respected in most states without active judicial oversight. Moreover, in regard to cost studies which constitute a critical element in developing an effective remedy in these cases, there simply is no other authoritative, impartial governmental entity that is capable of monitoring and regulating the delicate mixture of expert and political judgments that is involved in this enterprise" (Rebell 2006, 79).

not easily rule that achievement must be higher, because enforcement of such a ruling is difficult. In particular, the courts can order schools to close or can rule that diplomas be withheld if achievement is not at a sufficient level. But these remedies are what we might call the "nuclear option," since they effectively say that "if you do not ensure that the schools sufficiently help children, we will force you to do it by hurting the children even more until you solve the problem." Instead the courts almost always turn to calls for increased spending on schools, arguing as the plaintiffs do that increased funding will fix the achievement problems, or at least will not hurt. Again, in terms of simple spending, the courts face enforcement problems should the legislature fail to act, and here some courts have again threatened the nuclear option if the legislature does not act appropriately in spending.[4]

The fundamental problem, as made clear by the prior analyses, is that there is no reasonable or reliable way to define "adequate funding." The plaintiff discussions of the issue, cleverly, are couched in commonsense. The arguments about funding generally include three elements: (1) a demonstration of a problem that could be easily fixed with resources, such as school plumbing that is in disrepair; (2) a general statement that we all know from our own experience that having more money is "better" than having less; and (3) at times, but not always, a demonstration that a special program at a particular site shows positive learning effects. These elements provide the evidentiary base that enters into a variety of court judgments. But none of these elements indicate how much money is needed to provide

---

4. Such thinking even appears to occur at the local level when the state legislature does not provide sufficient local funds. Goodwin (2006) reports that New York City mayor, Michael Bloomberg, "admits he killed 21 planned schools because they are in districts of politicians he deems insufficiently attentive to his demands [to fund the court judgment on adequacy of funding]."

an adequate education. Nor do they indicate how much achievement will improve with any added spending.

Because the courts lack expertise, they are willing to turn to "experts" who have conducted "costing out" studies to hear the details on what is required. But these costing out studies have no scientific basis and have never been tested against reality (chapter 7). The consultants, almost always hired by interested parties, say themselves in their more candid moments that the analyses can be manipulated and indeed are only done because the relation between funds and student performance is unclear.

The irony of course is that substantial scientific evidence shows no consistent relation between money alone and student achievement (Hanushek 2003a). This finding also shows the difficulty facing the courts: if spending has a very small effect on achievement, it will take a very large amount of money to bring about any achievement goal. The larger the judicial appropriations, however, the less likely it is that the legislature and the executive will support the ruling, leading to both practical and constitutional issues.

The previous chapters also provide evidence that shows the problems with the courts' basic funding logic. Given both unrestricted funding and the latitude to make decisions, school districts have not demonstrated an ability to improve poor student performance (chapter 4). The sad story of Kansas City, which was told to dream its biggest dream and the state would finance it, yet could never improve student achievement, is the poster child for why money alone is unlikely to work. Kansas City is, of course, not alone, and the wide-ranging examples of New Jersey, Cambridge, Sausalito, and the District of Columbia reinforce the fact that Kansas City is not a singular example of bad policy.

If these districts were identifiably bad or corrupt, it might be possible to write off the evidence of bad performance and simply vow not to fund districts "like these." But, while they appear bad after the fact, they were given court and legislative support and funding throughout the process.

Moreover, it is also possible get high achievement—even for children from low-income families—without adding large amounts of resources (chapter 3). In all states it is easy to identify high-poverty schools that achieve much higher than is "expected" of them, based on the backgrounds of the students. But no evidence suggests money as opposed to more fundamental differences in their policies and operations accounts for such unexpectedly high performance.

The usual way the advocates of more spending deal in the courtroom with these disconcerting facts is to argue that these are special cases and that there is no reason that they have to be repeated. The tautological rebuttal of evidence that districts fail to spend extra money effectively is to state "money used wisely can be effective." This statement ignores the fact that districts have not generally shown an ability to use money wisely. Indeed, there is *no* broad-based evidence to show that added funds without other changes in programs and policies lead to more achievement.

The courts do not have the *expertise* or the ability to develop nuanced policies that recognize what goes on in schools. For example, the courts cannot dictate how districts use funds across their schools, even when the evidence shows that districts currently do not make spending decisions relative to identified student needs (chapter 6). Per-pupil spending differences in a wide range of urban districts regularly vary by multiple thousands of dollars, and moreover these districts do not provide extra resources according to poverty concentrations. Spending differences within New York City are larger than the differences between New York City and Westchester County, even though the latter differences played prominently in the *CFE* decision. The court can dictate equal spending, that is, something that can be directly monitored and enforced, but this ruling may not even satisfy spending equity principles if one considers concentrations of disadvantaged students.

Because the courts, and apparently the schools, do not know how to raise the achievement of all students to a high standard with any certainty, the courts have trouble ruling on the basis of outcomes because they cannot have any expectation that the ruling will be satisfied. Thus, simply requiring, for example, that at-risk students reach some achievement standard does not offer a way out for the courts because they know that even a good faith effort by the schools might not produce the desired result, and may simply invite further court cases or extended judicial supervision.

Neither can the courts readily dictate such essential elements of schools as how time is spent on math and reading and whether that time is productive (chapter 8). In simplest terms, even if some curricula or teaching methods are more productive than others, the courts cannot intervene in a practical manner. And in general, good teaching in any classroom does not cost more than bad teaching. Of course, as we discuss below, the legislature and maybe even the school districts are facing the same difficulties, because they also have trouble enforcing the dictates of various educational process matters, including the curriculum that is actually taught in classrooms or the quality of classroom interactions.

Doing Harm by Doing Good

It is not the case that court directives are "free" policies. Some argue simply that, if the court solution doesn't work, no harm is done and at least we can say that we tried.

The very deliberations and character of judicial decisions tend to *lock in* current ways of operating. The courts have been heavily influenced by consultants who tell them how much an adequate education will cost. These analyses are uniformly built on the extensions of current policies toward incentives, teacher salaries, and school organization and do not consider any inefficiencies that might exist (chapter 7). None of the consultants has ever, for example, suggested that different salary structures for teachers, say, with performance rewards, might enter into effective school policy. Indeed, a number of studies relied on by courts and legislatures explicitly reject providing just the minimum (or efficient level) of funds for the programs they deem good. In fact, what is defined as "costs" in the consultants' studies is merely some modified value of current district spending without regard to whether that spending is effective. It is a serious mistake to interpret the current spending as uniformly indicating what is required.

The courts *ignore* the broad evidence that the current achievement level can be produced much more cheaply. Students in private schools do at least as well as those in public schools, even though private school expenditures are considerably less (chapter 5). Private schools can do this because they strive to keep the cost of providing a quality education down so that they can attract consumers. But their success shows that more efficient schooling is clearly possible. By implication, improvements in outcomes could also be accomplished more efficiently than by simply expanding today's typical public school.

The courts, deciding a single case, do not have to consider any *trade-offs* or other activities of the government. While legislatures and governors regularly consider appropriations for schools in the context of spending on other activities of government (welfare, prisons and safety, roads, etc.) and in the context of the taxes needed to fund these, courts decide specific cases concerning schools. If, again, the cases represent violations of constitutional requirements, one could argue that these funds must come in front of all other uses of income, either public or private.

The level of judicial appropriations in the New York City case is instructive. Before any response, if New York City were a state, its spending would rank well within the top ten of the nation. The New York City judgment of $5.63 billion in annual operating expenditures and close to $2 billion in annual capital expenditures amounts to a new bill of more than a thousand dollars a year for every household across New York State. If funded through the income tax, state rates would have to increase by some 30 percent! But the court does not worry about how this will be financed.

In fact, Michael Rebell, the lead attorney for the New York City plaintiffs, argues that the courts are the best place to decide school appropriations precisely because they have no worries about the source of revenues or other competing demands. He states, "Cost questions in education inherently involve a judgmental dimension, and since the legislature often is itself an interested party in the resource allocation decisions that are involved in this process, the only authoritative governmental institution that has both the legitimacy and the ability to tackle this task is the judicial branch" (Rebell 2006, 74). This position is, of course, far from the intended role of the courts under typical interpretations of the separation of powers. It does, however, match the single interest politics of those pushing court cases and advocating dramatic increases in school funding.

While a large part of the population appears willing to fund success in the schools, funding failure has real costs in opportunities forgone and priorities distorted.

The Democratic Appropriations Process

The plaintiffs argue that education is too important to be left to the democratic appropriations process. The stated position is that judicial appropriations would be fairer and more appropriate, even though most states do not have elected judges who are answerable, at least in the short run, to the body politic.

The coalition behind judicial approaches is broad and varied. These are people with a strong self-interest: public school personnel, unions, and state departments of education; people with intense feelings about improving the schools, including parents; a variety of foundations that support the cases and their preparation; and other vocal parties with a genuine desire to improve the schools. These concentrated and identified common interests face a diffuse group with less readily identified interests (who, after all, is for inadequate education?).

Deciding on the right balance among different government programs and between public and private spending, along with structuring the schools and their incentives, is rightfully the province of the democratic appropriations process. Constitutions generally provide for basic rights, that is, floors on what is permissible. But when these provisions are interpreted to be very much higher so that they introduce new constraints that go considerably beyond what state governments are doing or have done historically, the roles are reversed.

This constitutional statement does not, however, imply that legislatures and governors always get it right. In fact, the dissatisfaction with the current performance of schools relates directly to decisions the political branches have made in the past.

The political branches are subject to many of the same forces as have led to the courts' recurring decisions on school finance matters. Indeed, the complexity of the issues, the uncertainties about the right set of reforms, and the pressures of self-interested parties have led to a variety of decisions that have not been altogether productive or effective with respect to schools (Moe 2001; Moe 2003).

We will never avoid politics in decisions about schools. The checks and balances of our constitutional governments are designed to control extreme forms of the expression of politics. Removing these normal checks and balances remains the central problem with the judicial appropriations process on school funding. The trial courts do face an internal check through the review by the appellate courts, but the evidence of court decision making leads to questions about the effectiveness of this check.

The entry of the courts into the appropriations process goes further, however. Once the courts have determined that there is a constitutional violation, legislatures are often paralyzed by the need to redraw the funding of the schools. The legislature cannot address other school policy issues of a more fundamental nature without first dealing with the financing. But the financing issues are not ones that can be easily dealt with, because the legislature must either find new funding sources or reduce other spending to meet the court demands for new, higher appropriations. Doing so frequently means reopening the delicate balance of school funding patterns across the state, a balance always difficult to maintain.

The inability to deal with other issues of educational policy (and other policy) is truly problematic. The standards and accountability movement, which culminated in the No Child Left Behind Act of 2001, is simply the result of frustration about the efficacy of input-based policies. A long history of policy experience—one reflected in a staggering amount of scientific research and evidence—shows clearly that policies aimed at increasing school resources and not at the true object of attention, student outcomes, are wasteful and ineffective. We cannot continue returning to these discredited policies.

An Alternative Perspective on Adequacy

Dealing with both the problems of our schools and the politics of achieving change is difficult. Our recommendations are ones that address both.

The previous discussion suggests the need for balance in the decision making about schools—tempering desires for improvement with a realism about policy options. It also suggests that noticeable changes, beyond simply more money, are needed if we are to improve our schools and our potential as a nation. We have outlined several approaches designed to put us on a path to improvement. They are, as history would teach us, easier to state than to implement. Nonetheless, the needs are very apparent, and we cannot let the chance for improvement slip away yet again.

1. *Our schools need strong accountability systems.*

Accountability in the schools involves a combination of clear and well-defined outcome standards for schools, of the accurate assessment and testing of student achievement against these standards, and of clear data reporting on the performance of each school.

One long-standing difficulty in making decisions about schools has been imprecise information about the quality and performance of schools. Partly, the difficulty is in separating the influence of schools on achievement from the influences of parents, friends, and others. For parents and other decision makers to make effective decisions about schools, they must know both where performance currently is and how it changes with different programs, incentives, and policies.

Separating the influences of schools and teachers from those of others can be done quite reliably with regular assessment data that is built on good tests of strong standards. Ensuring the availability of such information and using it both to inform the public and to develop incentives is important in meeting the performance challenges in the schools.

Each of the states is now involved in setting and enforcing accountability in schools. These efforts, partly the result of state initiatives and partly the result of the federal government's pushing through NCLB in 2001, have shown early signs of positive effects. But attempts to end these legislative actions have also grown louder. We need to strengthen these actions, not weaken them (Chubb 2005).

The substitution of input measures of school quality—spending, class sizes, credentialing of teachers, and the like—simply does not yield valid and reliable evidence. If we are interested in student outcomes, which we need to be, there is no substitute for focusing directly on achievement.

2. *The incentives to improve student outcomes must be strengthened dramatically.*

Schools currently face weak and confusing incentives to improve student outcomes. A number of natural improvements and extensions make sense.

First, part of accountability systems should be a combination of sanctions and rewards to provide direct incentives to meet the standards. NCLB mandates policy changes when failure exists, and states frequently go further. The incentives implied by these accountability systems must be focused directly on performance by teachers and schools.

Second, we place special emphasis on providing greatly expanded parental choice for schools. The expansion of choice achieves multiple goals. It provides incentives for all schools to do a good job, because they will lose students and revenue if they do not. It introduces democratic control of individual schools, since parents will be able to vote directly on school performance through their choice of schools, and thus they do not have to rely on bureaucratic decision making to get results. Finally, in schooling as in other sectors of the economy, we see that competition pushes toward improved performance.

The opponents of choice have managed to confuse the issue in several ways. They argue that choice takes money from the regular public schools. They argue that choice schools are not subject to government oversight and thus that any public funds for them could be siphoned off into unproductive schools. They argue that parents, particularly low-income parents, are not good at making decisions about schools. They leave out the simple fact that the aggressive attack on choice coincides with self-interested behavior and a wish to avoid any competitive pressure on the current public schools. These arguments against choice are not founded on empirical evidence.

While opponents of choice have been generally successful in limiting even experimentation with alternatives, the choice options that have appeared are starting to show success. Even though frequently hobbled by adverse legislation and finances, charter schools have made inroads on schools in most states. A few general voucher systems—in Milwaukee, Cleveland, and Washington, D.C., for example—have also capitalized on special circumstances that have permitted their introduction. From these experiences we are beginning to see that the antichoice arguments do not represent reality.

Third, because of the overwhelming importance of good teachers, rewards should follow good performance. In most states, however, the details of contracts are settled through collective bargaining at the local district level. Given this and given the diversity across local systems in different states, it is difficult to think that the state could control and mandate the exact form of all incentive contracts. It is, however, plausible to think that the state could set general boundaries on the incentive portions of contracts. In other words, local districts could develop their own contracts and salaries as long as they fit within some general guidelines of the state. For example, the state might specify that a certain portion of the salary budget must go into a bonus pool (as Florida has done) and might also put some bounds on how evaluations are done.

The current convention of paying all teachers (of a similar experience and education level) the same amount is simply incompatible with a desire to improve student outcomes. Policy and actions must recognize not only that we have distinct shortages of high-quality math and science teachers and other specialists but also that we need to upgrade the quality of teachers throughout the schools. Rewards should be linked to performance in the classroom, not to a perceived potential based on credentials, education, and other factors shown to be unrelated to student outcomes (Hoxby and Hanushek 2005).

3. *The operations of schools must be transparent so that all interested parties can readily understand what individual schools are doing and why.*

Under current operations, it is extraordinarily difficult to understand the operations, programs, and decisions of local schools. The kinds of details about activities and budgets generally do not allow even the most interested parents (and decision makers) to see what is happening. This fact in turn makes it difficult for parents to interact productively with their local schools.

Accountability focuses on reporting student outcomes and introducing rewards and sanctions for performance. But there is more information that can and should be provided.

Two kinds of information are essential for the oversight of schools by parents, decision makers, and the public. First, there needs to be "resource transparency" so that everybody knows what allocation decisions are being made. Second, there needs to be "programmatic transparency" so that judgments can be made about the instructional program that is put in place. Historically, it has perhaps been possible to argue that providing detailed information for schools was difficult and expensive, but those arguments have lost their force both as information is regularly produced for a variety of purposes and as presentation on the Web cuts the costs.

In relation to resources, budgets have been so opaque that not even experts can decipher how and why resources are allocated. This situation makes it almost impossible for anybody outside the schools to enter into intelligent conversation or enlightened decision making. The fact discussed above, that resources are not now related in any systematic way to student performance, undoubtedly relates to the fact that important information on resources and decisions is kept hidden. Governors, legislators, and the public need to insist on knowing exactly (1) how money finds its way to districts, (2) how money finds its way to students and schools, (3) where teachers come from, and (4) how teaching talent is distributed within districts (Hill 2005). Budgeting and accounting systems that obfuscate the true allocation—for example, by not reporting actual spending, as noted in chapter 6—do not promote good decision making.

We believe that there should also be a free flow of information about the reliability and effectiveness of the programs that a district undertakes. The proliferation of programs with little accountability for results simply contributes to the performance problems we face.

Because of the realities of the current school scene, we emphasize this kind of transparency, because choice and accountability are thwarted by lack of transparency, and by all forms of monopoly—including intellectual ones. We see the continuing, and tragic, use of programs and curricula that have been scientifically discredited. The "whole language" fiasco has become nationally known, but other manifestations of fuzzy curriculum and bad preparation exist (chapter 8).

It no longer can suffice for a school simply to assert that it is using an appropriate program. NCLB focuses on scientifically validated programs; to qualify for federal reading funds, for example, districts must use reading programs that are supported by science-based research—that is, employing clinical trials. This idea should be taken to the school level, and schools should post their reasoning and justification for their educational choices. The public should know.

Moving Forward

An important consideration is that each of the three elements of change should reinforce the others, and that they should be thought of as a package. Each element has an obvious and natural place in school decision making. Yet each on its own is subject to efforts to limit effectiveness. It is easier to eliminate one or more of the reform elements when thought of individually than when the elements form a package.

The opponents of any change in the current system argue that there is uncertainty about the best way to introduce accountability or incentives. They throw up the possibility that some reforms might not achieve their ends or that they might have associated unintended consequences. And they are correct. There is uncertainty about the best way to proceed—in large part because the opponents have been successful in blocking even the smallest experiments with change.

At the same time, the one thing that is certain is that the current system is not achieving its goals. All evidence indicates that simply doing more of the same will not carry us to where we want our schools to be.

Indeed, on a number of scores, there is dramatic evidence

that the current system is harmful. We know this, for example, about a range of reading and math programs still found in many schools. We know this from the ineffectiveness of the current salary structure.

The opponents of change continue to run aggressive campaigns to close any breaches and to defend the current structure, but it is clear to us that these reform efforts should be expanded and not rolled back. The constrained introduction of public charter schools across the nation should be broadened and onerous restrictions lifted. More experiments with vouchers—building on experiments in Milwaukee and the District of Columbia, as well as in New Orleans with Katrina relief policy—should be undertaken. Support should be provided for new teacher compensation plans—such as those popping up in Denver and Houston.

There remains much to be learned about alternative incentives and accountability. But this is not an argument for sticking with the current system, because the current system is not producing what we want and need.

These words apply to both the legislatures and the courts. Real improvement takes fundamental reform. It will not happen through more of the same.

Real adequacy is achieving learning results. It is not compounding bad decisions and institutional mistakes with further decisions that lock in these mistakes.

References

Chubb, John E., ed. 2005. *Within our reach: How America can educate every child*. Stanford, CA: Hoover Institution Press.

Goodwin, Michael. 2006. Mad Mike's school ax hurts kids. *New York Daily News*, March 1, 2006, 31.

Hanushek, Eric A. 2003a. "The failure of input-based schooling policies." *Economic Journal* 113, no. 485 (February): F64–F98.

———. 2003b. "The importance of school quality." In *Our schools and our future: Are we still at risk?* edited by Paul E. Peterson, 141–173. Stanford, CA: Hoover Institution Press.

Hill, Paul T. 2005. "Transparency." In *Reforming education in Arkansas: Recommendations from the Koret Task Force*, edited by Koret Task Force, 127–139. Stanford, CA: Hoover Institution Press.

Hoxby, Caroline Minter, and Eric A. Hanushek. 2005. "Rewarding teachers." In *Reforming education in Arkansas: Recommendations from the Koret Task Force*, edited by Koret Task Force, 155–166. Stanford, CA: Hoover Institution Press.

Moe, Terry M. 2003. "The politics of the status quo." In *Our schools and our future: Are we still at risk?* edited by Paul E. Peterson, 177–201. Stanford, CA: Hoover Institution Press.

———, ed. 2001. *A primer on America's schools*. Stanford, CA: Hoover Institution Press.

National Center for Education Statistics. 2005. *NAEP 2004: Trends in academic progress, three decades of student performance in reading and mathematics*. Washington, DC: U.S. Department of Education.

National Commission on Excellence in Education. 1983. *A nation at risk: the imperative for educational reform*. Washington, DC: U.S. Government Printing Office.

Organisation for Economic Co-operation and Development. 2005. *Education at a glance: OECD indicators 2005*. Paris, France: Organisation for Economic Co-operation and Development.

Peterson, Paul E., ed. 2003. *Our schools and our future: Are we still at risk?* Stanford, CA: Hoover Institution Press.

Rebell, Michael A. 2006. "Professional rigor, public engagement, and judicial review: A proposal for enhancing the validity of education adequacy studies." Presented at the Annual Meeting of the American Education Finance Association. Denver, CO.

U.S. Department of Education. 2004. *Digest of education statistics, 2003*. Washington, DC: National Center for Education Statistics.

INDEX

Abbott districts, xxvi, 131–38, 132n37
Abbott v. Burke, xxiii, 63n81, 105n6
academic performance index (API), 142
The Academic Achievement Challenge
(Chall), 319
adequacy cases, conclusions on, xvii–
xix, 75–76, 326, 353–54; court-
ordered remedies for, 66–71; courts
and, xv–xvii, 33–48, 44n46, 334;
federal court desegregation and, 37–
40, 39n14, 40n17, 41n20;
implications for, 251–55, 253n1; in
Kansas, 47, 53–54, 60–61, 65, 67–68,
335; in Massachusetts, 47, 71–73;
new direction for, 71–75; in New
Jersey, 44n26, 63–64, 63n81, 64n85,
68, 335; plaintiffs in, 235–36;
presumption of unconstitutionality
with, 48–66; proof of causation and,
57–66, 66n91; proponents of, 103–6,
106f; school districts and, 44–48,
44n46; in Texas, 47, 71, 72–75; in
Wyoming, 54–57, 65, 65n89

"adequacy movement," 34–35
African American(s), 3, 85;
achievement of, 110–11, 226–27;
males, 111n12; private schools, xxvii,
91–92; schools, 115–16; students,
144; test scores of, 225. *See also*
blacks
AIR. *See* American Institute of
Research
Ajax, Canada, 92
Alabama, xv–xvi, 43, 67, 83t, xvin3
Albany, New York, 30
American Federation of Teachers, 129
American Institute of Research (AIR),
27, 88, 265, 302–3, 303n34; analysis,
277, 280, 283; on CFE, 302–3,
303n34
ANB. *See* average number belonging
Andover, 196
Annenberg Institute for School Reform,
253n1
API. *See* academic performance index

Armed Forces Qualification Test, 116
Assessing Patterns of Resource Distribution, 253n1
Assessment Review Panel, 152–53
Atlanta, 91–92
Augenblick, John, 267–68, 270–71, 273, 279, 292, 305
Augenblick, Palaich, and Associates, 279, 292
Austin, Texas, 237, 241t, 242f, 243
Ausubel, David, 165
average number belonging (ANB), 297n30

Baltimore, 91, 237, 240, 254
Baltimore City Schools, 240
Barkis, Anne, 267–68, 305
Beale, Howard, 3
Benton Harbor, Michigan, 39, 40n17
Berry v. School District of Benton Harbor, 39, 40n17
Bill and Melinda Gates Foundation, 111
black(s), children, 7–8, 38–39; test results for, 116. *See also* African Americans
Black Panther Party, 140n42
Black Power, 139–41, 140n42, 151
Bloomberg, Michael, 27–28, 340n4
Booker, Cory, 134–35, 136
Bradford, Derrell, 131n36
Brazosport Independent School District, 93
Bronx, New York, 89, 202
Brooklyn, New York, 89, 91, 202
Brown v. Board of Education, 8, 19, 28, 37, 44, 116, 333
Buchanan, James M., 174
Buck Trust, 151–52
Buckley, John, 29
Buffalo, New York, 6
Bullock, Judge, 305
Burns, Marilyn, 151
Bush, George H.W., 7

California, xiv, 83t, 241, 314; high-poverty schools in, 88; Proposition 13, 43; school districts in, 43
California Academic Content Standards, 152, 153, 153n61

California Academic Performance Index, 143
Cambridge, Massachusetts, xxvi, 335, 341–42; community around, 122–23; decentralized practices at, 128–29, 128n30; enrollment at, 123; per-pupil spending in, 123, 124f, 126f, 129–30, 129n33; school district performance/spending in, 105–6, 106f; student test results for, 125, 126t, 129, 129n33
Campaign for Fiscal Equity (CFE), xxiv, 1–2; AIR/MAP and, 277–78, 278n21, 302–3, 303n4; costing out study by, 25–27, 48, 259n3, 265; lawsuit filed by, 19–21; as organization, 6, 16–17
Campaign for Fiscal Equity v. New York, 1–2, 8, 335, 345; defendants/plaintiffs in, 9–10, 339n3; filing of, 9–18; *I,* 51, 56–60, 60n75; *II,* 52, 57–61, 60n75; outcome of, 29–31, 34, 301–2, 337; trail, 19–25, 48–49
Campbell County School District v. Wyoming, 54–55, 295–98
Campbell 2006, 65n89
Canada, 92
The Catcher in the Rye (Salinger), 196
Catholic schools, 89–91, 197–200, 205–6, 222, 224, 225n12, 227
Center on Reinventing Public Education, 237
CFE. *See* Campaign for Fiscal Equity
Chall, Jeanne, 319
Chicago, 107, 236, 239
Chicago Public Schools, 251
children, black, 7–8, 38–39; disabled/disadvantaged, xxv, xxix, 4, 144, 285; French, 323; health/social services for, 58; minority/poor, 46–47; white, 7–8, 38–39, 110–11
Chubb, John E., 168, 226
Cincinnati, Ohio, 239, 240, 241t
City Journal, 134–35
civil rights, 10, 12, 37
Civil Rights Act (1964), Title VI of, 10, 12
Clark, Russell G., 107–8, 109, 113, 155
Clay, West Virginia, 92
Clemson University, 86
Clinton, Bill, 114

Clopton, Paul, xxvi, 259, 300
Clute, Texas, 93
Coate, Douglas, 133–34
coefficient of variation (cv), 246
Coleman, James, 225, 321
Coleman research, 225, 226, 321–22
College Board SAT test, 117, 118t
Columbia Falls Elementary School District No. 6 et al v. the State of Montana, 297n30
Columbia Financial Responsibility and Management Assistance Authority (Control Board), 114
Columbia University, Campaign for Educational Equity at Teachers College, 31
Law School, 14
Community School Board 6, 3–6, 19, 30
Comprehensive Test of Basic Skills (CTBS), 120n19
Control Board. *See* Columbia Financial Responsibility and Management Assistance Authority
Core Knowledge schools, 323–24
costing out studies, 48, 50n46; on adequate education, 257–59, 257n1; alternative outcome standards in, 264–69, 264n10, 266n13, 269n13; approaches to, 259–63, 263n9, 290–92; appropriate input prices in, 286–88; CFE's, 25–27; conclusions on, 304–8; cost function approach as, 262–63, 263n9, 291; cost-performance relationships in, 264n10, 266n13, 269–75, 274n17–18, 275n19; educators' wish list method as, 290; evidence-based approach as, 261–62, 291; inefficiency in, 276–78, 276n20; MAP's, 25–27, 265; maximum expenditure and, 281–82; minimum cost and, 278–82, 279n23, 281n23; opportunities v. outcomes in, 301–4, 314; professional judgment method as, 261, 290; projecting outcomes within, 282–87, 284n24; reliability/validity of, 263–90; resulting evidence of, 292–301, 294f, 294n27–28, 295f, 296f, 297n30, 298n31, 298t, 299n32,

299t; spending estimates in, 289, 289n25; "state of the art" approach as, 261–62, 291; successful schools method as, 262, 291
Costrell, Robert, 272n15
Council of the Great City Schools, 114n15, 119–20, 119n17, 120n18
court(s), adequacy cases and, xv–xvii, 33–48, 44n46, 334; capacity, xix–xxii; decisions, xxii–xxiv, 36, 65–71; on educational funding/policies, 35–36, 37–48, 330–54; equity cases/state, 35, 40–44, 41n20, 333–35; federal, 37–40, 39n14, 40n17, 41n20; legal/practical issues confronting, 36; Massachusetts, 36; New York, 5, 43, 48–49; -ordered remedies, 66–71; role of, 37–38, 175–76; in school policymaking, 333–35; state, 40, 45–48; Texas, 36; Wyoming, xviii, xxv, 295–300, 296f, 298n31, 298t, 299n32, 299t, 300n33. *See also* desegregation
CTBS. *See* Comprehensive Test of Basic Skills
Cubberly, Ellwood P., 170n88
Cunningham, George, 104
Cuomo, Mario, 1, 4, 9, 13
Curley, James, 171n89
cv. *See* coefficient of variation

D'Alessandro, Bobbie, 129
Daley, Richard J., 171n89
Dallas, 241t
Dayton, Ohio, 202
DCPS. *See* District of Columbia Public Schools
Decker, Thomas, 289
DeGrasse, Leland, courtroom of, 11–18, 27–29; decisions by, 19–25, 302
Democratic Party (Manhattan), 10–11, 15–16
Denton, Peter, 133
Denver, 236, 247–48
Department of Education, 30
desegregation, 35, 37–40, 39n14, 40n17, 41n20, 110
Detroit, 38, 40n17
developmental appropriateness, 163
Dietz, John, 263n9

"Different Ways of Knowing," 128
Dinkins, David, 3, 4
District of Columbia Public Schools (DCPS), xxvi, 114, 341–42, 354; administrators, 119; Dunbar High School in, 115–16; enrollment at, 121–22; test results for, 116–17, 116n16, 117t, 118t, 121–22, 121n20, 122n22
District of Columbia State Education Office, 121
Dunbar High School, 115–16, 156
Duncombe, William, 268, 285

EdSource, 88
education, academic achievement and, 104n3, 284, 284n24; access to, 4; adequate, 257–59, 257n1; class sizes and, 23, 62; complexity of, xxi–xxii, 4; curricular incoherence in, xxix, 317–18; democratic appropriations process in, 346–47; "effect sizes" and, 284n24; equal, 1; equity cases in, 35, 40–44, 41n20, 333–35; finance, 269n14; funding disparities in, 5–7; infrastructures for, 39, 108; K–8, 207–8; K–12, 33–36, 34n2, 62–63, 329–54; per-pupil spending in, 34–35; preschool, xx; sound basic, 20–25, 28–29, 48, 57–58, 60, 265; state funding of, 1, 6–7, 9–18, 21–25, 28–29; states and public, xvii, 1–2, 41–48, 103–4. See also Progressive Education
Education Management Accountability Board, 122n22, 130n34
Education Reform Act, 125
Education Trust (2002), 86–87, 86n1
Education Trust West, 241
Education Week, 142n44, 259n3
efficiency, 195–200, 275n19, 276n20, 279n23, 281n23
equity cases, 35, 40–44, 41n20, 333–35
Evangelical Protestant schools, 197–99, 222, 222n8, 224
Evans, William, 226, 300
Evers, Williamson M., xxvi, 259
Excellent Education for Everyone, 131n36, 133
Exeter, 196

Farrell, Herman, 11
Faville, Brent, 257
Feiden, Douglas, 17–18
Fermanich, Mark, 266, 300
Figlio, David, 226
Finch, Peter, 3
Finding Forrester, 196
Fort Worth, Texas, 237, 241t, 242f, 243, 248
Freedom of Information Law, 17
Freeman v. Pitts, 61
full-time equivalent (FTE), 238

Gardner, Howard, 128, 156
GDP. See gross domestic product
Gibson, Kenneth A., 135
Giuliani, Rudy, 16
Google, 197
government, growth, 104n2; trade-offs by, 344
Graham and Parks Alternative Public School, 127
Great Neck, New York, 7
Greeley, Andrew, 225
Grogger, Jeffrey, 226
gross domestic product (GDP), 157
Guin, K., 246

Hague, Mayor, 171n89
Hall, Stanley, 164n76
Hancock, et al v. Commissioner of Education, 272n15
Hanushek, Eric, xxviii, 22–23, 63, 177
Harlem, New York, 92
Harrington Elementary School, 128
Harris study, 86n1
Hart, Betty, 320
Harvard University, 122, 125, 127–28
Hedges, Larry V., 63
Herbert, Bob, 17
Heritage Foundation, 88
"HIgh School and Beyond" survey, 225
High School Proficiency Assessment, 138
Hill, Paul, xxvii
Hirsch, E. D., Jr., xxviii
Hofer, Thomas, 225
Houston, Texas, 239, 241t, 242f, 243, 248
Hoxby, Carol, 85

Huff, Carol, 11

Iannoccone, Laurence, 168–69
independent school districts (ISD), 246
Intel, 197
ISD. *See* independent school districts

Jackson, Robert, 3–6, 9–10, 16, 30–31
Jefferson, Thomas, 114
Jencks, Christopher, 225, 226–27
Jenkins III. See Jenkins v. Missouri
Jenkins v. Missouri (Jenkins III), 39–40, 61
Jersey City, New Jersey, 137–38
Johntz, William F., 150
Jose P. v. Ambach, 3–4, 17
judicial activism, 4, 337–45
judicial branches, xvii, 5

Kansas, 83t, 92, 306; adequacy cases in, 47, 53–54, 55, 60, 65, 67–68, 335; per-pupil spending in, 35
Kansas City, Missouri, School District (KCMSD), 61, 155, 335, 337, 341–42; per-pupil spending in, 38–40, 39n14, 40n17; revitalization money and, 108–9, 108n10; rulings against, 107–8; school district performance/ spending in, 105–6, 106f, 107–13, 107n9, 108n10, 109n11, 111n12, 112f; student test scores in, 111, 111n12, 112n13
Kansas Legislature, 53
Kansas State Supreme Court, 53–54, 55, 267
Katrina relief policy, 354
KCMSD. *See* Kansas City, Missouri, School District
Kentucky, xv–xvi, 49, 83t, 104, 266
Kentucky Supreme Court, 266
King Open School, 128
Kirst, Michael W., 145, 170
Klein, Chancellor, 27
Klein, Joel, 28
Koret Task Force, xxiv, xxix–xxxi, 329–30
Kozol, Jonathan, 7–8

language arts, 314
Lartigue, Casey, 114n15

learning, discovery, 163, 319; styles, 165, 165n80
learning disabled/disadvantaged, xxv, xxix, 4, 144, 285
Lee, Valerie, 89
legislature(s), 5, 25; appropriation power of, 69–71, 336–45; powers of, 36, 46; proof of causation and, 57–66; state, 340n4
LEPC (Legislative Education Planning Committee), 267
Levittown Union Free School District v. Nyquist, 5, 9, 12
Levy, Harold, 15, 20
Limited English Proficiency, 223
Lindseth, Alfred, 18, 257
Little Rock, Arkansas, 40n17
Llaudet, Elena, 223
Long Island, New York, 5
Los Angeles, 107, 116n16
Los Angeles Times, 142, 142n43, 148–49
Los Angeles Unified, 241
Lukemeyer, Anna, 268, 285
Lutheran schools, 197–98, 222

MacInnes, Gordon A., 132n39
MacLaury, Bruce K., 120n19
Malanga, Steven, 134–35
Management Analysis and Planning (MAP), 277, 280, 283, 302–3, 303n34, 306; on CFE, 302–3, 303n4; costing out study by, 25–27, 265; report by, 20–21
Manhattan, 3, 10–11, 34, 89, 202. *See also* Washington Heights
MAP. *See* Management Analysis and Planning
Marin City, California, 139, 144, 148, 150, 156. *See also* Sausalito, California
Marin Community Foundation, 151–52
Massachusetts, 83t, 130, 272, 306; adequacy cases in, 47, 71–73; court decisions in, 36; per-pupil spending in, 34–35
Massachusetts Comprehensive Assessment System (MCAS), 125–27, 127t

Massachusetts Institute of Technology (MIT), 122
mathematics, 111, 121; ethnicity and, 222–23; proficiency, 123–24; U.S. achievement in, 315–16, 316*f*
MCAS. *See* Massachusetts Comprehensive Assessment System
McDuffy v. Secretary of Education, 72, 125
Milliken II remedies, 38–39, 40n17
Milliken v. Bradley, 38, 61
Milwaukee, 207–8, 354
Minneapolis, 44n26
Minorini, Paul, 178
Mission City, Texas, 92
Missouri, 28, 38–40, 39n14, 40n17, 83t, 107, 107n9, 110, 113, 198
Missouri Board of Education, 113
Missouri Department of Elementary and Secondary Education, 107n9
Missouri Mastery and Achievement Tests, 110
Missouri Synods, 198
Missouri v. Jenkins, 38–39
MIT. *See* Massachusetts Institute of Technology
Moe, Terry M., 168, 226
Montana, 47; school funding in, 306; spending history of, 296–301, 296f, 297n30, 298n31, 298t, 299n32, 299t, 300n33
Montana Supreme Court, 297n30
Montoy v. Kansas, 35n4, 53
Morantz, Alison, 112
Moynihan, Daniel, 104n2
multiple intelligences, theory of, 128
Municipal Reform, 167–73, 168n86, 170n88, 171n89
Murphy, John, 39
Myers, John, 267–68, 271, 272n15, 273, 305

A Nation at Risk, xix, 332
National Assessment of Educational Progress (NAEP), 63, 74, 85; data, 220–23, 220n6, 221t, 222n8; gains/results, 94, 116; tests, 331–32, 331n1
National Center for Education Statistics (NCES), 62–63, 223–24

National Center on Education and the Economy, 119n17, 120n18
National Commission on Excellence in Education, 332
National Education Association (NEA), xvi, 167, xvin4
National Educational Goals Panel, 94
National Longitudinal Survey of Youth, 226
NCES. *See* National Center for Education Statistics
NCLB. *See* No Child Left Behind Act
NEA. *See* National Education Association
Neal, Derek, 226
Neeley v. West Orange- Cove, xviii
Network, 3
New Jersey, xxvi, 83t; adequacy cases in, 44n26, 63–64, 63n81, 64n85, 68, 335; Newark school district performance/spending in, 105–6, 106f, 131–39, 140f; per-pupil spending in, 34–35, 52–53
New Jersey Assessment of Knowledge and Skills, 136
New Jersey State Board of Education, 138
New Orleans, 91, 354
New York, 1, 57, 66, 83t, 285; budget deficits of, 2, 25–27; courts, 5, 43, 48–49; equity cases in, 42–43; judges in, 10–11, 34; per-pupil spending in, 34–35; on school funding, 1, 6–7, 9–18, 21–25, 28–29, 58, 64, 246
New York City, 1, 92, 314; Catholic schools in, 89–91, 197–200, 205–6, 226n11; elite establishment of, 6; equal education in, 8–31; per-pupil spending in, 34, 44n26, 342; school funding in, xx, 6–8, 9–18, 21–25, 28–29, 52, 57–60; schoolchildren, 2, 6–7; sound basic education in, 20–25, 28–29, 48, 57–58, 60, 265. See also *Campaign for Fiscal Equity v. New York*
New York City Board of Education, 4, 60
New York City Board of Regents, 58
New York City Council, 30

New York City Independent Budget Office, 23
New York City Public Schools, 20, 57–60
New York City School District, 58
New York Constitution, 10, 12, 338
New York Court of Appeals, 5, 43, 52, 56–57
New York Daily News, 10
New York Supreme Court, 9–11, 66
New York Times, 17, 22
New York's City Hall, 30
Newark, New Jersey, curriculum/testing in, 132–33, 132n38–39, 136–38, 137f; graduation rate at, 136–38, 137f; school district performance/spending in, 105–6, 106f, 131–39, 140f; Shrag on, 133, 135
Newsweek, 66
Newton, Huey, 139n42
"The New York Adequacy Study: Determining the Cost of Providing All Children in New York an Adequate Education," 302
No Child Left Behind Act (NCLB), xxx, 56, 264, 268, 282, 284, 303; accountability/influence of, xiii–xiv, 314, 349; introduction of, 334–35
North Central Comparison States, 296–301, 296f, 297n30, 298n31, 298t, 299n32, 299t, 300n33
North Dakota, 83t; schools in, 267–69, 279, 292; spending history of, 296–301, 296f, 297n30, 298n31, 298t, 299n32, 299t, 300n33; student performance in, 293–94, 294f, 294n27–28, 295f
North Dakota Department of Public Instruction, 289

Oakland, California, 254
Odden, Allan R., 63, 266, 280–81, 300
OECD (Organisation for Economic Co-operation and Development), 331–32
Ontario, Canada, 92
Open Court, 150
Ostrom, Vincent, 170

parents, 319–20; communication/involvement of, 215–16, 217t, 319–20; habits/speech patterns of, 320–21
Parent-Teacher Associations (PTA), 161n69–70
Pataki, George, 13, 15, 24, 26–27
Paterson, New Jersey, 137
Patterson, Mary Jane, 115
Pearson, Josephine, 148
Pendergast, Boss, 171n89
Peterson, Paul, xxvi, 257
Philippi, West Virginia, 93
phonics, 319
Picus, Lawrence O., 63, 266, 300, 305–6
Pilot School, 127, 128n28
PISA. *See* Programme for International Student Assessment
Pittman, Sir John, 150n58
Pittsburgh, 92
poverty, 19, 46–47, 92–93; California schools with high, 88; learning and, 80–82, 81f, 82t, 86n1; schools, high-performance/high-, 79–95, 86n1, 342; South Carolina's achievement proficiency and, 80–86, 81f, 82t, 83t, 84t
Praxis teacher-readiness test, 120
Preston, Betty, 113
Princeton University, 226
Programme for International Student Assessment (PISA), 332
Progressive Education, 125, 151–52; child-centered, 164–67, 164n75–76, 165n80, 167n85; doctrines of, 156–57; history of, 164n75
property taxes, 40–41
PTA. *See* Parent-Teacher Associations
public relation firms, 16–17
Public School 287, 30
Publishers Weekly, 7

QPA (Quality Performance Accreditation), 267

racial discrimination, 10, 14, 44
racism, institutional, 7–8; Wayland on, 19–20
RAND study, 94
Read, Judge, 24

reading, achievement, 314–16, 315f, 316f, 322–25, 324f, 325n3; eighth grade, 116n16; proficiency, 123–24; programs, 120n18; U.S. achievement in, 315, 315*f*

Rebell, Michael, 279n23, 339n3; on education finance, 269n14; lawsuits litigated by, 3–6, 8–9, 14–18, 26, 31, 345

Regents diploma, 24, 338

Regents Learning Standards, 48, 52, 60n75, 264–67, 264n10, 266n13, 303

Republican Party (New York), 13

Rich, Wilbur, 131n36, 135

Risley, Todd, 320

Rochester, New York, 6

Rodriquez v. San Antonio, 41, 41n20, 333

Rone, Dana, 136–38

Rouse, Cecilia, 226

Roza, Marguerite, xxvii, 246

Sacramento, California, 144, 241t

St. Albans, 196

St. Louis, 44n26, 109, 109n11

St. Paul, Minnesota, 44n26

Salinger, J.D., 196

San Francisco, 144, 241t

Sausalito, California, xxvi, 155, 335, 341–42; class sizes at, 141; curriculum at, 145–51, 146n49, 146n50; learning disabled/ disadvantaged at, xxv, xxix, 4, 144, 285; performance at, 149–54; school district performance/spending in, 105–6, 106f, 139–54, 141f, 143f; suburb of, 139; teachers at, 147–48, 147n52, 148n53; violence at, 148, 148n54

Savage Inequalities (Kozol), 7–8

school(s), accountability of, 348–51; African American private, xxvii, 91–92; changes/reforms, 2, 353–54; choice/vouchers, 349–50, 354; finance case law, 35; free common, 52, 58, 338; funding in Montana, 306; high, 331; high-poverty/high-performance, 79–95, 86n1, 342; middle, 315; national/state surveys

of, 86–89, 86n1; operational transparency of, 351–53; policymaking/courts, 333–35; principals, 239; secondary, 331; time, productive use of, 313–14, 320–26, 324f, 325n3; time, unproductive use of, 314–16, 318–20; U.S. attainment, 331–32, 331n1; U.S. policies, xiii–xvii

school district(s), accountability/interest groups and, 161–63, 161n69–70; adequacy cases and, 44–48, 44n46; allocation of funds by, 235–55; in California, 43; Cambridge, Massachusetts, 105–6, 106f; case studies of, 107–54; central office spending by, 244–46; comparative analysis of, 154–58; conclusions on, 174–78; district level spending patterns by, 246–49, 246f; experienced teachers and, 240–42, 241t; fiscal practices of, 249–51; high-poverty/high-performance, 79–95, 86n1, 342; high-spending/low-performance, 103–78; KCMSD performance/spending in, 105–6, 106f, 107–13, 107n9, 108n10, 109n11, 111n12, 112f; in Long Island, 5; Newark, New Jersey, 105–6, 106f, 131–39, 140f; organizational structure of, 159–61, 159n67; performance/spending, 105–6, 106f; politics of, 158–73, 158n65; Sausalito, California, 105–6, 106f, 139–54, 141f, 143f; special program funds for needy populations of, 242–44, 242f; staff allocation by, 238–40; teaching practices of, 163–67, 164n75; Washington D.C., 105–6, 106f, 202. *See also* independent school districts; Municipal Reform

schools, private, xxvii; administrative simplicity of, 205–9; African American, xxvii, 91–92; Catholic, 89–91, 197–200, 205–6, 222, 224, 226n11, 227; class size at, 208–9; conclusions on, 227–29; co-production at, 209–20, 213t; cost-sensitivity of, 200–201, 200n4; educational expenditures at, 201–4,

201n5; efficient, 195–200; elementary, 205; Evangelical Protestant, 197–99, 222, 222n8, 224; homework at, 217–18; Lutheran, 197–98, 222; organizational solutions at, 204–9; parental communication/involvement at, 215–16, 217t, 319–20; peer culture at, 212–14, 213t; religious, 197–200; significance of, 218–20; size of, 204–5; social capital at, 215; student achievement at, 220–23, 220n6, 221t, 222n8; systemic comparisons of, 224–28, 226n11; teachers at, 203, 215, 217t; two-tier v. multi-tier system at, 206–8, 207t

schools, public, 195; administrative simplicity of, 205–9; case studies on, 92–94; Catholic and, 89–91, 197–200, 205–6, 222, 224, 226n11, 227; class size at, 208–9; conclusions on, 227–29; co-production at, 209–20, 213t; cost-sensitivity of, 200–201, 200n4; educational expenditures at, 201–4, 201n5; elementary, 205; homework at, 217–18; organizational solutions at, 204–9; parental communication/involvement at, 215–16, 217t, 319–20; peer culture at, 212–14, 213t; significance of, 218–20; size of, 204–5; social capital at, 215; student achievement at, 220–23, 220n6, 221t, 222n8; systemic comparisons of, 224–28, 226n11; teachers at, 203, 215, 217t; two-tier v. multi-tier system at, 206–8, 207t

Schwab, Robert, 226

Seattle, 237, 241t, 254

Serrano v. Priest, xiv, 43, 178, 333

Shanker, Albert, 129

Shrag, Peter, 44, 115; on Newark, 133, 135; on teachers, 176n92

Sidwell Friends, 196

Silverstein, Justin, 267–68, 305

Simpson, Thacher and Bartlett (law firm), 14, 18–19

Smith, F. D., 323–24

Smith, James, 20–21, 25–26

Sobol, Thomas, 9, 22

Social Communities That Work, 253n1

social promotion, 157n64

Society of Education, 225–26

South Carolina, 47; achievement proficiency/poverty in, 80–86, 81f, 82t, 83t, 84t; on preschool education, xx

South Dakota, spending history of, 296–301, 296f, 297n30, 298n31, 298t, 299n32, 299t, 300n33; standards classification of schools in, 83t

South Marin County Education Task Force, 151–52

Sowell, Thomas, 91–92

Spitzer, Elliot, 15–18, 19, 29

Standard & Poor's, 26–27

Standard & Poor's School Evaluation Service, 266, 277–78, 278n21

"Standards Movement," 46–47

Stanford University, 88, 145

Stanford-9 composite scores, 117, 118t, 120n19

state(s), constitutions, xvii50; courts, 40, 45–48; courts/equity cases, 35, 40–44, 41n20, 333–35; funding of education, 1, 6–7, 9–18, 21–25, 28–29; high-poverty/high-performance, 79–95, 86n1, 342; public education and, 1–2, 41–48, 103–4

Stone, Joseph, 226

student(s), xvi; achievements of, 220–23, 220n6, 221t, 222n8, 284, 284n24; African American, 144; charter school, 122n22; funding in Buffalo, 6; performance in North Dakota, 293–94, 294f, 294n27–28, 295f; test results for Cambridge, Massachusetts, 125, 126t, 129, 129n33; test scores in KCMSD, 111, 111n12, 112n13; white suburban, 111n12, 112

Sugarman, Stephen, 178

Sutherland, Asbill and Brennan (law firm), 14, 16, 18–19

Syracuse, New York, 6

Target, 197

teacher(s), 252–53; alternative methods of paying, 62; blaming, 316–18, 317n2; at private schools, 203, 215,

teacher(s) (*continued*)
217t; at public schools, 203, 215,
217t; qualified, 21–22; -readiness
test, 120; salaries of, 23, 39, 62, 174,
287–88; in Sausalito, California, 147–
48, 147n52, 148n53; school districts/
experienced, 240–42, 241t; Shrag on,
176n92; unions, 135, 172
"Teaching for Understanding Project,"
128
TERC (Technical Education Research
Center), 129, 129n31
Texas, xviii, 83t, 92–94; adequacy cases
in, 47, 71, 72–75; court decisions in,
36; education funding system in, 41,
41n20, 242–44, 242f, 246–47, 247f;
per-pupil spending in, 35
Texas A&M study, 248
Texas Supreme Court, 73–74, 338
"three city study," 202, 205
Title I legislation, 86, 223–24, 250
Torgesen, Joseph, 324–25, 325n3
Transparency international ranking,
157
Twin Falls, Idaho, School District, 93

UFT. *See* United Federation of
Teachers
unions, teacher, 135, 172; trade, 3, 16.
See also specific unions
United Federation of Teachers (UFT),
16, 20
United States, 9, 79, 157, 280–81;
economy, 331; math achievement in,
315–16, 316f; reading achievement
in, 315, 315f; school attainment in,
331–32, 331n1; school policies of,
xiii–xvii
University of California at Berkeley, 88
University of Southern California, 305
University of the District of Columbia,
116
University of Wisconsin, 226
U.S. Constitution, Fourteenth
Amendment of, 9, 44, 333
U.S. Department of Education, 90, 197,
200, 213–14, 225

U.S. Supreme Court, 37

Vacco, Dennis, 13–15
VanderHoff, James, 133–34
Verstagen and Associates, 266–67,
272n15
Violence in schools, 148, 148n54
vocabularies, 325

Walberg, Herbert, xxv
Wal-Mart, 197
Ward, James Gordon, 174n91
Washington, D.C., school crisis in, 114;
school district performance/spending
in, 105–6, 106f, 202. *See also*
District of Columbia Public Schools
Wayland, Joseph F., 14–15, 18; on
racism, 19–20; views of, 21, 27–28
Weingarten, Randi, 20
Wellesley, 272n15
Wenders, John T., 177
West Orange-Cove Consolidated
Independent School District, 263n9
West, Paul, 257
Westchester County, New York, 246,
342
white(s), children, 7–8, 38–39, 110–11;
suburban students, 111n12, 112; test
results for, 116
"whole-word approach," 319
Wichita, Kansas, 92
Wildavsky, Aaron, 178
Will, George, 66
Williams, Anthony, 122
Wilms, Douglas, 225, 226
Wolkoff, Michael, 257
Wyoming, 83t, 155n63; adequacy cases
in, 54–57, 65, 65n89; court decisions
in, xviii, xxv, 65, 295–300, 296f,
298n31, 298t, 299n32, 299t, 300n33;
per-pupil spending in, 35, 35n4
Wyoming Constitution, 54, 65, 338
Wyoming Supreme Court, 54–55,
65n89, 295–96, 297n30

Yale University Law School, 3
Yinger, John, 268, 285
Yonkers, New York, 6, 40n17
Yseta Independent School District, 93

EDUCATION next BOOKS

Education Next Books address major subjects related to efforts to reform American public education. This imprint features assessments by Hoover Institution fellows (including members of the institution's Koret Task Force on K–12 Education), as well as those of outside experts.

Assessments from the Hoover Institution's Koret Task Force on K–12 Education

Courting Failure:
How School Finance Lawsuits Exploit Judges'
Good Intentions and Harm Our Children
Edited by Eric A. Hanushek
(published by Education Next Books, 2006)

Charter Schools against the Odds
Edited by Paul T. Hill
(published by Education Next Books, 2006)

Within Our Reach:
How America Can Educate Every Child
Edited by John E. Chubb
(published by Rowman & Littlefield, 2005)

Our Schools and Our Future
. . . Are We Still at Risk?
Edited by Paul E. Peterson
(published by Hoover Institution Press, 2003)

Choice with Equity?
Edited by Paul T. Hill
(published by Hoover Institution Press, 2002)

School Accountability
Edited by Williamson M. Evers and Herbert J. Walberg
(published by Hoover Institution Press, 2002)

A Primer on America's Schools
Edited by Terry M. Moe
(published by Hoover Institution Press, 2001)